I0799850

IMAGES
of America

AROUND IVA SOUTH CAROLINA

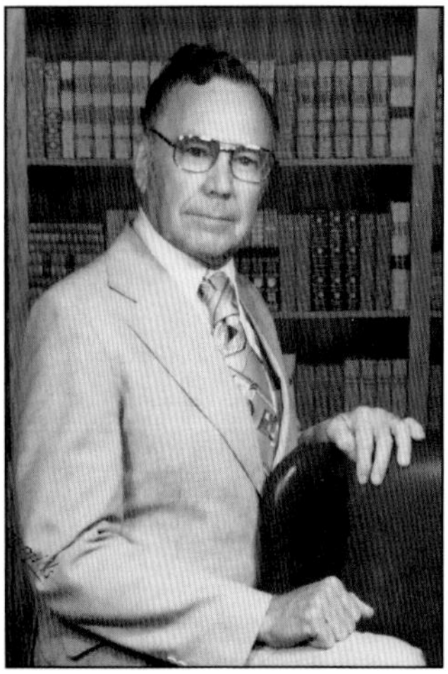

Rodney E. Bowman
(January 20, 1911–
April 5, 1991)

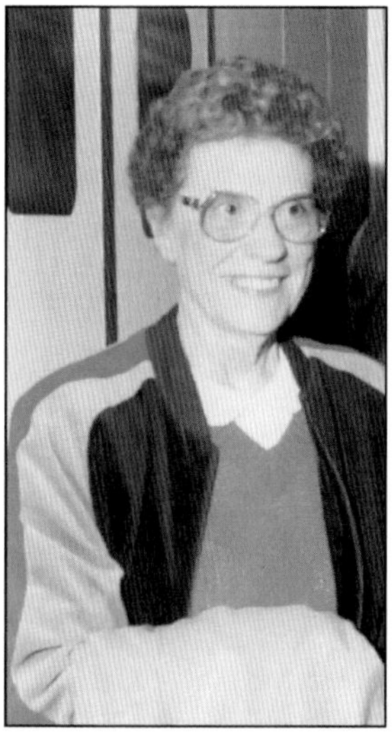

Ethyl Hall
(May 14, 1913–
October 4, 1998)

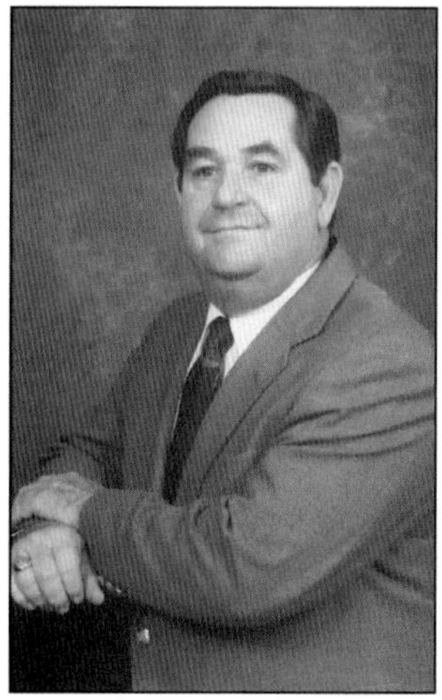

Julian L. Maxwell, Jr. (April
10, 1944–July 2, 1998)

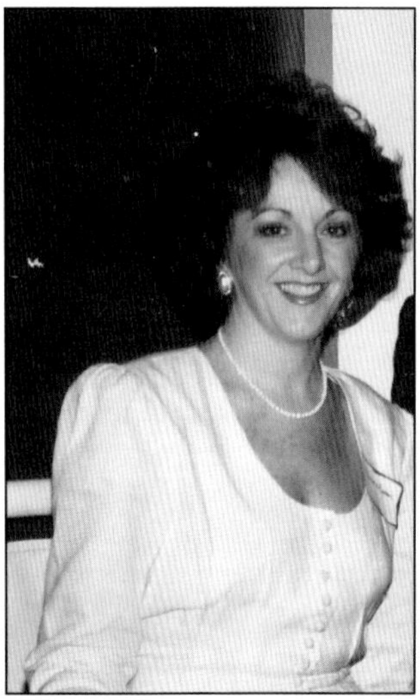

Elaine E. Evans
(August 12,
1948–September 30, 1997)

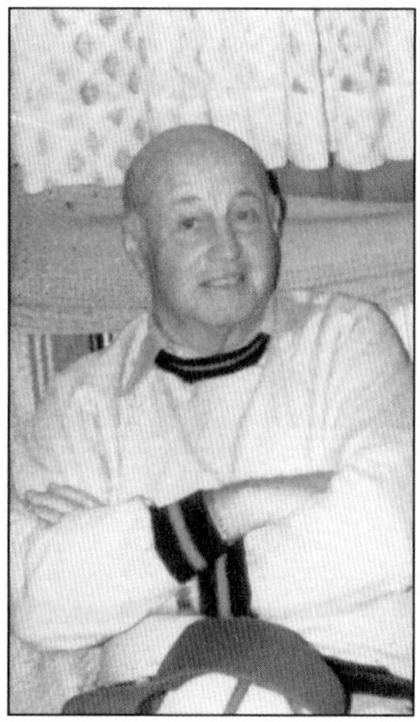

James A. Compton
(January 23, 1920–February
28, 1990)

This book is dedicated to the faithful members of REVIVA who made this possible, and to the memory of five of our beloved members.

IMAGES
of America

AROUND IVA SOUTH CAROLINA

REVIVA

ARCADIA
PUBLISHING

ISBN 978-0-7385-0043-0

Published by Arcadia Publishing
Charleston, South Carolina

Printed in the United States of America

For all general information contact Arcadia Publishing at:
Telephone 843-853-2070
Fax 843-853-0044
E-Mail sales@arcadiapublishing.com
For customer service and orders:
Toll-Free 1-888-313-2665

Visit us on the Internet at www.arcadiapublishing.com

Contents

ACKNOWLEDGMENTS

Many thanks go to the dedicated volunteer members of REVIVA, Iva's Community Improvement Association, who made this historical pictorial book possible for all to enjoy. It was quite a task, and what a learning experience it was!

Many photos were furnished to REVIVA years earlier when Pendleton District Historical Society made copies of old photographs for the Iva community and provided copies for REVIVA to put on exhibit in the REVIVA museum, which can be seen there even today.

We extend our appreciation to all those involved. The sub-committee spent hours, days, and months working on this project, and they weren't even sure they would ever get this completed; however, Ms. Jackie Pettigrew Sorensen, the co-chairman of the group, continued to challenge the team to "keep on working until it is done."

REVIVA's Historical Pictorial
Sub-Committee

Thanks go to the co-chairpersons: Jackie Pettigrew Sorensen, Yvonne Bowman McGee, Alice Ozmint Campbell, and Aileen McMahan Alexander. Thanks also go to the others who assisted: Josh Gray, Lyn Hughey, Walter Hughey, Carl Evans, Amy June Burton, Roger Burton, Kevin Metz, Varina Simpson, Hank McKee, Fred Whitten, and all others who provided photographs and information. Finally, our special thanks go to Kimmberly Cook, who got us over the "finish line."

Introduction

At one time, this land in South Carolina was where the American Indians traveled along the creeks and rivers, fishing and hunting for game, such as wild turkey, deer, and rabbit, which are still in abundance today. They made their homes and raised their families along this beautiful Savannah River region. Today, people continue to do these things, but now they fish and hunt for pleasure, using the rivers and lakes for leisure, and the nearby cities for recreational activities and work.

Small settlements sprang up along the rivers in the early pioneer days of our country's history, then extended out. Just a few miles apart, and situated along the roads, were villages such as Alice, Barnes, Dean Station, Twiggs (which became Starr), Moscow, Moffettsville, Antreville, Lowndesville, and Cook's Station (which was later called Iva). Generally, each village had a store, a grain mill or cotton gin, blacksmith shops, a tannery, or cottonseed oil mills. Moffettsville was the first place in this section to have a post office built, and its mail was received from the main post office at Ninety Six, South Carolina. The post office at Moffettsville served until September 30, 1901. The first postmaster was James H. Davidson, and the last one was W.T.A. Sherard. During the early days, products were shipped by barge from river ports, such as Hardscrabble, which was located along the Savannah River. From the river ports, the shipments were carried down to Hamburg, South Carolina, and Augusta, Georgia, where the railroad from Charleston ended. In 1886, the railroad was completed to this section of the state. Settlers moved from the rural areas to develop communities along the railways, and this resulted in the demise of outlying communities such as Generostee and Moffettsville. During this time, Dr. Augustus G. Cook of Moffettsville (the prominent landowner and local physician) bought property from Mrs. Betsy Brown, who owned a large plantation. Dr. Cook moved his family into a two-story wooden house, located near where the old Iva Drug Store now stands. He named the depot Cook's Station, and it operated as a shipping point on the Savannah Valley Railroad. The name had to be changed when it was discovered that there was another station on the line named Cook's Station. One of the railroad men suggested that the whole community be named Iva, in honor of Iva Cook, Dr. Cook's daughter. This was the beginning of a settlement that went from being a farming community in the 1700s to a railroad shipping point in the 1800s, and which later became an industrial mill village when Jackson Mill was built in 1906. At that time, there were less than 200 workers because Iva had been an agriculture area, but the mill built homes and offered incentives to encourage people to move into the community and work in the cotton mill, which operated for well over 90 years.

Some of the adventures of the past 200 years of history of Iva are touched on in this book, as well as points of interest from Antreville, Starr, and Lowndesville. Antreville is located near the Discovery Route, 7 miles from Iva. Starr, Iva, and Lowndesville are located on S.C. Highway 81 South on the National Heritage Corridor Nature Route.

Lowndesville was first chartered by the South Carolina Legislature on December 21, 1839. There was a post office officially called Lowndesville as early as August 17, 1836. It was said that the town was named after the Lowndes family of the Charleston area, possibly that of William Lowndes, the United States congressman. February 15, 1924, was a very windy day. A grass fire started beside the Charleston & West Carolina railroad tracks and spread to the far end of town, burning a barn, a cottonseed oil mill, and several dwellings. The fire destroyed much of the community. Lowndesville is located in Abbeville County, and is 7 miles from Iva. This town contains several old homes, a general store, and several picturesque churches. It remains a pretty little community near the beautiful water of Richard B. Russell Lake, which is one of the U.S. Army Corps of Engineers lakes built on the Savannah River.

Antreville is a quiet agricultural crossroad community, 8 miles east of Iva along highways 184 and 28. Originally Centreville, its name was reinvented when the postmaster sent in the post office name to be registered. Due to poor penmanship, it became Antreville. The Shiloh Methodist Church and the Gable House are two examples of historical buildings of Antreville. The Gable House was on the border of Anderson and Abbeville Counties. The Gables claim that Anderson County really got its start there. Many years before becoming known as the Gable House, it was called Temple of Health because of mineral springs behind the house that were said to be of medicinal value. The Temple had stood since General Andrew Pickens signed the last treaty with the Cherokees in 1777. It also served as a stagecoach stop and as an inn, and General Pickens stopped many times there while going back and forth from Abbeville to his home in Oconee County. Highway 28 became known as General's Highway. John C. Calhoun also traveled along this highway while going to Clemson from his home in Abbeville County. The Gable House, the home of Levi and Jeanette Latham Gable, was so sturdily built, with 12-foot logs, that Mr. Asa Hall used to take his wife there during storms. This house and a General Mercantile store beside the house stood until a few years ago when the home was moved to Historic Homes Park in Georgia.

Starr is a small settlement 6 miles north of Iva. Initially called Twiggs, it originated around 1838, and in 1888 it was renamed Starr, in honor of Captain W.W. Starr, a railroad official of the C & WC railroad. The property came from a land grant of 712 acres in 1799, which was later purchased by several businessmen. Three of the earliest families were the Gentrys, the Stuckeys, and the Joneses. Josephine Stuckey, daughter of Thomas and Mary Ann Stuckey, was the first postmistress of Twiggs. Starr could boast, in the early days, of having four practicing doctors: Dr. J.N. Land, Dr. Clarence Dean, Dr. George Pettigrew, and Dr. Goodman Bare.

Starr became a thriving farming community. It depended on barges to get its products, which were mostly cotton, wheat, and corn, to and from the markets. These crops were transported from the port of Hardscrabble, an early settlement situated near the mouth of Generostee Creek, and also, at one time, a river port for the Starr-Iva area. A channel was dynamited, in the Savannah River at Hardscrabble, to form this river port, from where farm products could be shipped to Hamburg, South Carolina (where the railroad from Charleston ended), and Augusta, Georgia. Hardscrabble port was washed away in August 1908, and it was never rebuilt. Soon after, bridges were built to take the place of ferries and barges, near Harper's Ferry and Sander's Ferry, to cross the Savannah River. With the coming of the railroad in 1886, things changed and businesses began shipping by rail, and small communities near the rivers vanished.

Starr's greatest claim to fame, probably, was the Pruitt House, which was well known for its hospitality and scrumptious meals. It also served as a boardinghouse for teachers, and as an inn for travelers. It burned in 1950. Starr has many beautiful homes that were built around the turn of the century. In later years, industrialization brought many changes, and some people left the farms to seek employment in larger cities. Considered a "bedroom community," Starr, however, remains relatively untouched and continues to have many beautiful farms and homes.

One

How It All Began

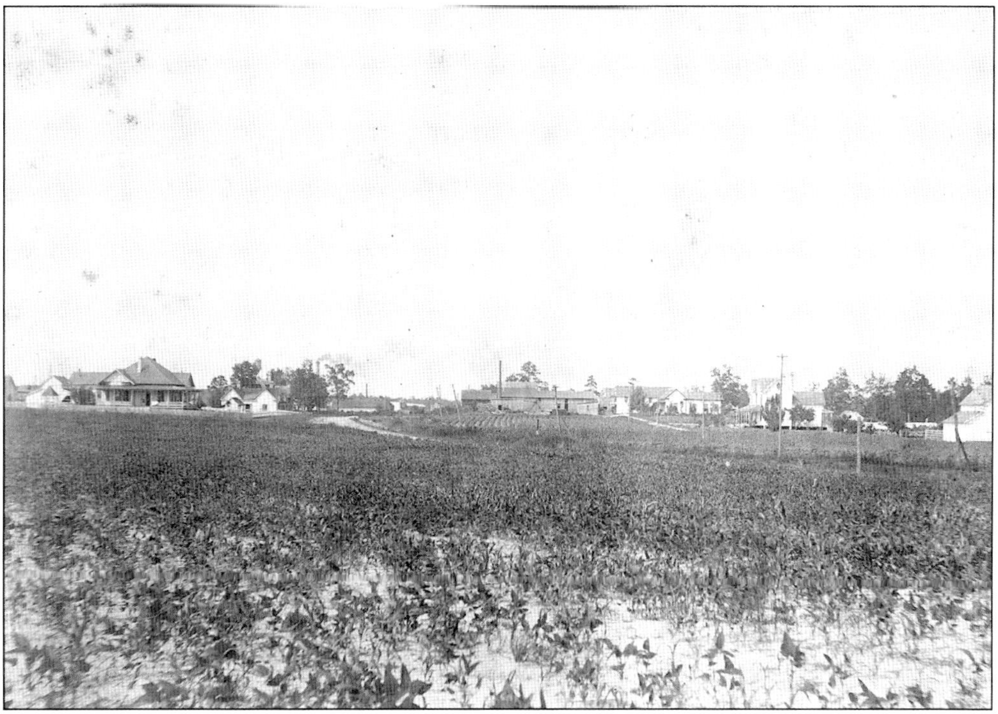

This view of the home of Iva Cook Bryson (left) looks northeast toward Iva. The dirt street in front is S.C. Highway 81, which is now the Heritage Corridor/Savannah River Scenic Highway. In the center of the picture is J.B. Thomas & Son Warehouse, which is still in operation today. The cotton field in foreground became a ball field until 1969 when Anderson County School District 3 administrative office was built here for the Starr-Iva schools. The Cook home is now occupied by Ernest and Elsie Evans, relatives of Iva Cook Bryson.

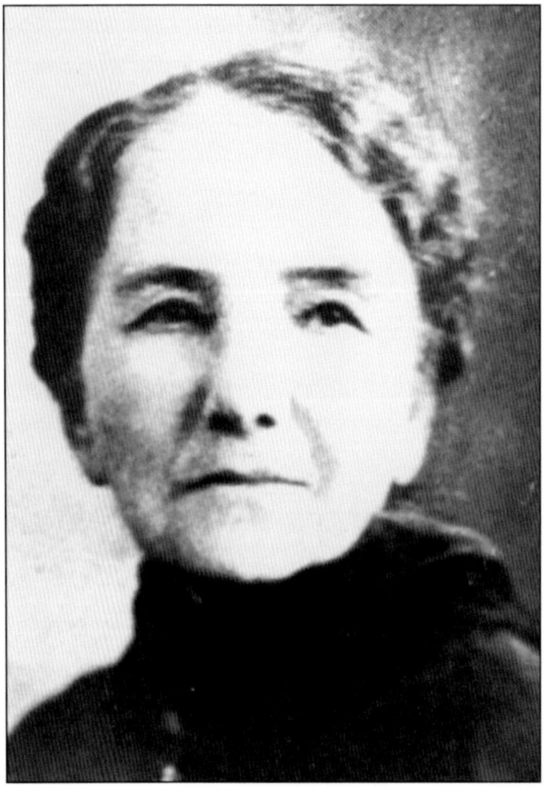

The town of Iva was named after Iva Cook (January 30, 1867–March 30, 1946) by Dr. Augustus Cook, her father. Her mother was Mary Clinkscales. Miss Cook married David Bryson in 1917, and they lived in the Cook home until her death. She was the author of *Woman's Work in the Associate Reformed Presbyterian Church.* Considered to be a rare book, it is now kept in the vault of the Erskine College Library in Due West, South Carolina.

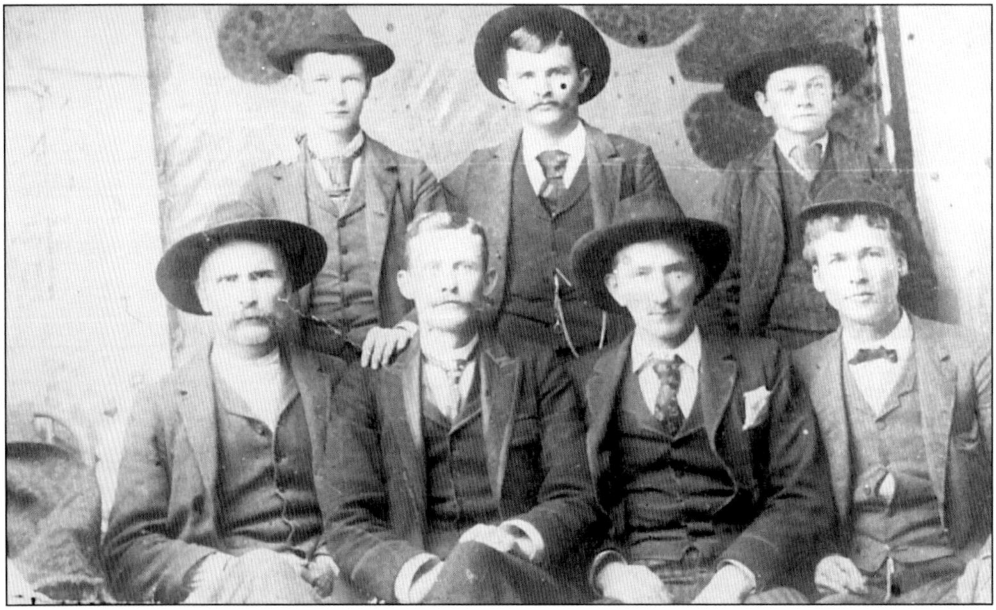

Some men of Iva are shown here, from left to right, as follows: (front row) Gus Cook, the founder of Cook's Station, which was later known as Iva; Pringle Cook, who operated one of the first mercantile businesses in town; Reese Watt, a former postmaster of Iva; and Frank Hanks; (back row) Loren McKee, a farmer in the community; Lemuel Reid, a former postmaster; and Henry McKee, a local farmer.

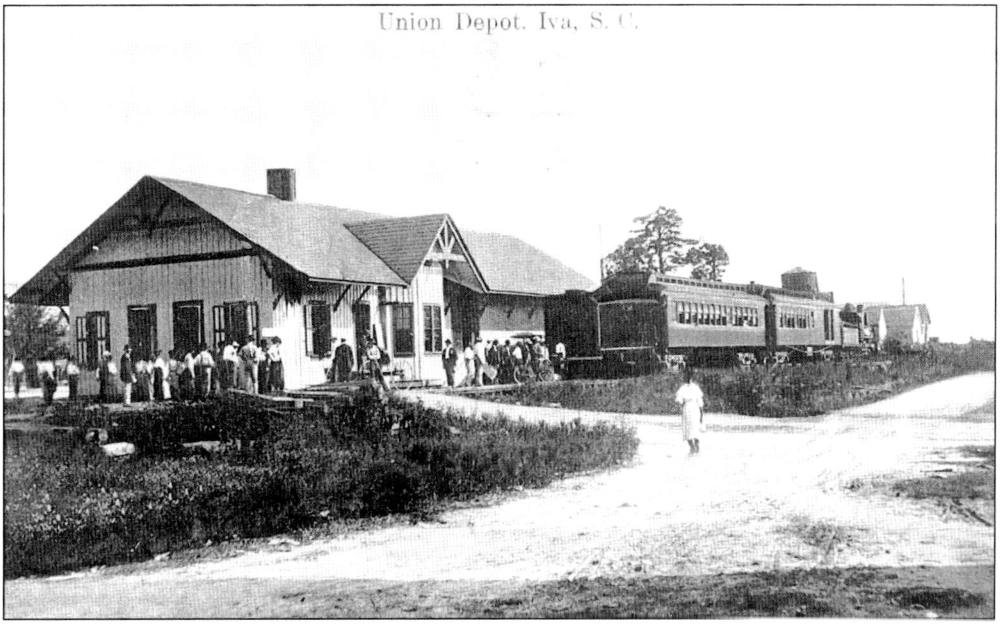

The Union Depot of Cook's Station, located in Iva, was later known as the Iva Railroad Station. This depot station served, for many years, as a receiving and disbursing station for the traveler who made two trips daily from Anderson to McCormick, South Carolina. The station was later moved, and the building seen here is now the private home of Mr. and Mrs. Walter Jones.

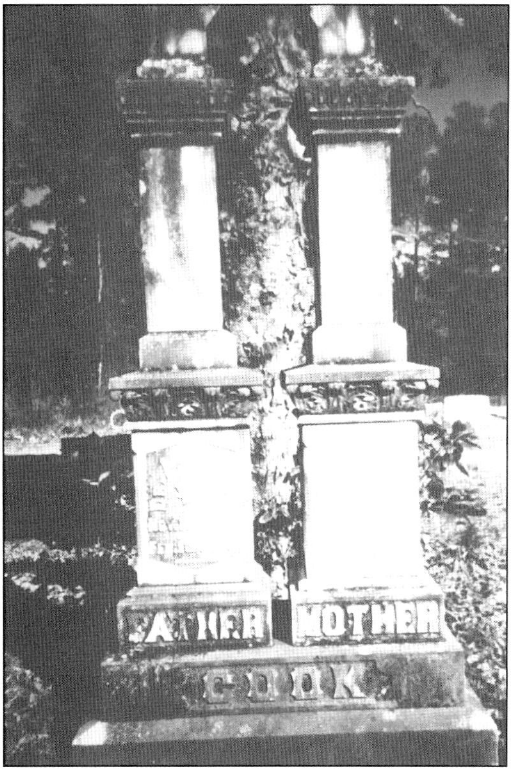

This monument at the gravesite of Dr. and Mrs. Augustus Cook, parents of Iva Cook, is located in the cemetery at Generostee Associated Reformed Presbyterian Church, which is situated on Parker Bowie Road outside of Iva. Across the road from this church was the Cooks' first home. Dr. Cook was a very prominent landowner and community leader.

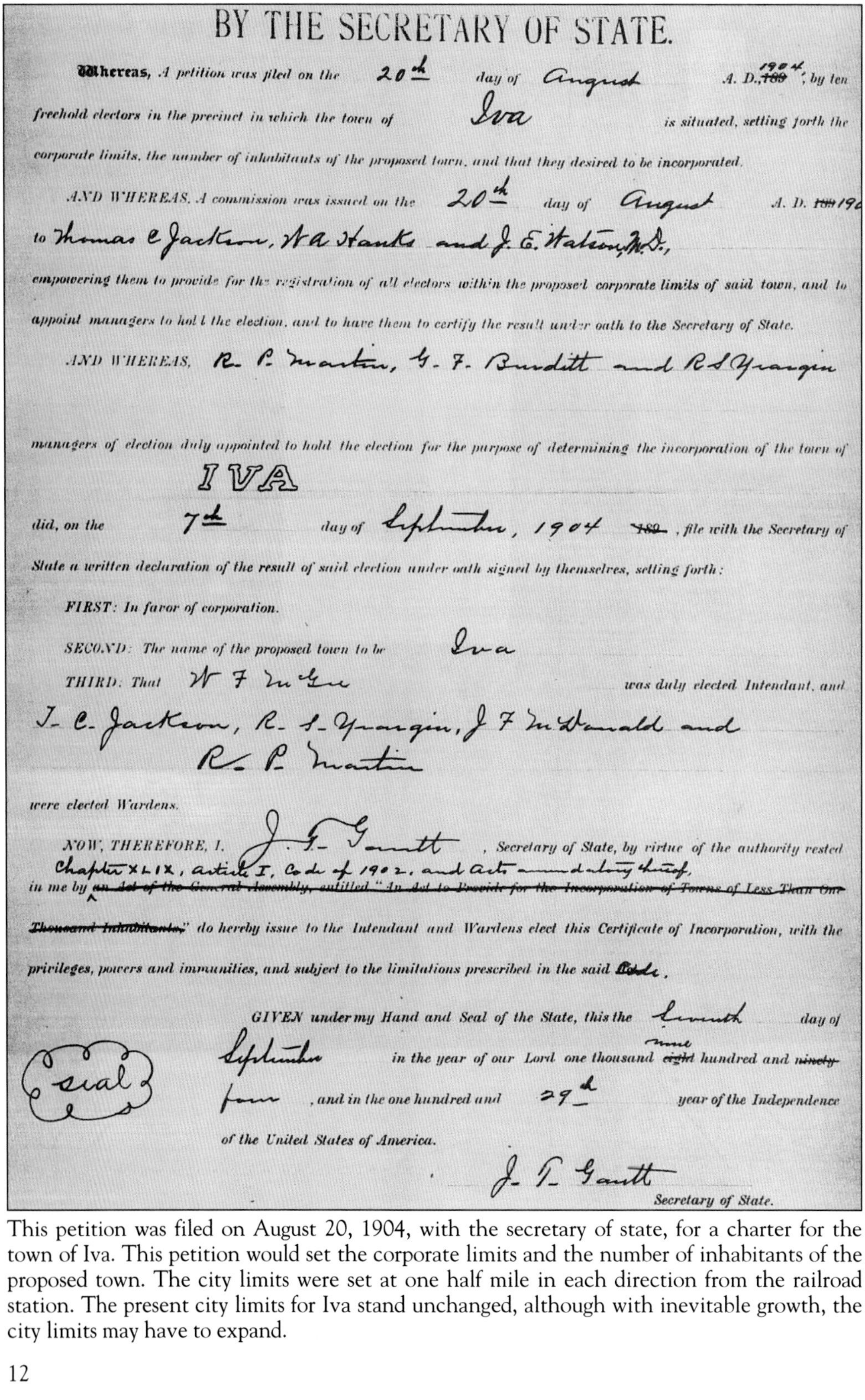

BY THE SECRETARY OF STATE.

Whereas, *A petition was filed on the* 20th *day of* August *A. D.,* ~~189~~ 1904*, by ten freehold electors in the precinct in which the town of* Iva *is situated, setting forth the corporate limits, the number of inhabitants of the proposed town, and that they desired to be incorporated.*

AND WHEREAS, A commission was issued on the 20th *day of* August *A. D.* ~~189~~ 190[illegible]
to Thomas C Jackson, A A Hanks and J. E. Watson, M.D.,
empowering them to provide for the registration of all electors within the proposed corporate limits of said town, and to appoint managers to hold the election, and to have them to certify the result under oath to the Secretary of State.

AND WHEREAS, R. P. Martin, G. F. Burditt and R S Yeargin
managers of election duly appointed to hold the election for the purpose of determining the incorporation of the town of
IVA
did, on the 7th *day of* September, 1904 ~~189~~*, file with the Secretary of State a written declaration of the result of said election under oath signed by themselves, setting forth:*

FIRST: In favor of corporation.

SECOND: The name of the proposed town to be Iva

THIRD: That W F McGee *was duly elected Intendant, and*
T. C. Jackson, R. S. Yeargin, J F McDonald and R. P. Martin
were elected Wardens.

NOW, THEREFORE, I, J. T. Gantt*, Secretary of State, by virtue of the authority vested in me by* Chapter XLIX, article I, Code of 1902, and acts amendatory thereof, ~~an Act of the General Assembly, entitled "An Act to Provide for the Incorporation of Towns of Less Than One Thousand Inhabitants,"~~ *do hereby issue to the Intendant and Wardens elect this Certificate of Incorporation, with the privileges, powers and immunities, and subject to the limitations prescribed in the said* Code.

***GIVEN** under my Hand and Seal of the State, this the* Seventh *day of* September *in the year of our Lord one thousand* ~~eight~~ nine *hundred and* ~~ninety~~ four*, and in the one hundred and* 29th *year of the Independence of the United States of America.*

Seal

J. T. Gantt
Secretary of State.

This petition was filed on August 20, 1904, with the secretary of state, for a charter for the town of Iva. This petition would set the corporate limits and the number of inhabitants of the proposed town. The city limits were set at one half mile in each direction from the railroad station. The present city limits for Iva stand unchanged, although with inevitable growth, the city limits may have to expand.

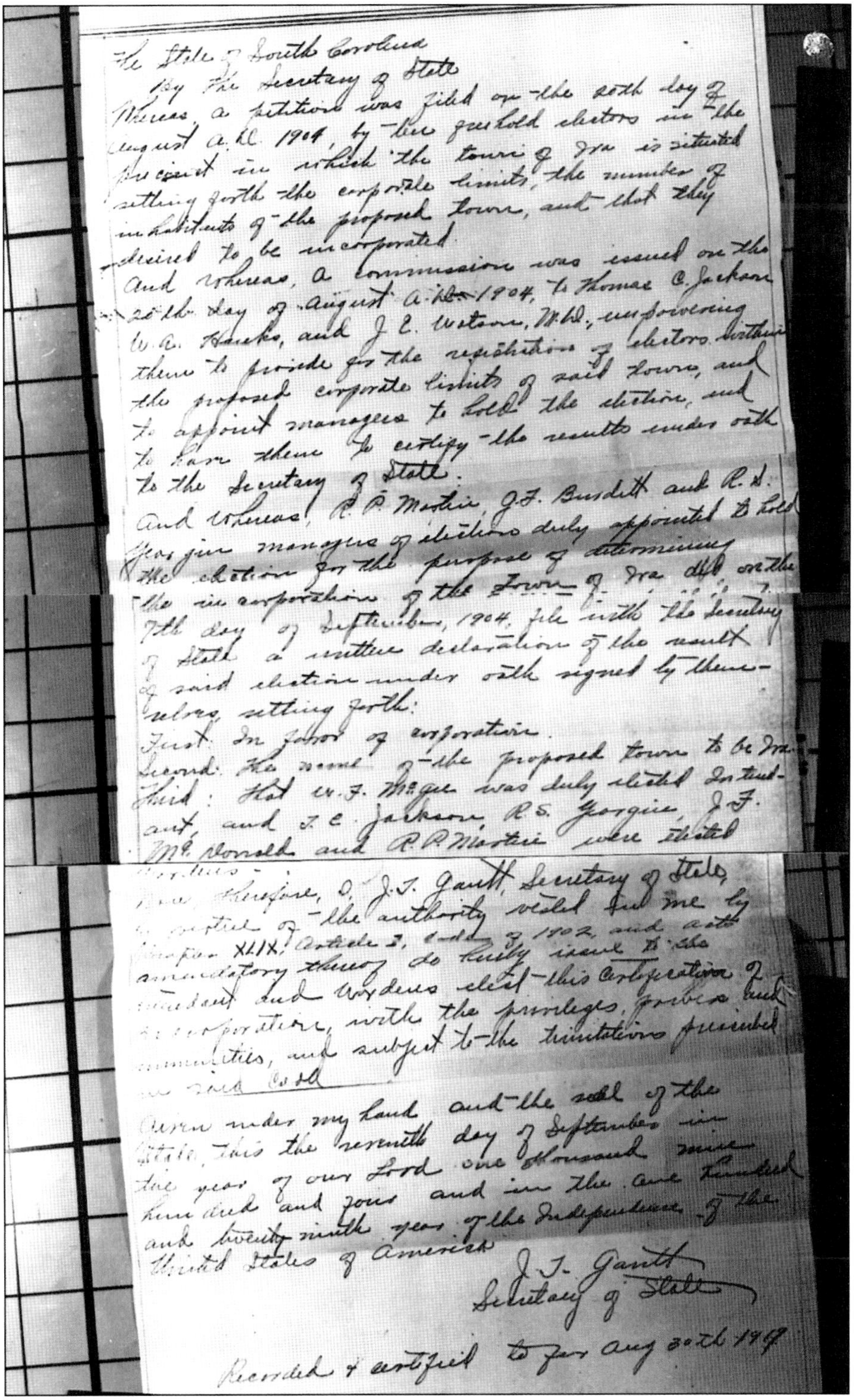

The State of South Carolina
By the Secretary of State

Whereas, a petition was filed on the 20th day of August A.D. 1904, by the freehold electors in the precinct in which the town of Iva is situated setting forth the corporate limits, the number of inhabitants of the proposed town, and that they desired to be incorporated.

And whereas, a commission was issued on the 20th day of August A.D. 1904, to Thomas C. Jackson, W.A. Hawks, and J.E. Watson, M.D., empowering them to provide for the registration of electors within the proposed corporate limits of said town, and to appoint managers to hold the election, and to have them to certify the results under oath to the Secretary of State.

And whereas, R.P. Martin, J.F. Burdett and R.S. Yeargin managers of election duly appointed to hold the election for the purpose of determining the incorporation of the town of Iva did on the 7th day of September, 1904, file with the Secretary of State a written declaration of the result of said election under oath signed by themselves, setting forth:

First: In favor of corporation.
Second: The name of the proposed town to be Iva.
Third: That W.F. McGee was duly elected Intendant, and T.C. Jackson, R.S. Yeargin, J.F. McDonald and R.P. Martin were elected Wardens.

Now, therefore, I, J.T. Gantt, Secretary of State, by virtue of the authority vested in me by [illegible] Chapter XLIX, Article 3, Code of 1902, and acts amendatory thereof do hereby issue to the Intendant and Wardens elect this certificate of incorporation, with the privileges, powers and [illegible] communities, and subject to the limitations prescribed in said Code.

Given under my hand and the seal of the State, this the seventh day of September in the year of our Lord one thousand nine hundred and four and in the one hundred and twenty-ninth year of the Independence of the United States of America.

J.T. Gantt
Secretary of State

Recorded & certified to fees Aug 30th 19[illegible]

This is a copy of the original charter for Iva. W.F. McGee was the first mayor of Iva. The first aldermen were T.C. Jackson, J.F. McDonald, R.S. Yeargin, and R.P. Martin.

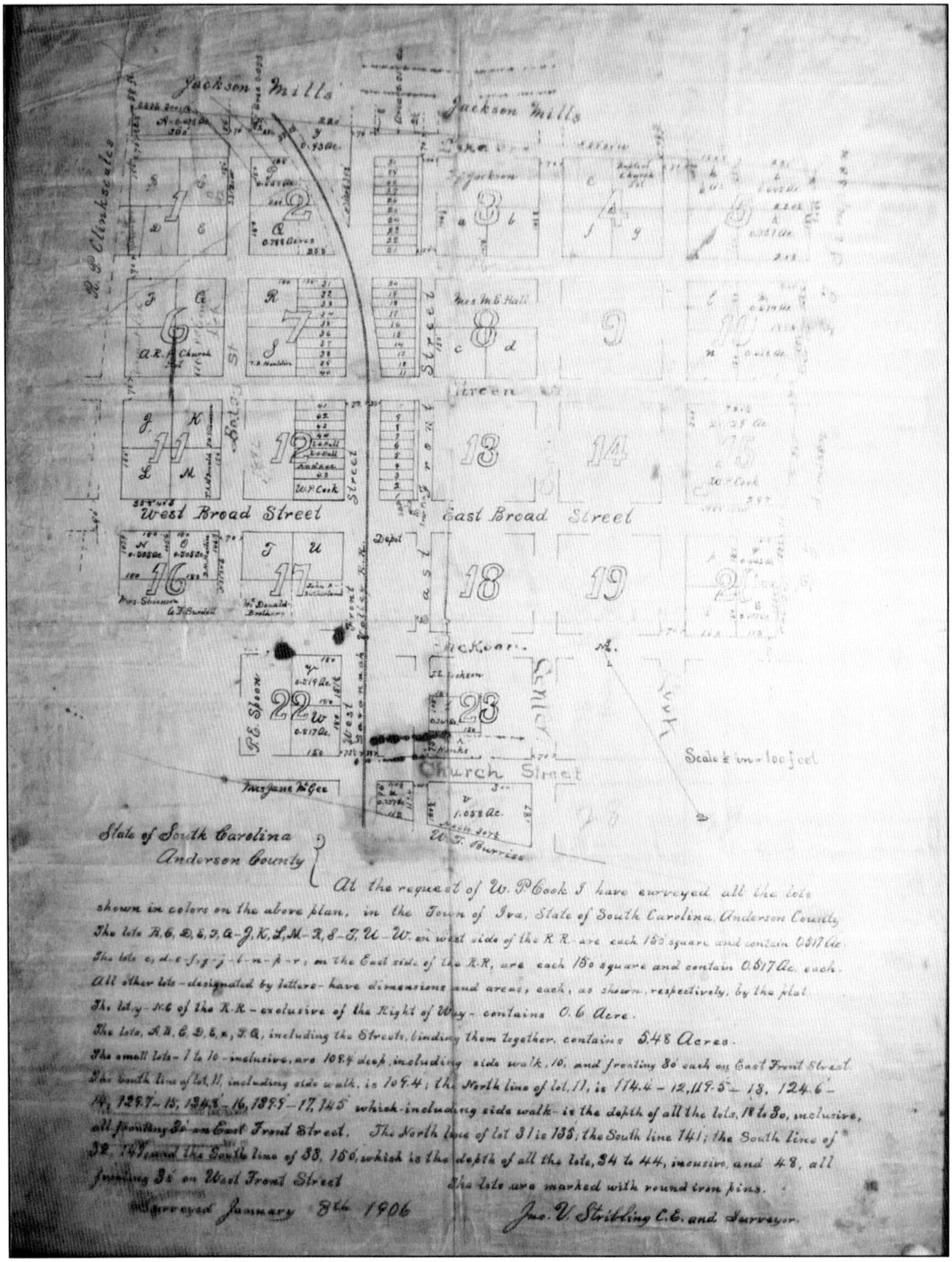

This hand-drawn map shows the streets of Iva as they were, some years ago.

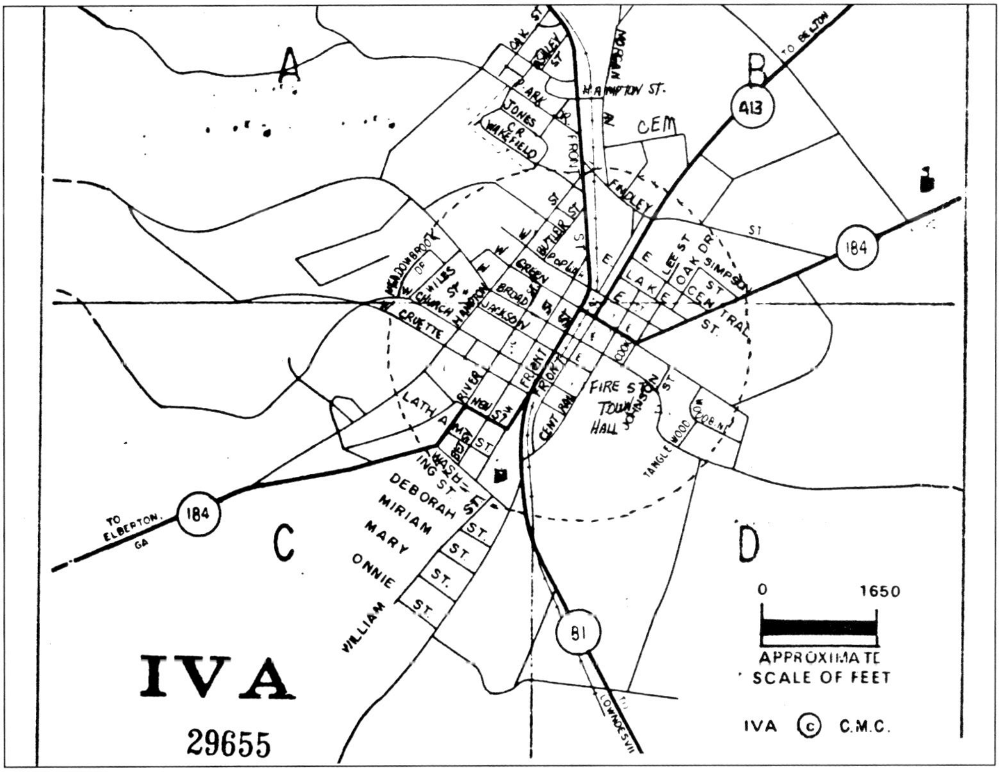

This is a scale drawing of Iva that shows the names of streets. This was used by the Postal Service after the zip code went into effect for the town of Iva.

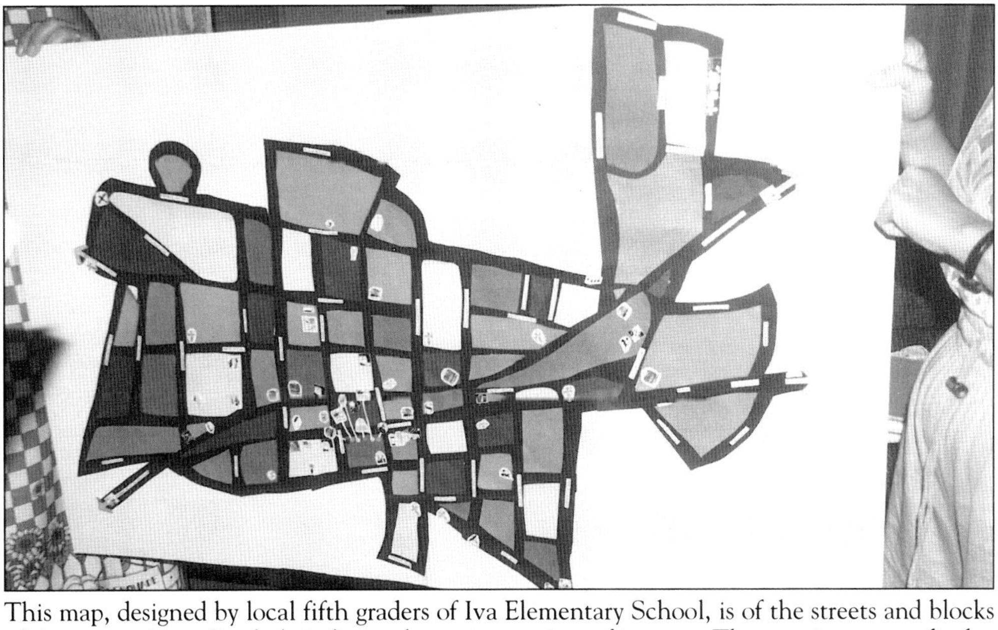

This map, designed by local fifth graders of Iva Elementary School, is of the streets and blocks of the town of Iva. Symbols indicate the various points of interest. The map is now on display in the REVIVA building in Iva. Involvement in this project helped to create interest in the community for the children who participated.

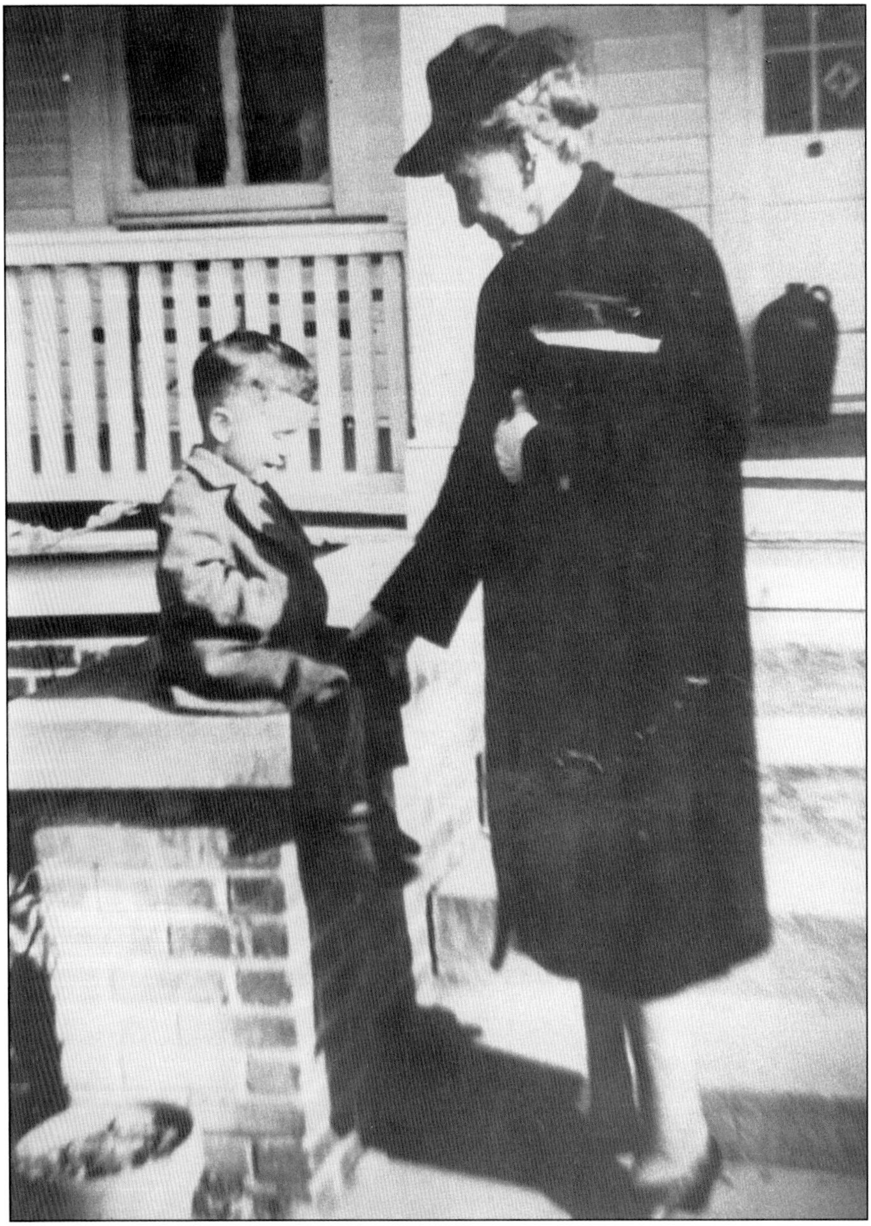

Iva Cook Bryson is seen here in front of her home in Iva as she chats with Charles Evans, her grand-nephew, who grew up to become a minister and serve as a missionary overseas. Although Mrs. Bryson had no children of her own, she was a great influence on others, young and old alike, as a dedicated Christian. A story, relating to Mrs. Bryson, is told by Aileen Alexander, a former student at Iva High School. The senior class was presenting *Aunt Samantha Rules the Roost*, and Mrs. Alexander was playing Aunt Samantha, a spinster and a very strong-willed person. The costumes required were from a certain era, and someone suggested Mrs. Bryson be asked if she could lend a helping hand. Mrs. Alexander was invited into Mrs. Bryson's home to select several dresses, hats, high-top shoes, handbags, shawls, and undergarments. Mrs. Alexander played the role of Aunt Samantha very smartly dressed, and all due to Mrs. Bryson's kindness.

Two

All Around Iva

Jackson Mills

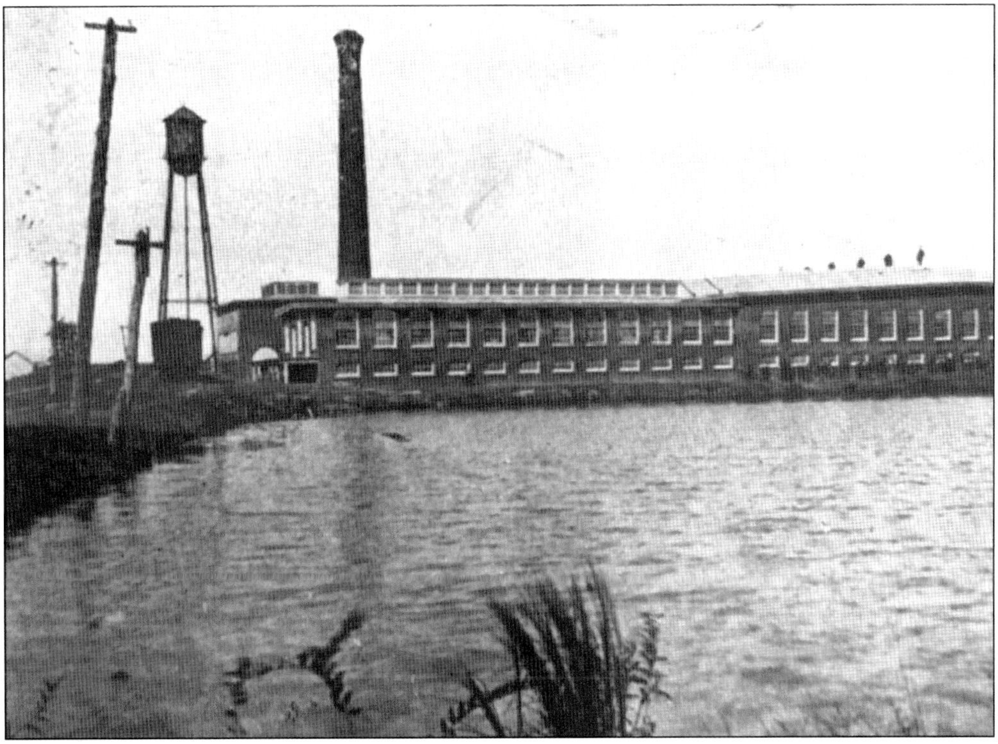

Jackson Mill was once one of the most outstanding cotton mills in the South. The mill was organized, c. 1904, by Thomas C. Jackson, who served as treasurer and manager, D.P. McBrayer, and others. Alfred Moore served as president. The mill once had 150 cottages for its 1,500-or-more inhabitants in Iva. This was a major growth spurt for the Iva community, occurring as the industrial revolution took off.

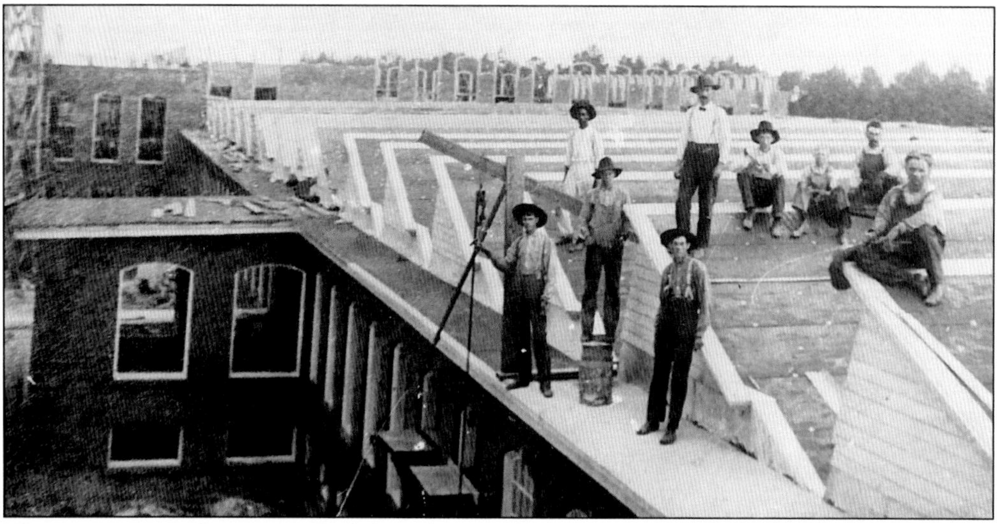

This picture was taken in 1905 while Jackson Mill No. 1 was under construction. Local people were hired by the stockholders of the new plant, and because there was no electricity at that time, all of the work was completed using manual labor and hand-operated tools. Jackson Mill No. 2 was built some years later at Wellford, South Carolina. There have been major improvements and additions to the mills at various times.

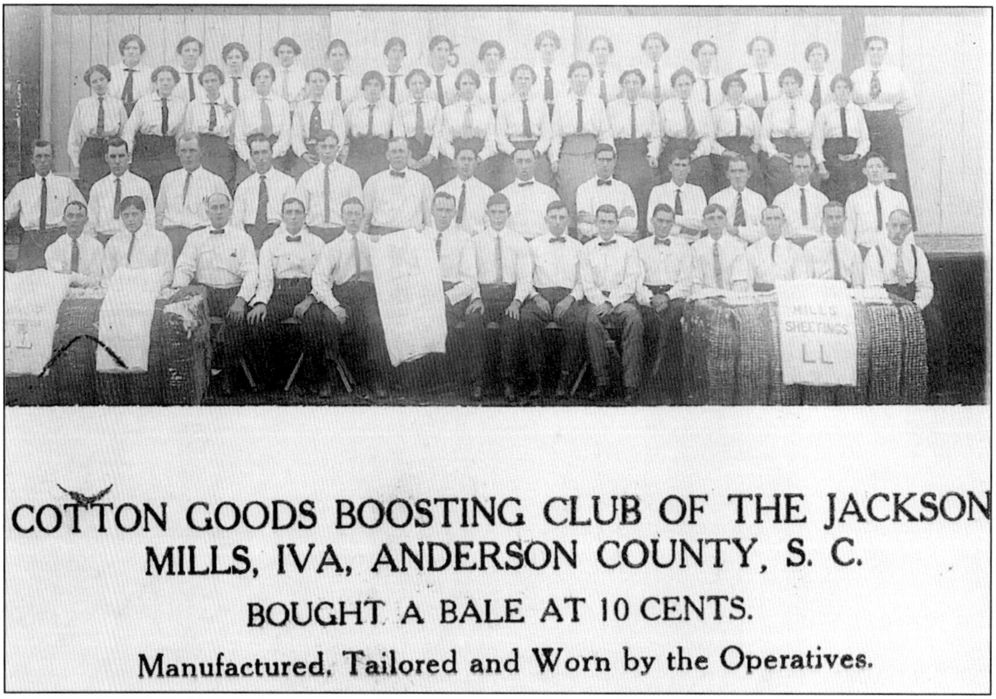

This group of mill employees tailored and wore the outfits that are pictured. Some of the Jackson Mill workers shown here in no particular order are Robert McBride, Melvin Jones, George Gibson, Styles Cobb, Ernest Guest, Sam Gambrell, Porter Parnell, Reece Parnell, Addis Ellis, Mr. Kellar, Charlie Hall, Cleburn A. Wiles, Ernest Seigler, Lura Simpson McBride, Allie Hall, Yancy Burton Sutherland, Lois Jones Simpson, Susie Wiles Harris, Marie Campbell Montgomery, and Theola Burton Wiles. Can someone give "REVIVA" the names of others?

During the early days of textiles, many men were hired to play baseball and given employment to work in the mill. The Jackson Mills once had an excellent baseball facility, with covered bleachers, located on New Street in Iva. The mill team always had sharp-looking uniforms, and people of all ages enjoyed going to the games.

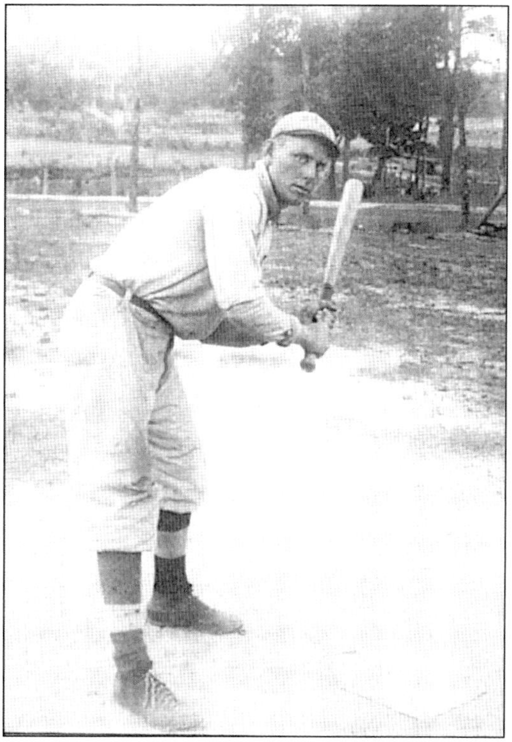

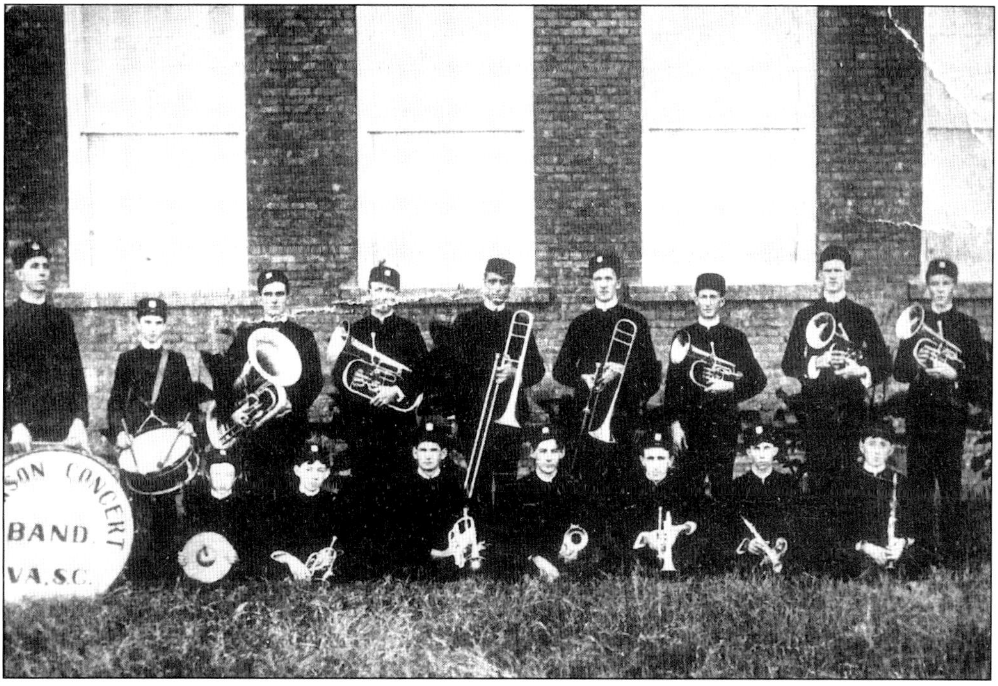

The Jackson Mill Concert Band was another asset for the Iva community. Back then, the mill took a great deal of interest in their town and surrounding community. This band was one of several organizations formed by Jackson Mill. Having musical or athletic abilities helped to ensure success in obtaining a job at Jackson Mill.

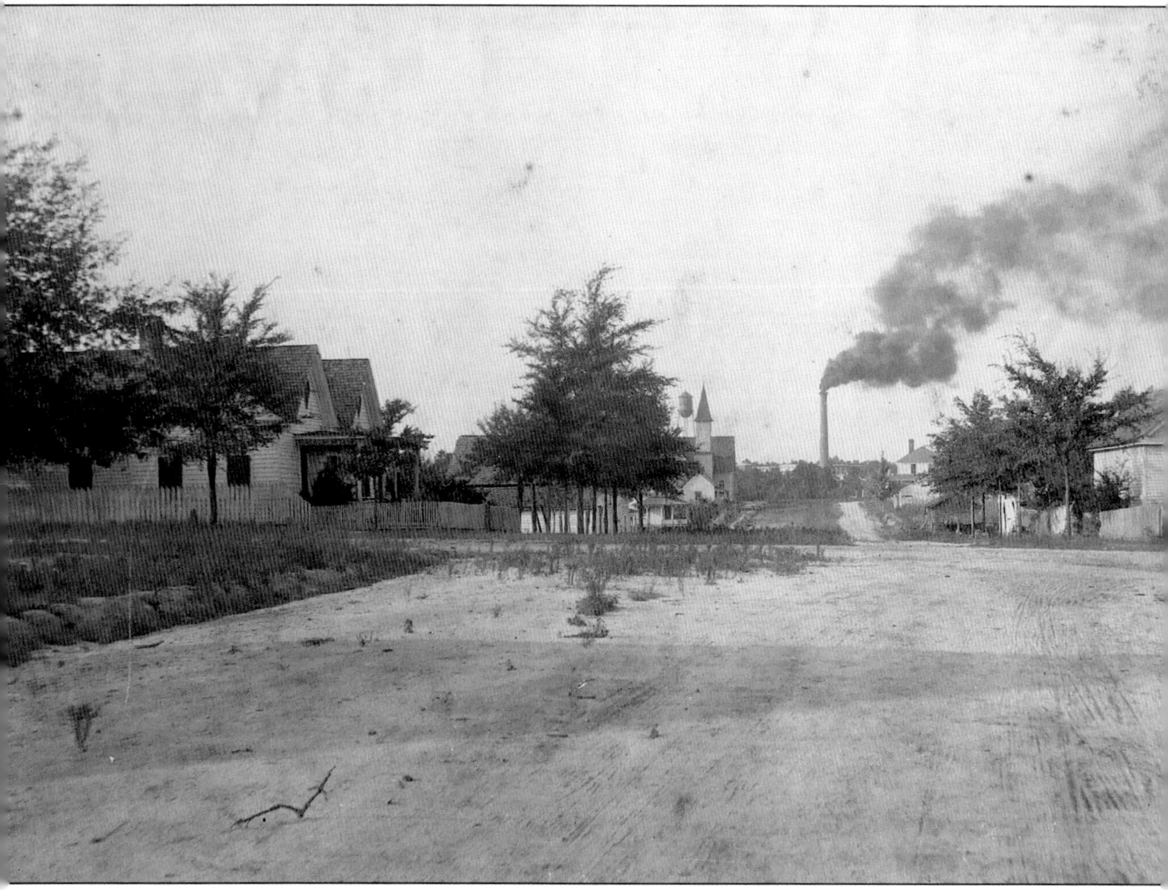

Jackson Mill Village homes are pictured here, with the mill smokestack in the background. This scene is at the intersection of Betsy Street and Jackson Street, looking toward the Iva Associate Reformed Presbyterian Church (center left) and the mill. The old Iva High School (not visible in this photo) was on the left of this intersection, where the new Iva Community Center now stands. The white-frame Associate Reformed Presbyterian Church is now a beautiful brick structure with a social hall and a manse. The frame house on the left burned, and the brick home of B.H. and Annette Holley is now located on this site.

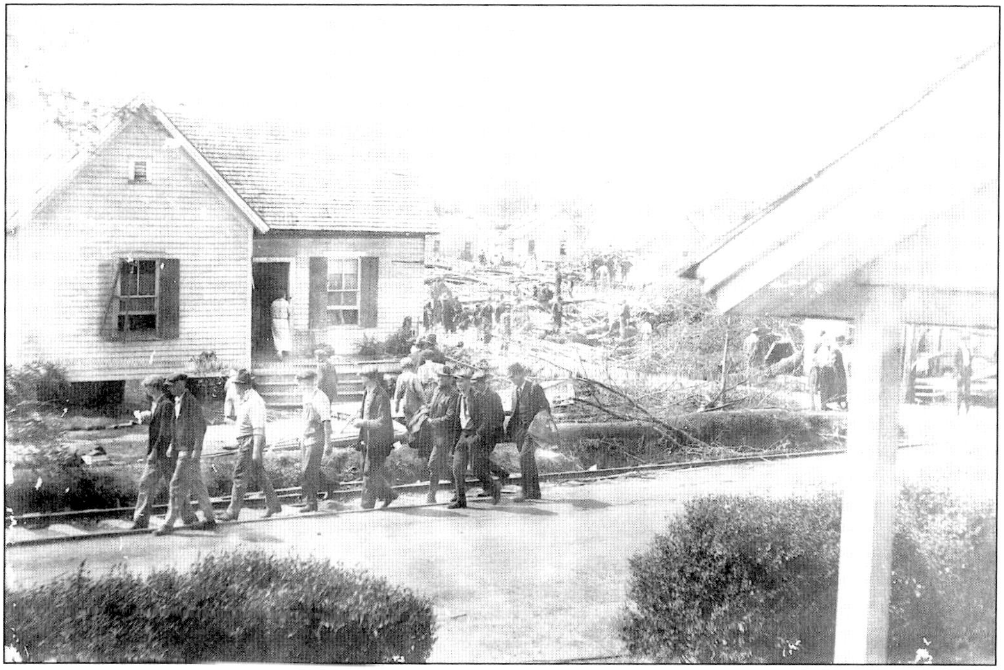

A group of men are seen here *c.* 1908, carrying iron rails to build a spur railroad track to Jackson Mill. This spur track was necessary to allow the train to bring coal to fire the furnace that made the power for the mill. The track also transported raw materials into and finished products out of the plant.

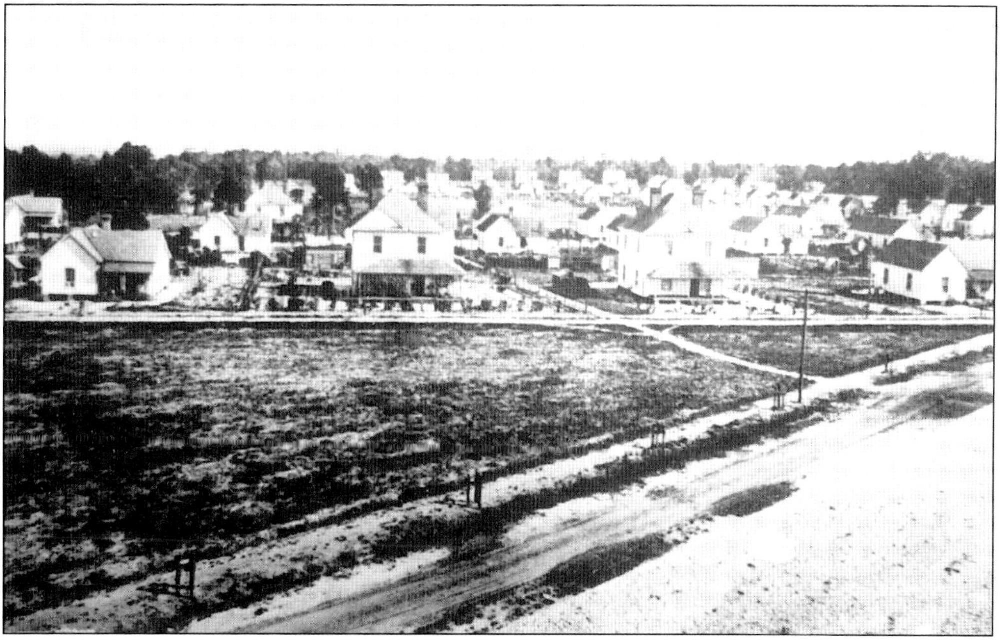

This picture shows the meeting of agriculture and industry, with the combination of the Jackson Mill Village and a field of cotton in the foreground. Cotton, called "King Cotton," was the number-one cash crop in the South, and so it was an advantage to live near a cotton mill. The mill would buy bales of cotton directly from the farmers.

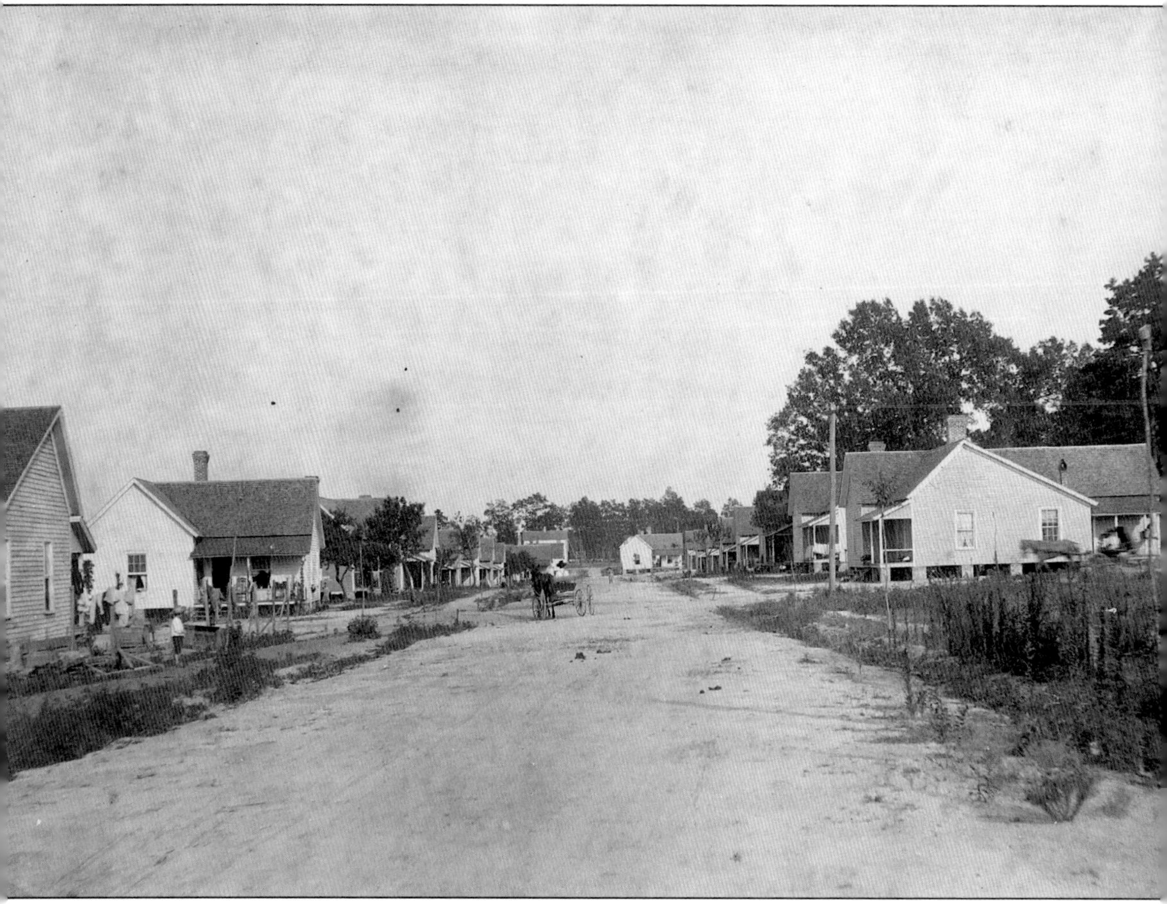

This picture shows housing at Jackson Mill during the horse-and-buggy days. The workers' houses were three or four rooms. The second hands' (now called shift supervisors) houses were five or more rooms. A big two-story house above the mill, on Morgan Avenue, was for the superintendent. Water and sewage were furnished, and rent was 25¢ per week, per room. In the early 1950s, the mill houses were sold to employees.

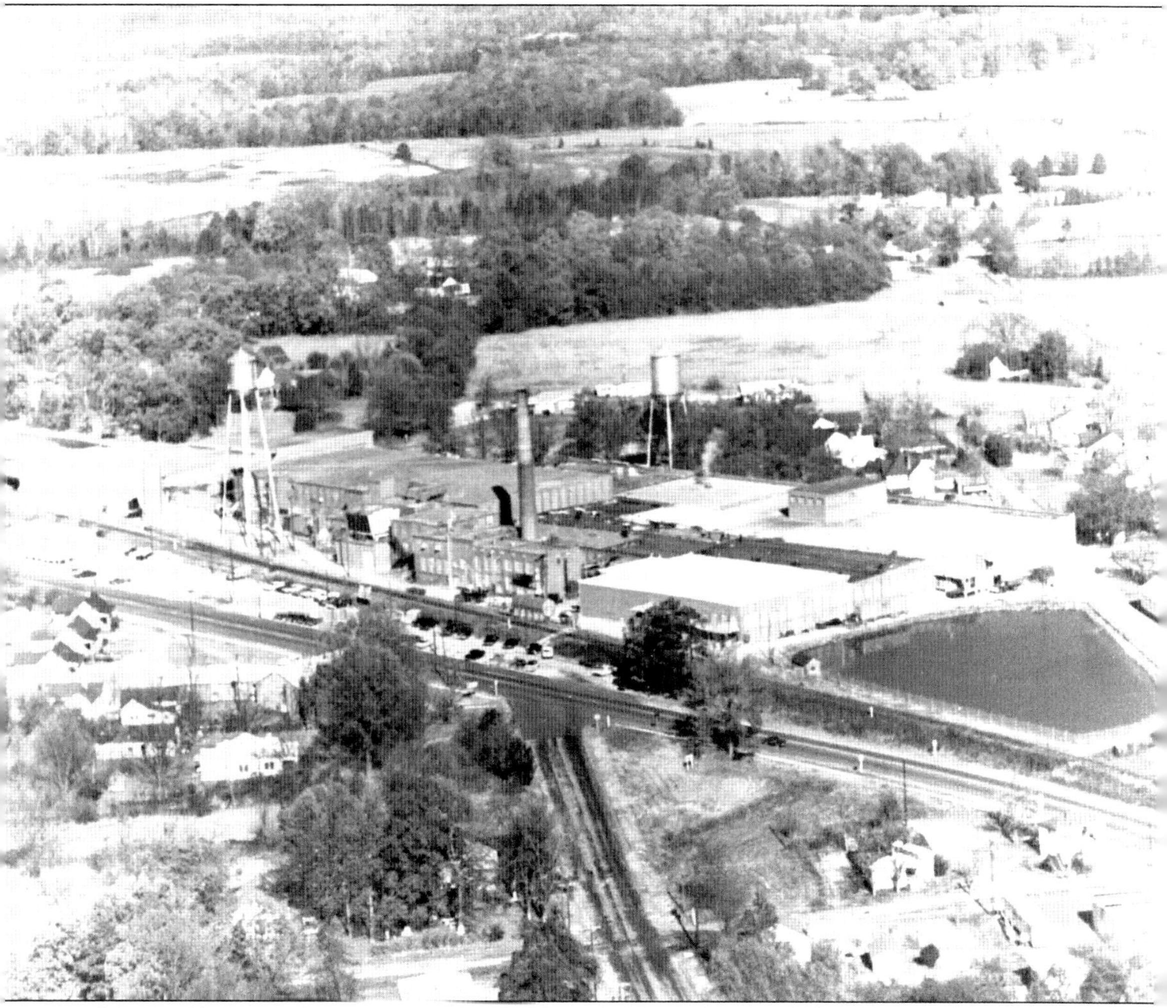

Jackson Mill is seen here, as it looked in later years, when it employed over 490 people from Iva and the surrounding area, as well as from Georgia. One time, the bridge across the Savannah River to Hartwell, Georgia, was damaged and put out of commission for auto travel for many months. During this time, Jackson Mills employees from Iva would meet their Georgia co-workers at the bridge, where they would walk across, and then ride to the mill. This cut down on a detour of many miles by car.

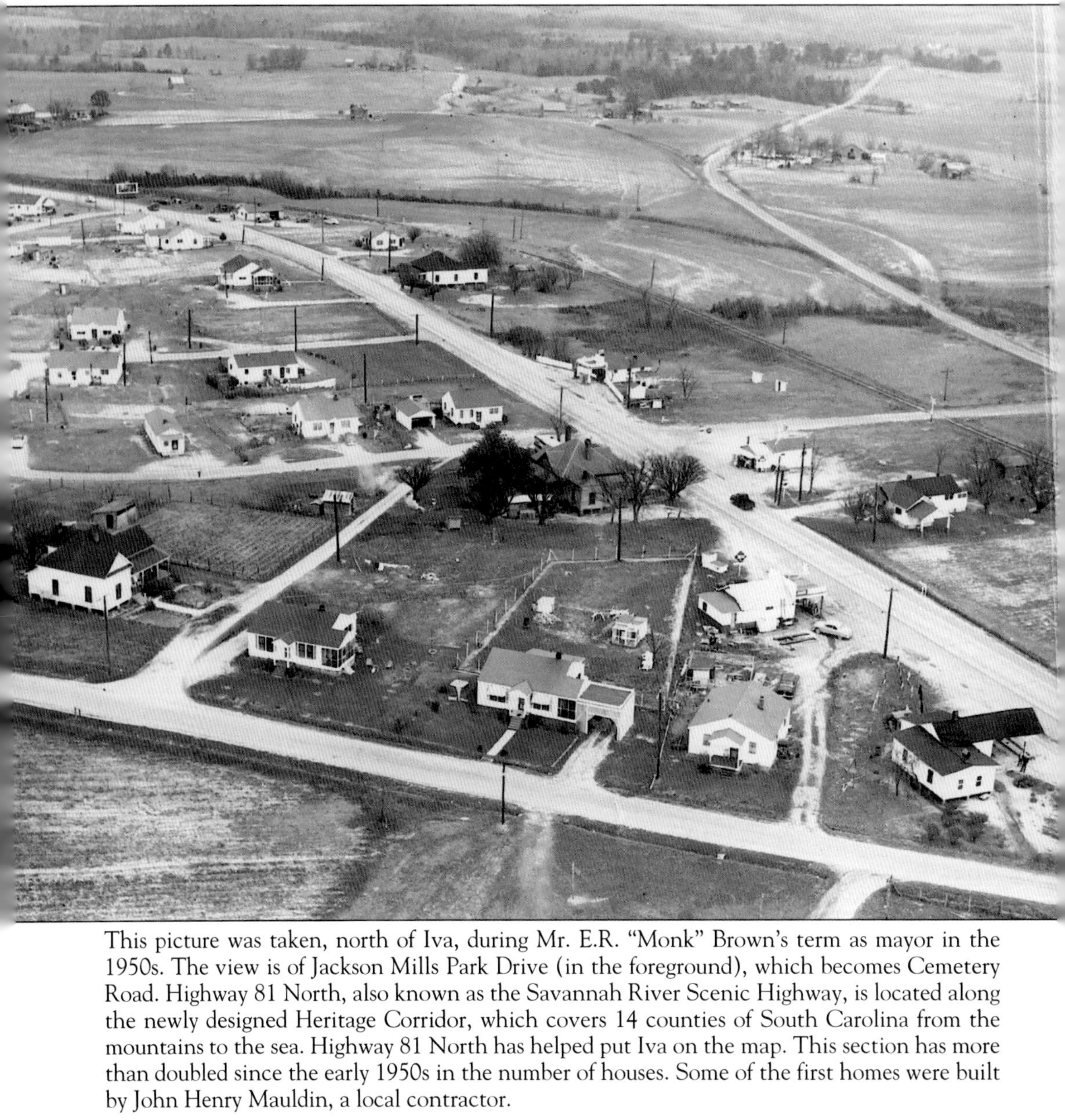

This picture was taken, north of Iva, during Mr. E.R. "Monk" Brown's term as mayor in the 1950s. The view is of Jackson Mills Park Drive (in the foreground), which becomes Cemetery Road. Highway 81 North, also known as the Savannah River Scenic Highway, is located along the newly designed Heritage Corridor, which covers 14 counties of South Carolina from the mountains to the sea. Highway 81 North has helped put Iva on the map. This section has more than doubled since the early 1950s in the number of houses. Some of the first homes were built by John Henry Mauldin, a local contractor.

Three

Merchants and Area Businesses

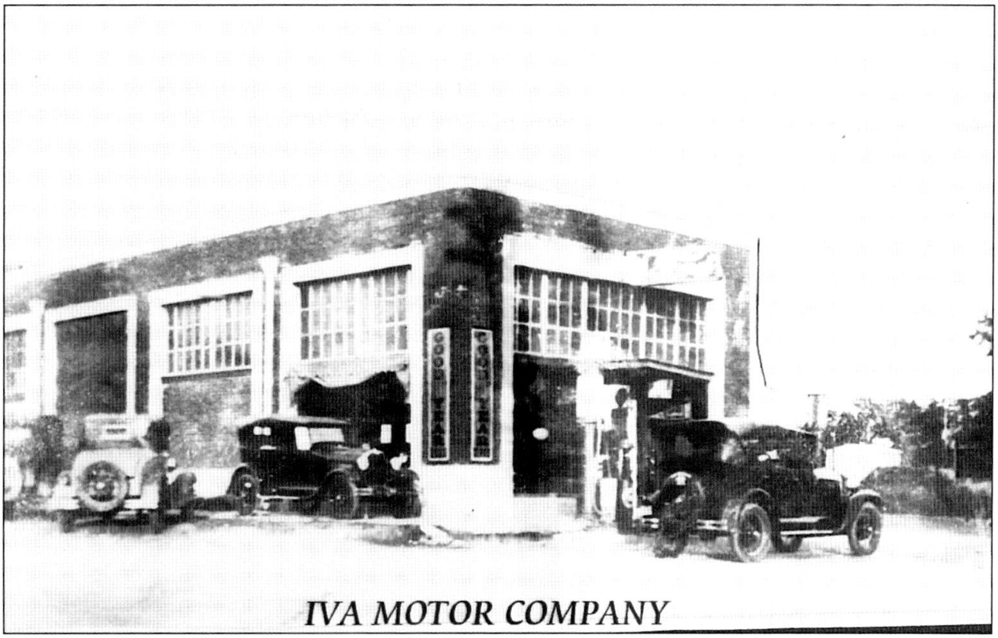

This building housed the Iva Motor Company in the early 1920s. It once housed a jail, and the barred windows and concrete floor remain in the back of the building. "Hawk" Evans tells how the mileage on the cars would get checked. According to Mr. Evans, they were to drive the cars on a special route and see how far a gallon of gas would go, then more gas would be brought to them and they would drive the cars back to the motor company. In 1953, the Epstein family, from New York, opened a blouse plant here. In 1999, a new occupant, Poly Plastics Iva, was welcomed.

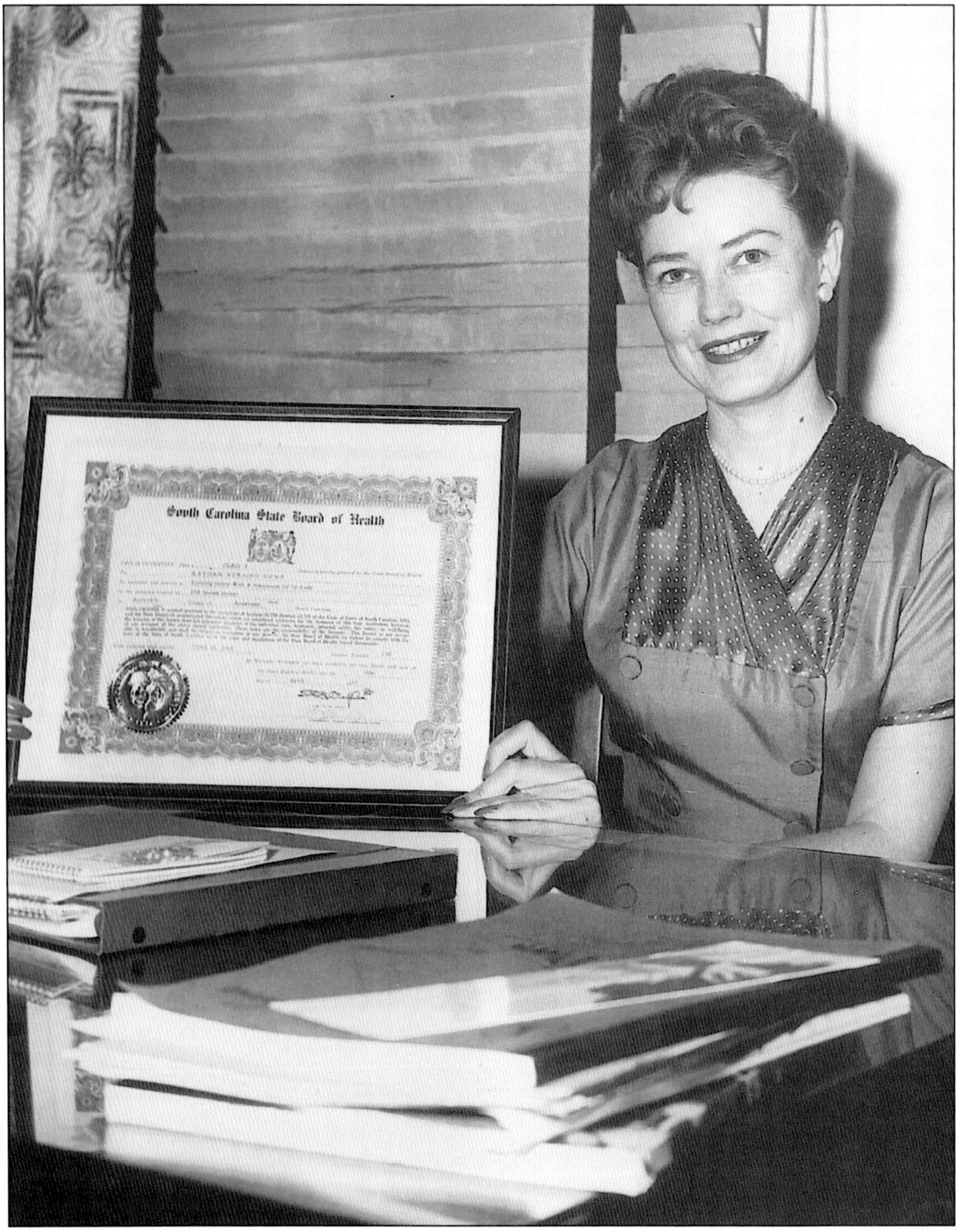

Lillian Latham, a native of Iva, is the former owner of Golden Acres Nursing Home, which opened in 1960 in Iva. Golden Acres Nursing Home was the first nursing home in Anderson County. In 1962, Ms. Latham renovated St. Mary Hospital, on James Street in Anderson, into her second nursing home facility, known as Latham Nursing Home. Ms. Latham's sister Lonita Dunn was the first administrator, assisted by Dwaine Latham (their brother). Annie Cox Cannon was the first patient admitted to the home.

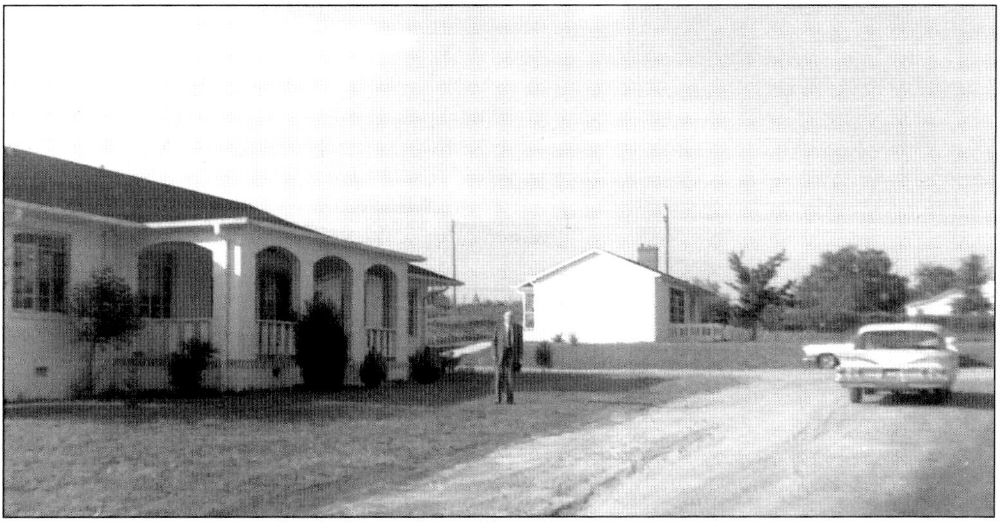

During the late 1950s, Ms. Latham was appalled to learn that an aging relative was a patient in the State Hospital in Columbia, for the one reason that there was a lack of suitable nursing facilities elsewhere. Ms. Latham was motivated by this to establish Golden Acres Nursing Home, which was the first "Class One" facility in Anderson County, located on Broad Street in Iva. The business, with ten patient beds, was purchased by Lillian Latham from Dr. C.S. Breedin in March of 1960. In approximately five years, she added 16 beds, and today there is a new 60-bed facility that was built between 1994 and 1995. Ms. Latham sold the business on May 31, 1995, and it is now known as Willow Creek.

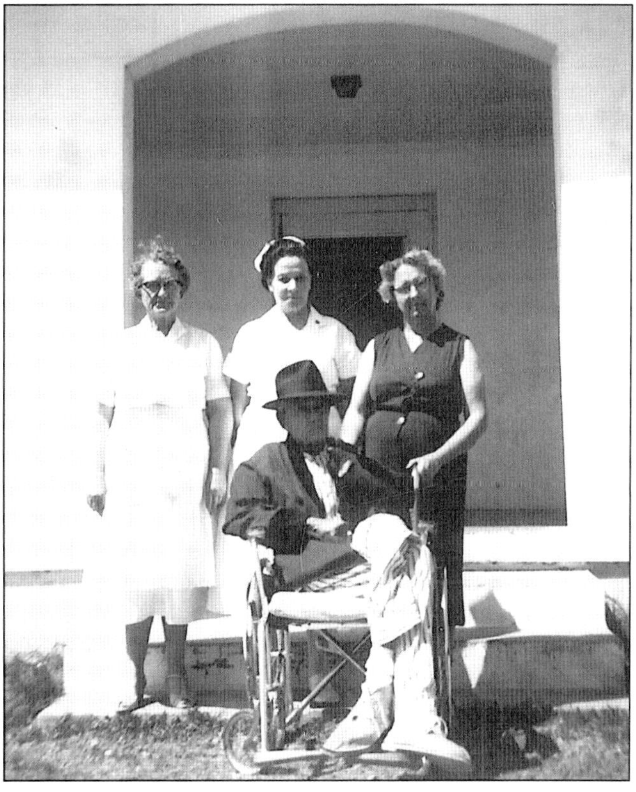

Pictured here, from left to right are, as follows: Mrs. Mary C. Latham, vice president of Latham Nursing Home and the mother of Lillian L. Latham; Mrs. Maude Stilwell; Sandra Jacob, RN; and John Latham (seated in wheelchair), who was Miss Latham's uncle, as well as being the first admitted male patient. Pallie Yeargin, not pictured here, was the first female patient, and Mrs. Elizabeth Tucker, not pictured here, was the first administrator for the facility.

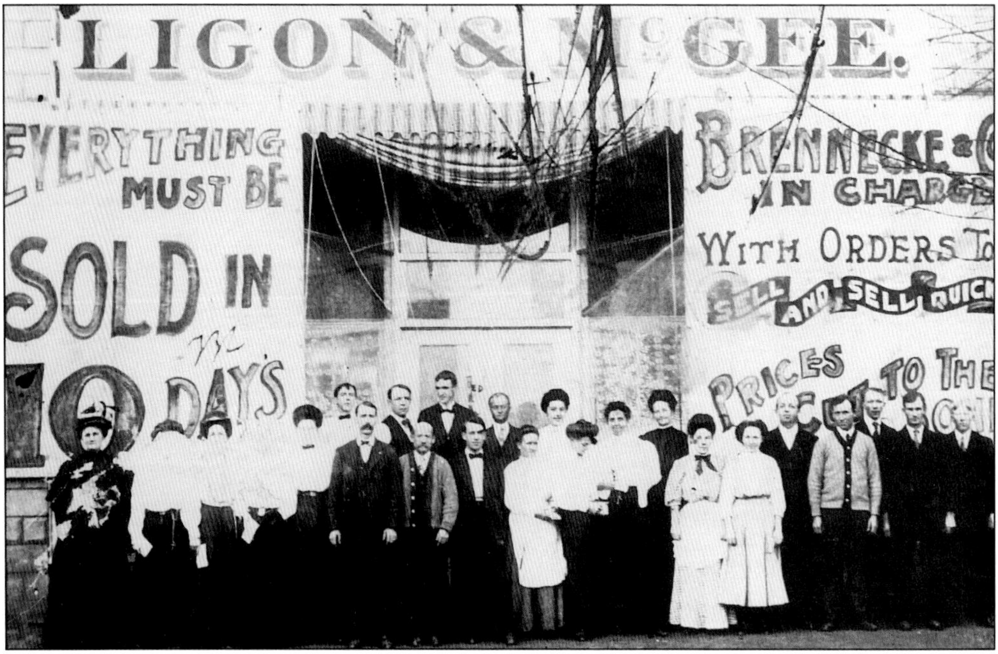

Ligon & McGee, the general merchandise store, held a prominent place in the growing community of Iva. Following an advertised sale, Mr. McGee moved to Anderson, and Joe Ligon operated a thriving general mercantile store for many years. Shown below, on a very cold day, are men (no ladies, for some reason) coming out for "bargains" during the auction sale of Ligon & McGee, around 1909.

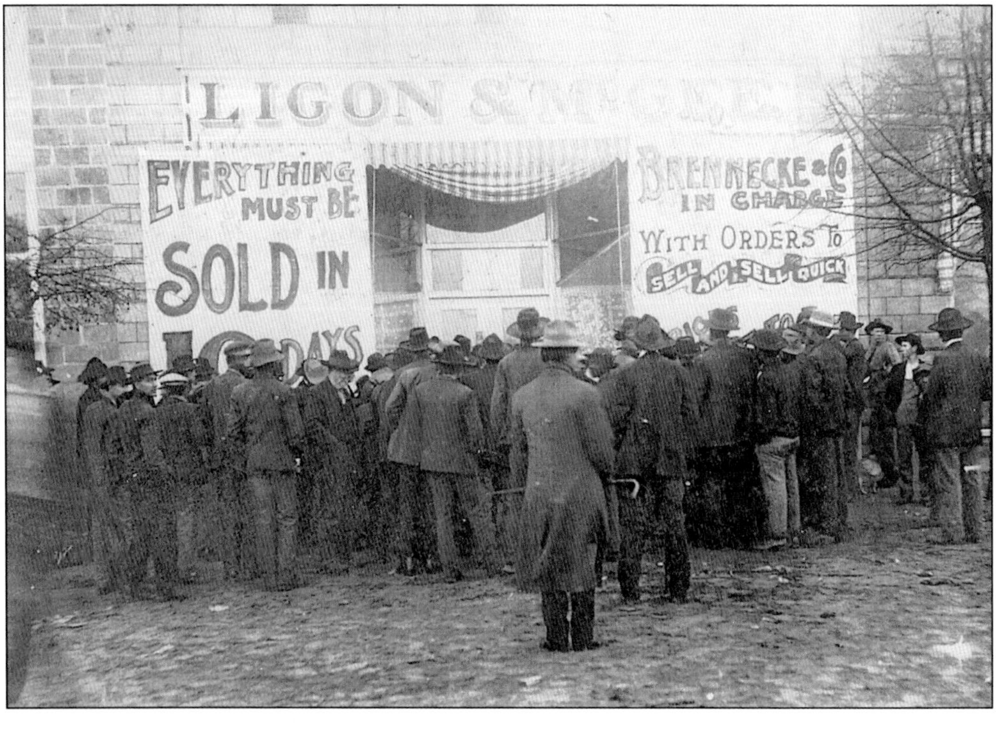

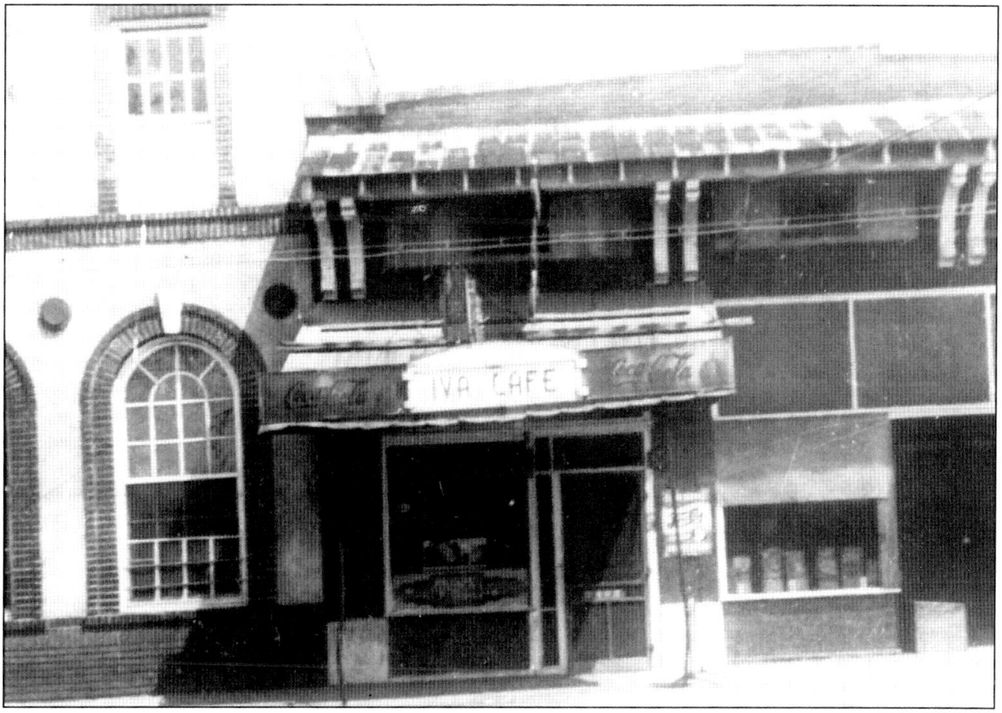

The Iva Café was owned and operated by Maurice and Christine Scott Lopez. Opened in 1935, the business moved next door (right) in 1949 and operated there until 1978. It served as a meeting place for youth, similar to that of the *Happy Days* television series, and it even offered curb service.

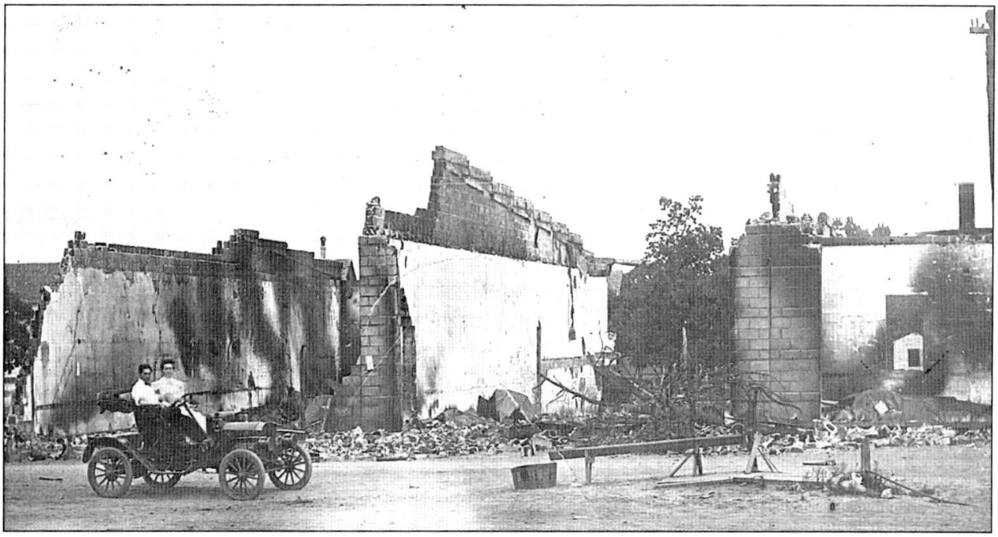

This is the first automobile to come to Iva. Several Iva citizens were treated to an unusual sight on the morning of May 12, 1904, when this automobile came through Iva from Hartwell, Georgia. The occupants of the car were several businessmen from Hartwell. It took two hours to make the trip from Hartwell, but "Dat thing was shore hittin it." It is interesting to note that the burned buildings in the background are where Brown's 5 & 10 variety store, once known as "The Brick Range," now stands on East Jackson Street.

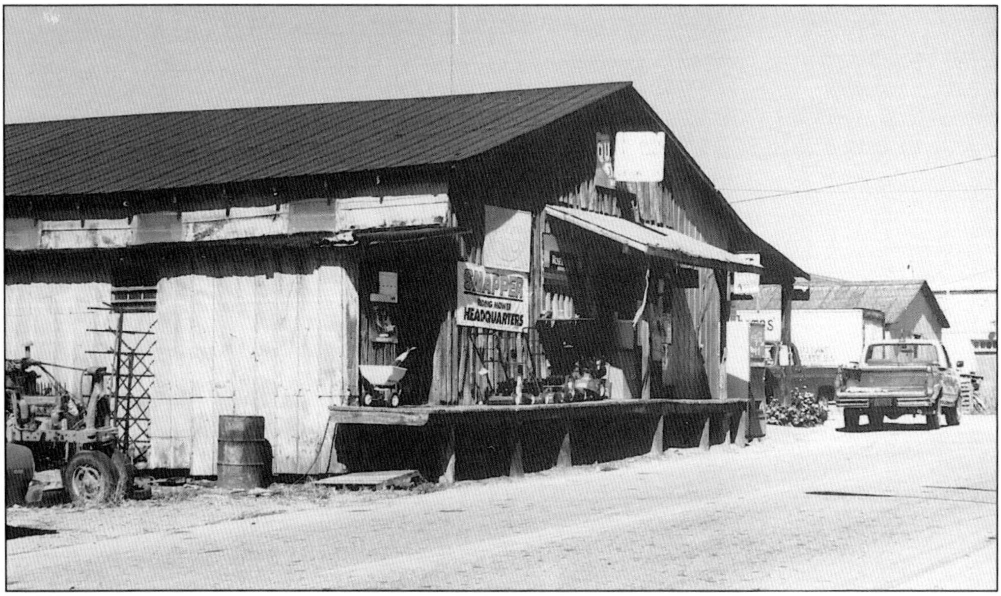

J.B. Thomas & Son Warehouse opened in 1896. It has been in the Thomas family for three generations, and under its current operators, Walter and Helen Wiles Thomas, it is still in operation today. The warehouse, located in Iva on the corner of West Front Street and East Front Street, serves farmers and many others from far and near. Supplies of all kinds can be found and sold here.

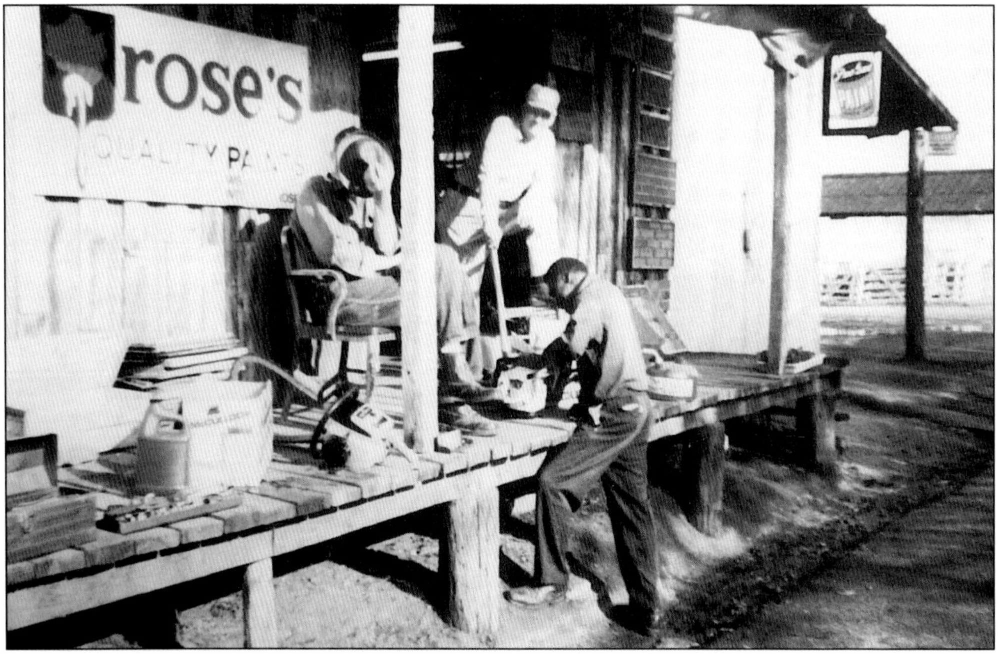

From left to right, Raymond Ozmint (with the hat over his face), Walter Thomas, and Wallace Allen are shown shooting the breeze at J.B. Thomas & Son warehouse in 1978. This store is an interesting place to go, and people go there for bedding plants, seeds, farm machine parts, and building supplies. Occasionally, someone may stop by to exchange ideas regarding their gardens and crops.

A real "pot-belly stove" still heats the J.B. Thomas & Son Warehouse/hardware store in downtown Iva during the winter to keep customers warm. This is their only means of heating. Years ago, these heaters were used in schools and churches, but today they are relics. A visit to this store can be a very interesting experience, as well as an opportunity to "go back in time."

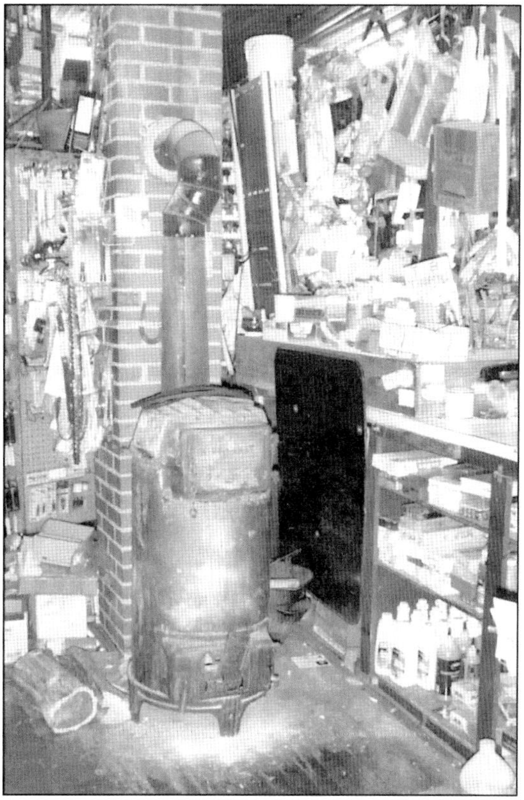

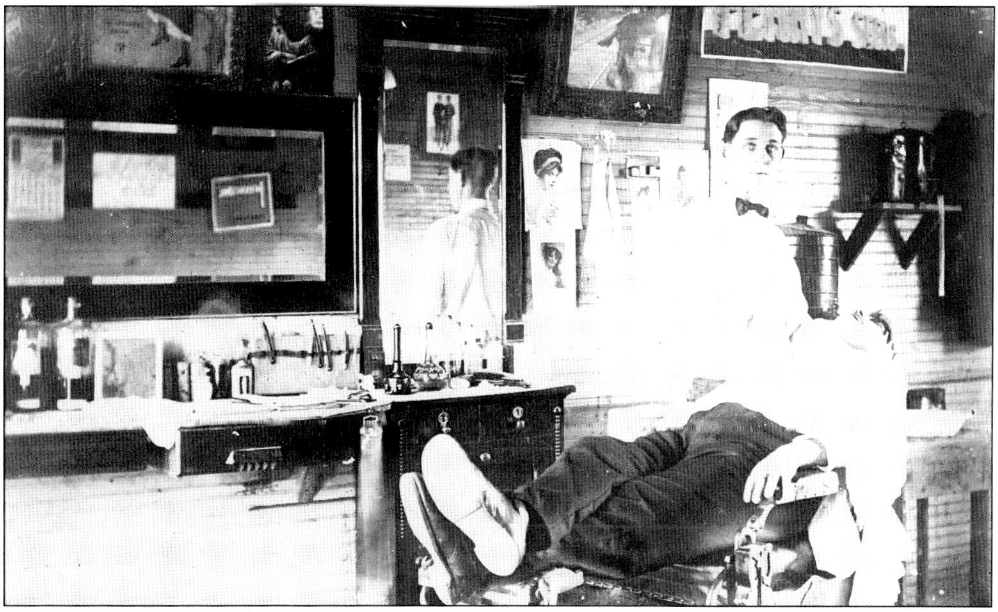

Mr. Lon Bryant owned a barbershop in Iva in the early 1920s. His shop was located on the corner next to Smith's store, just behind the old Dixie store. He cut hair for adults and children, boys and girls. He moved to Calhoun Falls, South Carolina, in 1937 and later moved to Lowndesville, South Carolina, where he lived until his death in 1962.

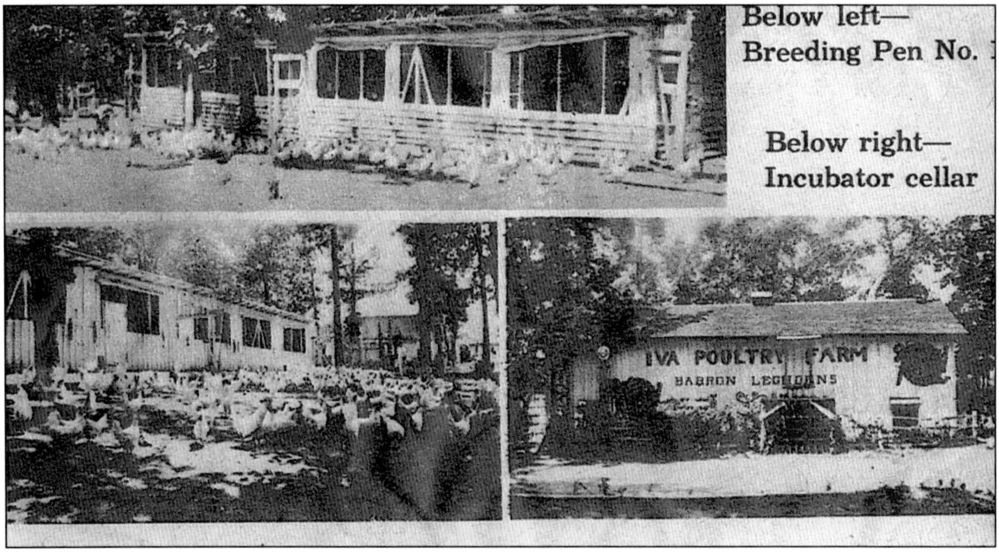

The Iva Poultry Farm, located in Iva, was owned and operated by T.C. Gray. Mr. Gray had built up one of the largest and most modern poultry farms in the state, with over 5,000 chickens in the hatchery at all times.

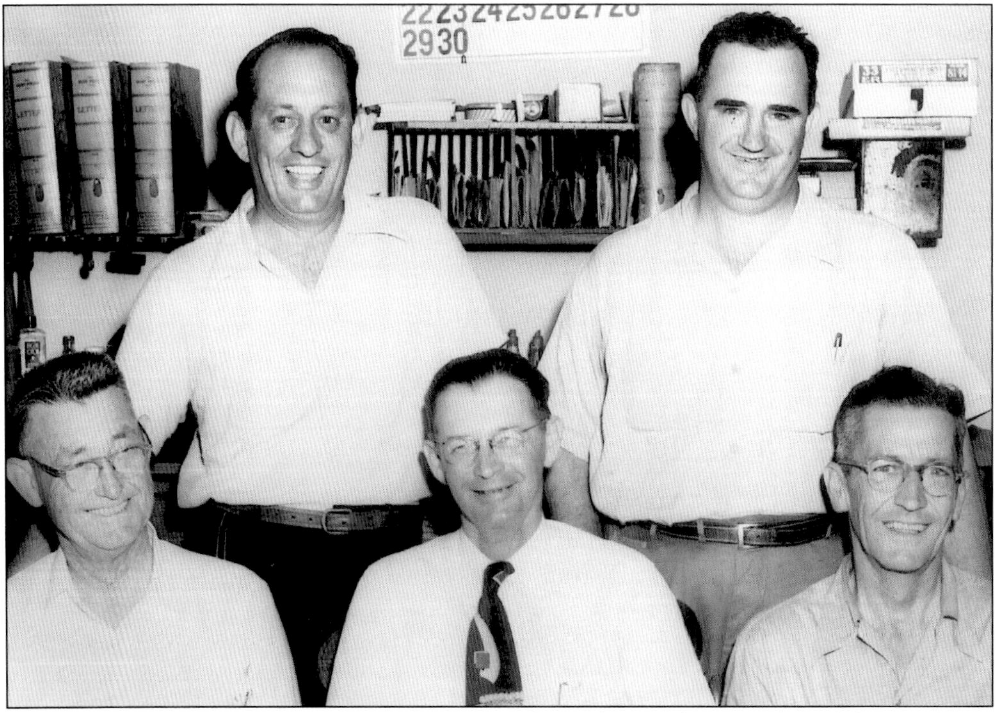

Members of the Iva Town Council of 1952 are shown here. They are, from left to right, as follows: (front row) Grover C. Smith Sr.; E.R. Brown Sr., mayor; and Ellis Loftis; (back row) Ethel Dixon and Ernest Evans. Ernest Evans is the only living member of this town council group. Today, Iva's council still consists of a mayor and four council persons.

Jesse James Cook was the owner of Cook's Bus Line for many years. The business operated from 1927 until the mid-'60s. It made daily runs from Iva to Calhoun Falls to Anderson, making numerous stops along the way. Many people, during this time, depended on the bus line as their only means of transportation. Mr. Cook was married to Bessie Terry Cook, and they had two children, Cleo Todd and Dell Cook. J.J. Cook was a U.S. postal carrier until his death in 1968.

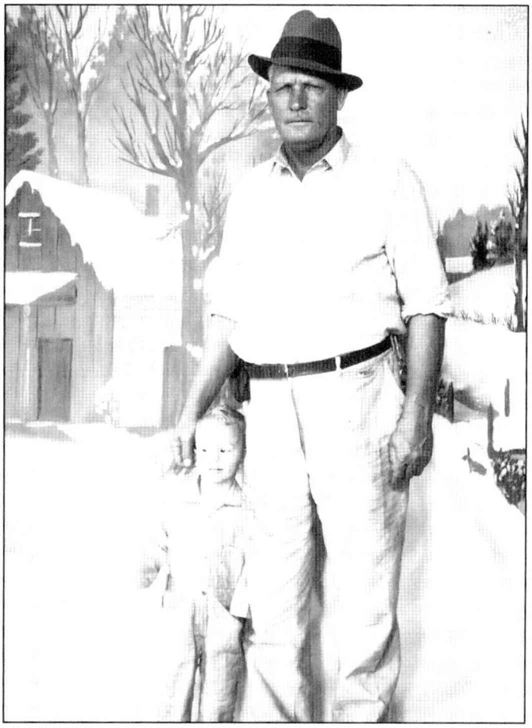

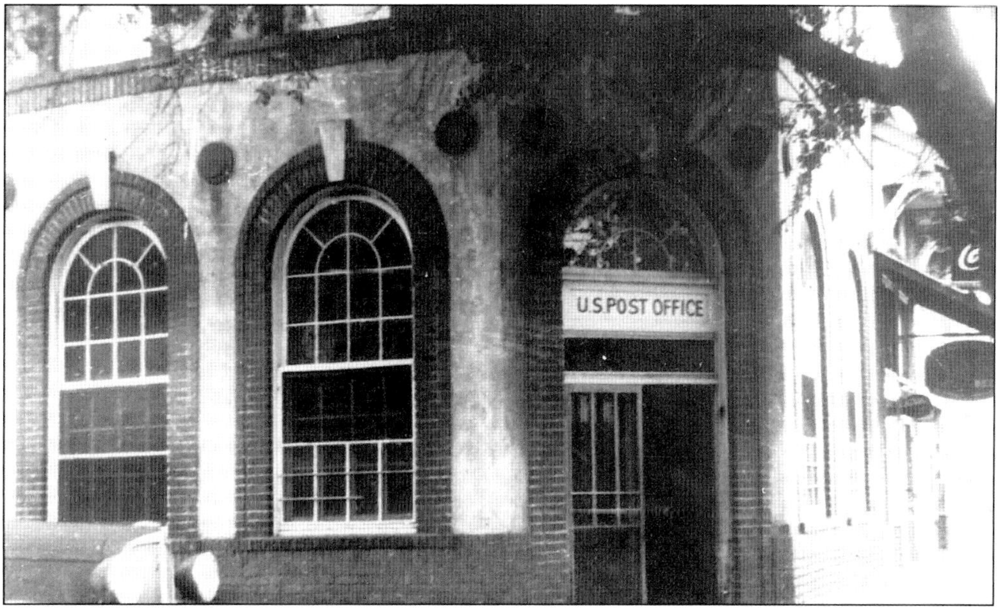

The Iva Post Office was located on the corner of Front Street and Broad Street in Iva, as shown here, for many years. In 1962, a new post office was erected. The post office for Iva has had several locations. The first post office operated from a building across from Cook's store. W.P. Cook was the first postmaster. The post office later moved to the corner between Erwin's supermarket and Iva Gulf Station. Another move took the office to where Brown's 5 & 10 Variety store is today. The next move was to the corner of Front and Broad Streets. In 1962 a new post office was built on Green Street, where it is located today.

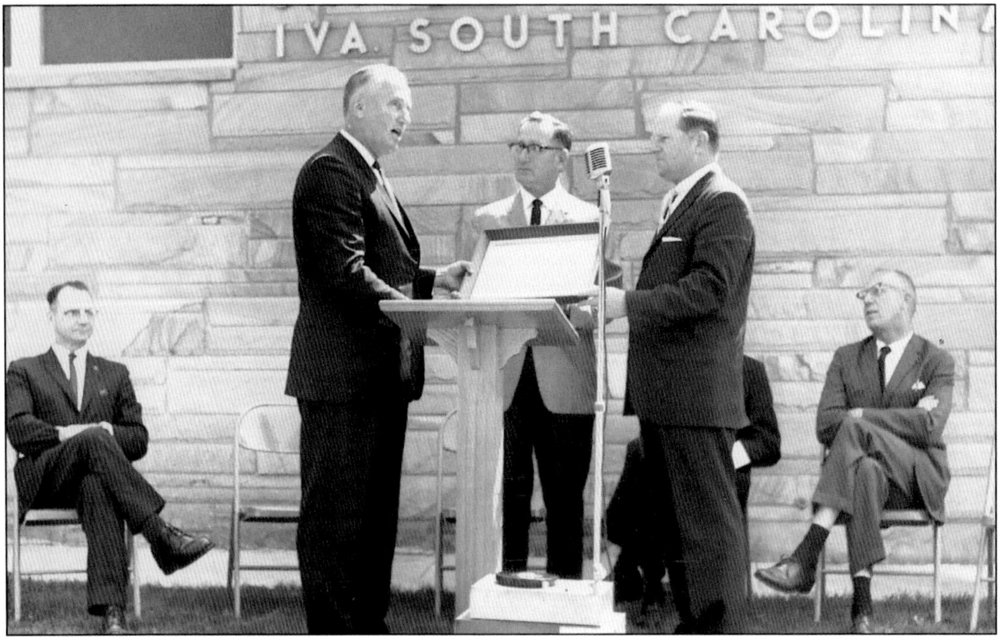

The dedication of the new post office was held in 1962. A "Citation for Excellence" award was presented to W.S. Simpson, postmaster (center), and the postal personnel. To the left of Mr. Simpson is C. Banks Gladden, regional director of the Post Office Department, and on his right is W.J. Bryan Dorn, U.S. representative. A new post office was erected during Mr. Simpson's 30-year tenure.

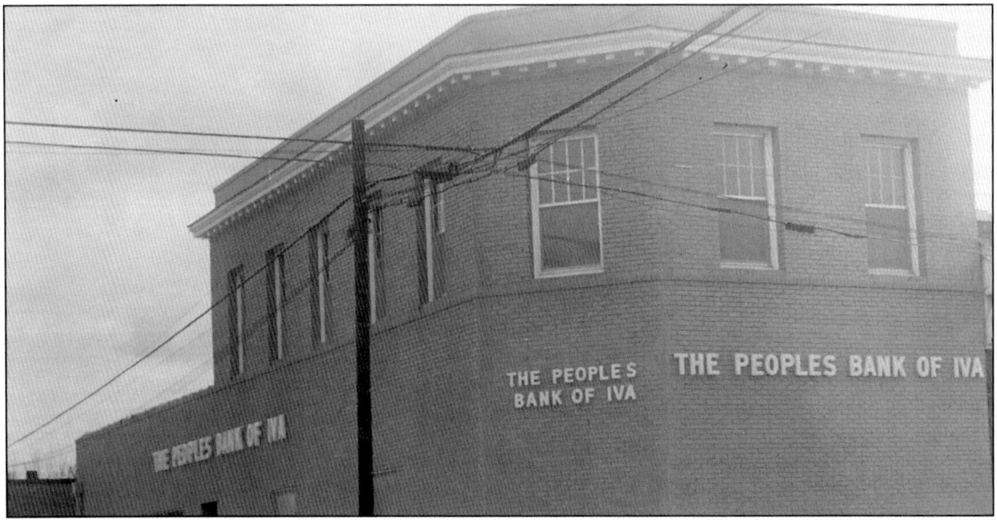

The Peoples Bank of Iva, with James P. Patterson as president, began as a small one-story building (back section) that was built in 1950. This bank now has four offices, with the home office located on Front Street in Iva, and three others in Anderson. A new office in Anderson will be open before the year 2000. Chairman of the Board J.R. McGee served as president for over 35 years, with Shawn Reid McGee becoming president of the bank in 1997. This building above now houses the REVIVA office, and it serves as a museum for many interesting exhibits, as well as history of the area, and as an Information Visitors Center located along the Heritage Corridor route.

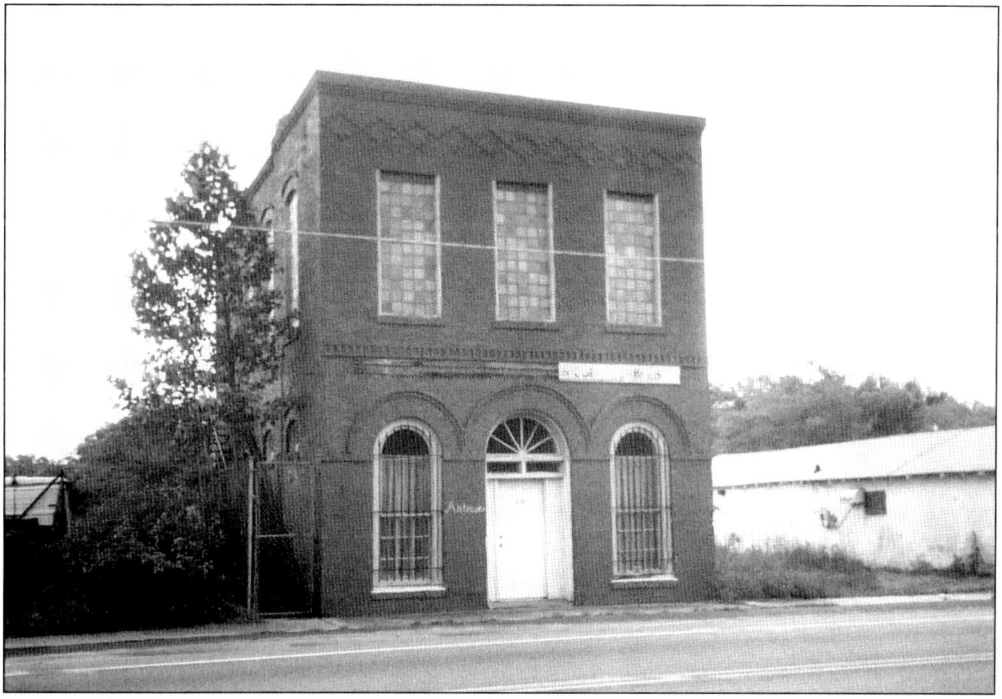

This well-known building in Starr was originally The Planter's Bank. It was organized by Albert Bowie in 1905, and the first teller was W.A. Hudgens. Later, the building was used as the post office, after the bank closed in the 1930s. The second story was used by Dr. Land, who was the first physician in Starr, and it was also used as a Masonic Lodge for a while. At a later stage, the building housed a broom factory and an antique shop. Today, the building stands unoccupied.

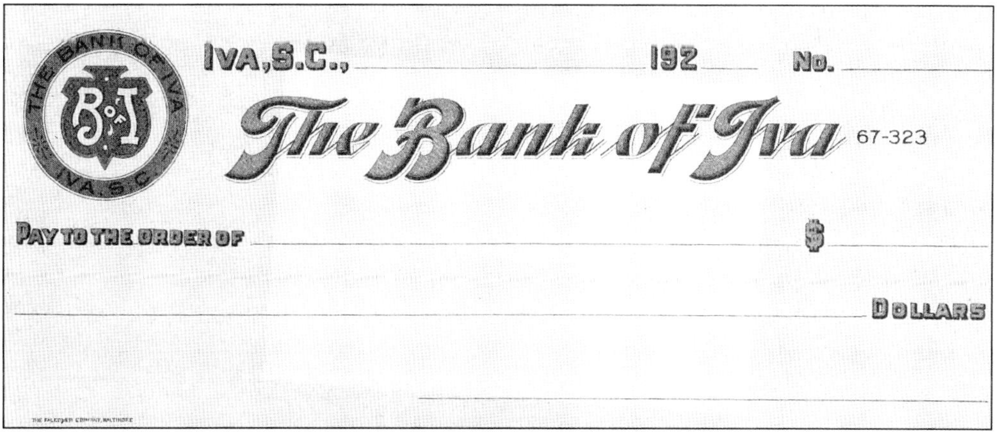

Pictured here is a copy of a check from The Bank of Iva, dated in the 1920s. "Your money in this bank is insured against all loss by robbery or fire. We pay interest on savings deposits." This was the logo for the first Bank of Iva, which was organized on February 15, 1905. The first officers were T.C. Jackson, president; Dr. J.E. Watson, vice president; and H.R. Sherard, cashier.

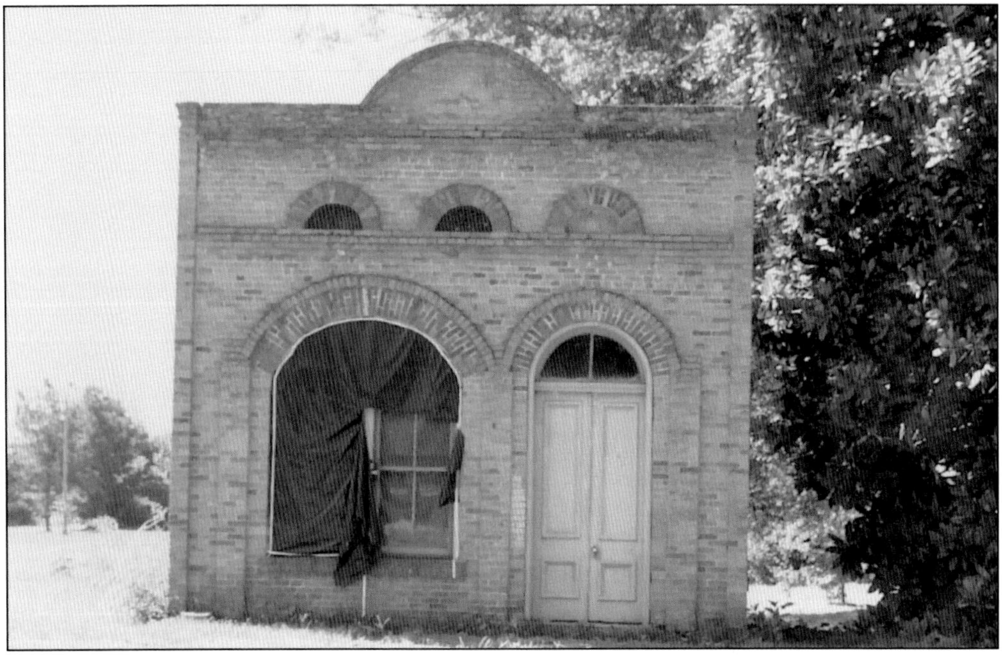

The Lowndesville bank, built in 1890, later became the post office, and although it is still standing, the building is no longer occupied. It may become a Heritage Corridor stop in the future.

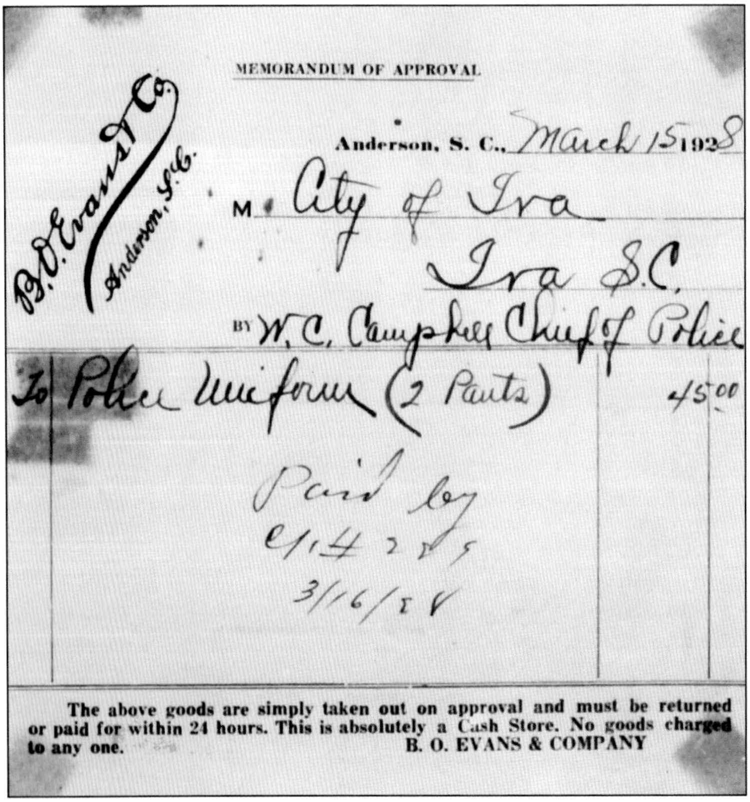

MEMORANDUM OF APPROVAL

B. O. Evans & Co. Anderson, S.C.

Anderson, S. C., March 15 1928

M City of Iva

Iva S.C.

BY W. C. Campbell Chief of Police

To Police Uniform (2 Pants) 45.00

Paid by

3/16/28

The above goods are simply taken out on approval and must be returned or paid for within 24 hours. This is absolutely a Cash Store. No goods charged to any one.

B. O. EVANS & COMPANY

This voucher shows the price of police uniforms in 1928. Today, in 1999, a pair of pants costs $38, and a shirt costs $26. Police uniforms, now, are issued twice a year. The winter issue consists of three shirts, two pairs of pants, one tie, one cap, one coat, and a pair of shoes. All this will cost around $300. Police Chief Campbell, whose name appears on the 1928 voucher, later became Anderson County deputy under Sheriff W.A. Clamp.

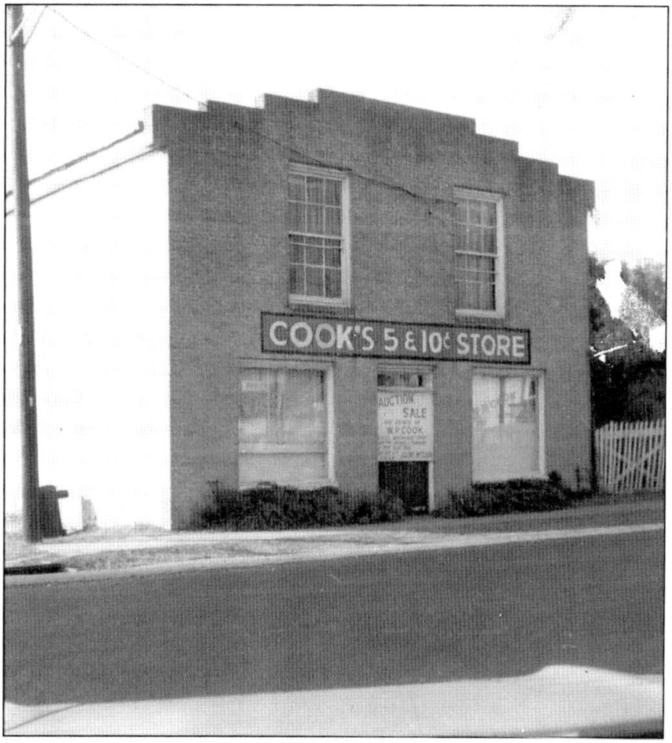

Cook's 5 & 10¢ store served Iva for many years. The store was owned and operated by the Cooks throughout its entirety. Miss Essie Cook, Dr. A.G. Cook's granddaughter, was the last owner and operator. Pictured below is an auction that took place when the business closed its door for the final time.

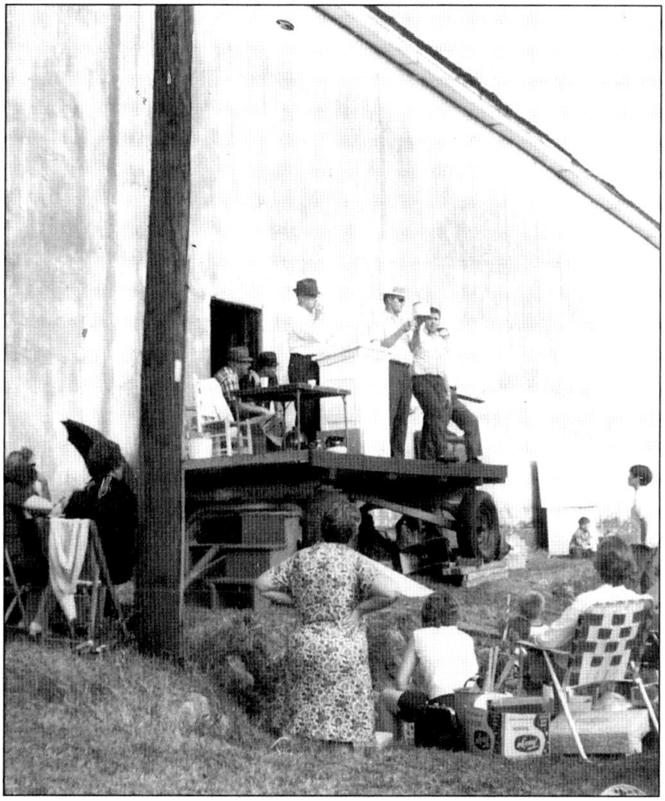

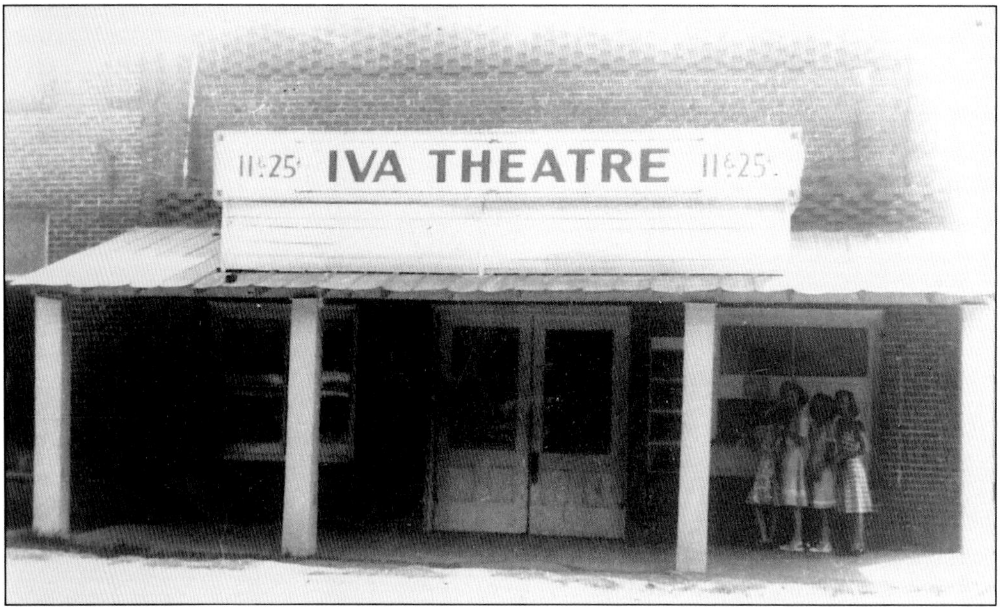

Iva has had several theaters. One of these was a tent theater in the late 1930s and early 1940s. Boys were known to slip under the tent after the show had started. Another theater was located on Lake Street, near Old Mill Hall. The third theater was where Brown's 5 and 10¢ is now, and in the later 1940s, this theater was where Iva Bingo is now. The last theater was located on the corner of Front and Green Streets, and this building was later known as Wakefield Grocery, then Marty's Auto Mart.

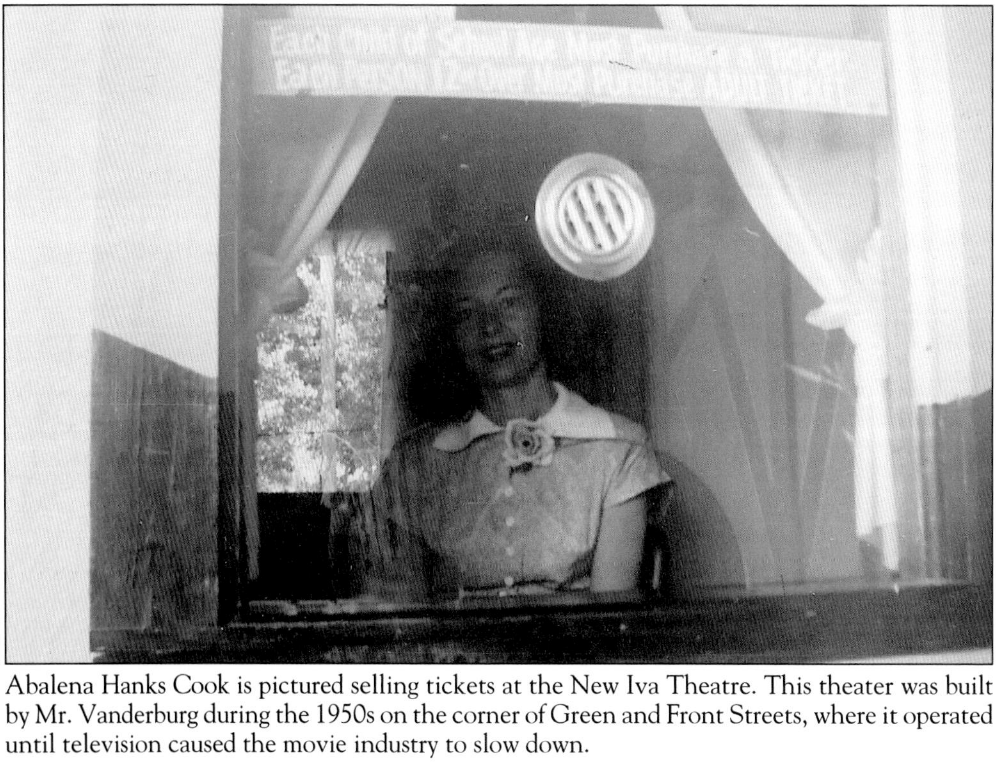

Abalena Hanks Cook is pictured selling tickets at the New Iva Theatre. This theater was built by Mr. Vanderburg during the 1950s on the corner of Green and Front Streets, where it operated until television caused the movie industry to slow down.

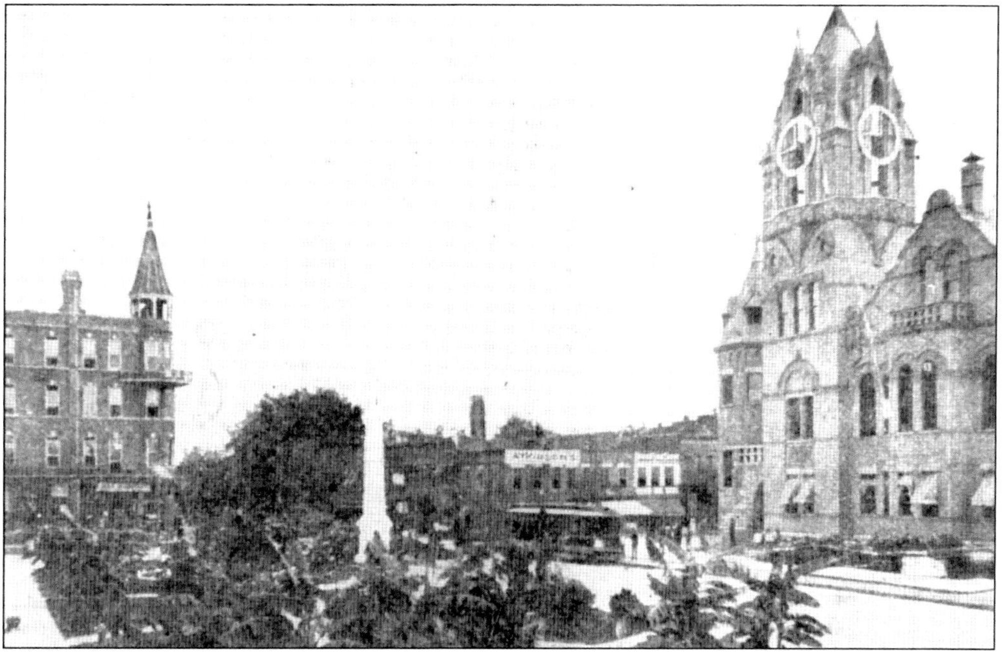

The city of Anderson is the county seat of Anderson County. It was named for General Robert Anderson, a Revolutionary War soldier. The Chiquola (later Plaza) Hotel opened with a grand ball in the 1890s. It featured a four-story atrium over its lobby, rising to a skylight at the roof. This building, of a classic Victorian architectural design, was the finest hotel between Charlotte and Atlanta.

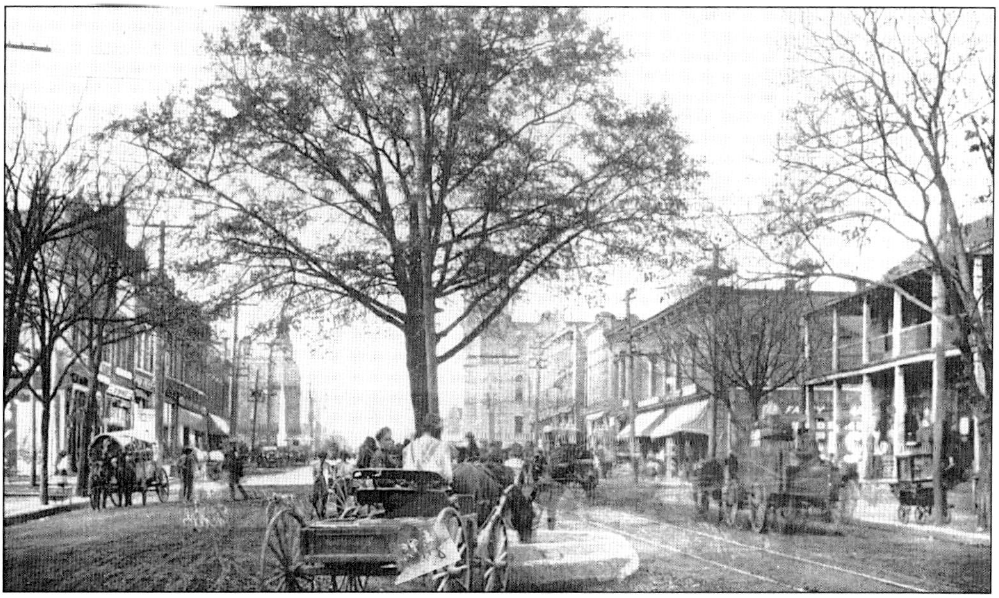

This photograph depicts early days on Main Street in Anderson. The first courthouse was built in 1828, and its builder, Robert Wilson, was the grandfather of Jeptha Forbes Wilson of Iva. The cornerstone for the next courthouse was laid on October 20, 1897. This time capsule was opened on July 5, 1991, and its contents are now in the Anderson County Museum. The "new" courthouse opened in 1991.

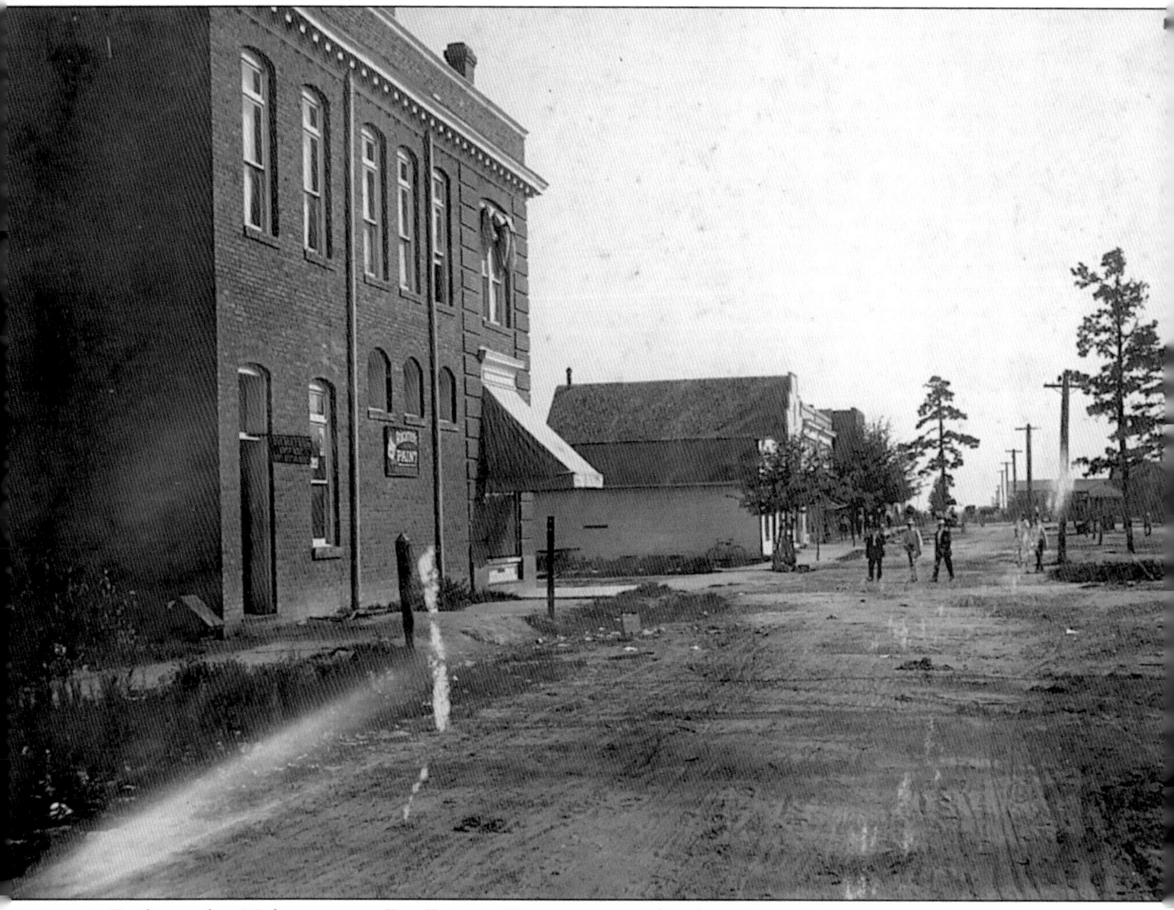

Early in the 20th century, Dr. Ernest Watson opened a drugstore in Iva. Located on the corner of Broad Street and Front Street, Dr. Watson's Iva Drug Store advertised family remedies, Nunnally's candy, fancy stationary, and school supplies. Dr. Watson sold the drugstore to Dr. Charles D. Evans in 1912. Later, the store was moved farther up on East Front Street, where more room was available. Dr. Evans operated the store until he was 85 years old, at which time he turned the business over to his son, Ernest W. Evans. When Ernest retired, the store was operated by his daughter, Elaine Evans, until her death in 1997. Elaine brought many new and pretty items into the store. Doctors used the upstairs of the old drug building for offices. The old building still stands today.

Four

Agriculture of Iva and the Surrounding Communities

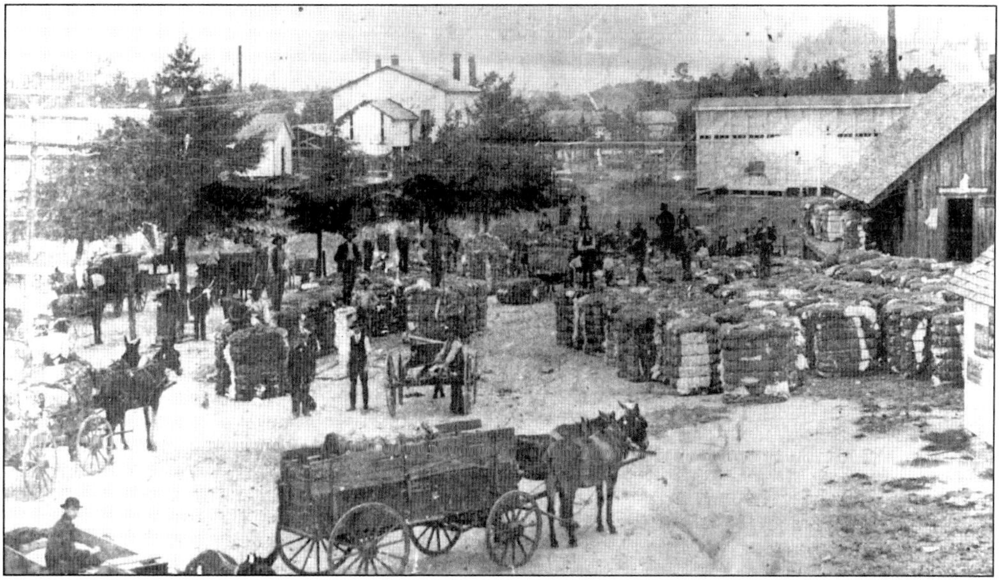

There was a cotton gin in operation in Starr in the early 1900s. Mr. W.L. "Bill" Mouchet bought the property in the early 1930s, and he operated the gin until his death. Mr. Mouchet's son, John Rhett, continued its operation until his own death in 1965. The family sold the property to a Mr. Campbell. Eventually, the property was purchased by Brooks McGee, who set up a new gin in an adjoining area. He operated this gin for several years, but today it is no longer in operation.

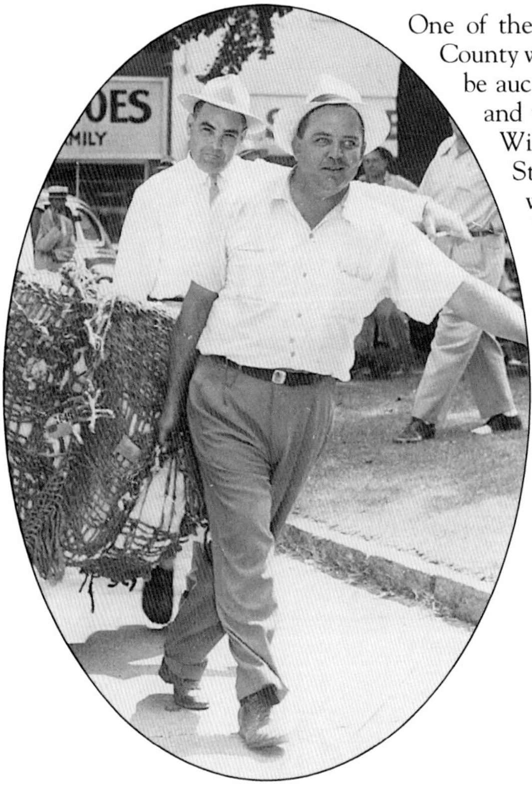

One of the goals of the cotton farmers in Anderson County was to get the first bale each fall, which would be auctioned off on the town square in Anderson and would bring an exceptionally good price. J. Willis McGee, who had a large farm between Starr and Iva, is seen here proudly showing his winning bale. He was one of the farmers who bought and sold mules at the McGee barn.

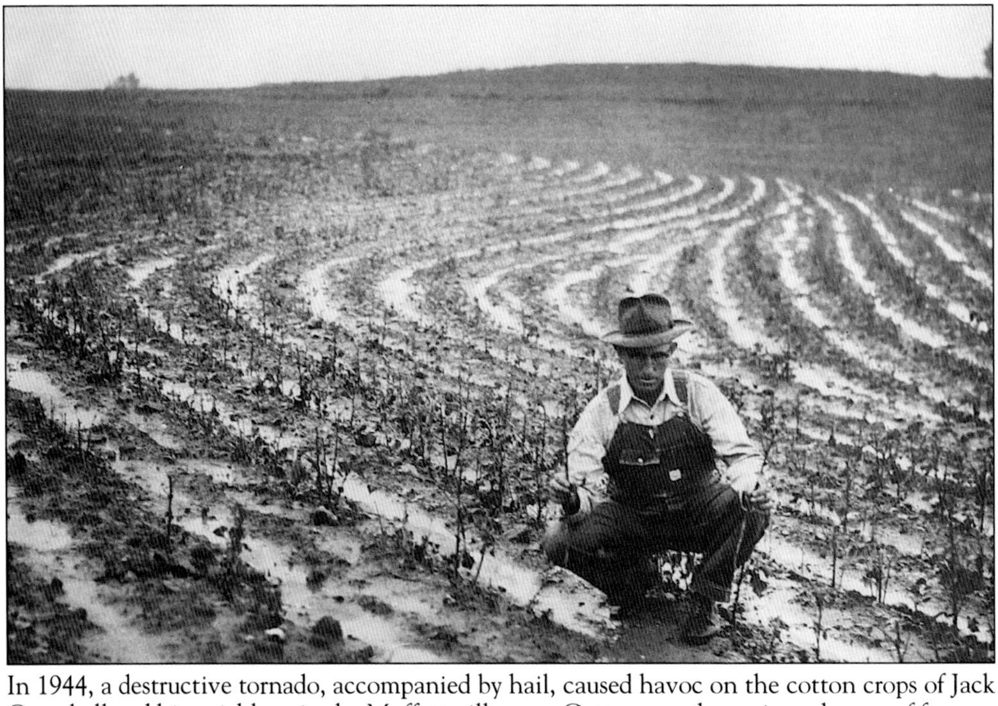

In 1944, a destructive tornado, accompanied by hail, caused havoc on the cotton crops of Jack Campbell and his neighbors in the Moffettsville area. Cotton was the main cash crop of farmers at that time. Some farmers were very fortunate to have had crop insurance.

This is the result of a tornado that destroyed the home and farm of Mr. and Mrs. Robert Burdette in 1944. The trees and cotton stalks were stripped of their leaves and cotton, and even the chickens were plucked of their feathers. Many odd and freakish sights were seen. People from surrounding areas came to see the damage and to lend a helping hand in any way they could. Mr. and Mrs. Burdette were not injured, just badly frightened.

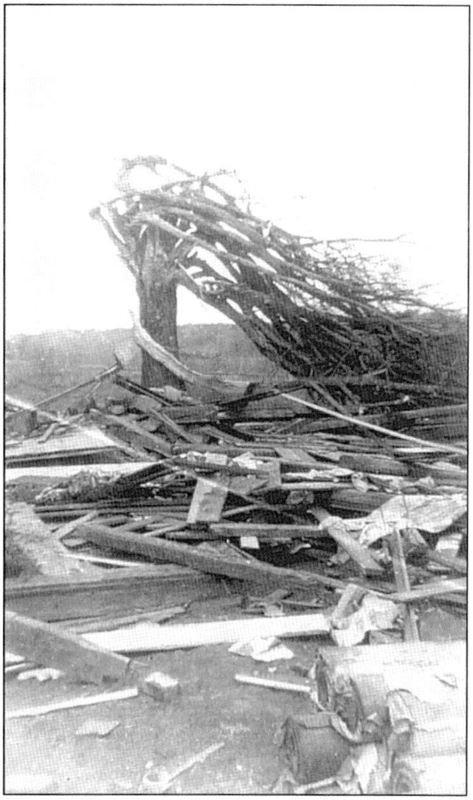

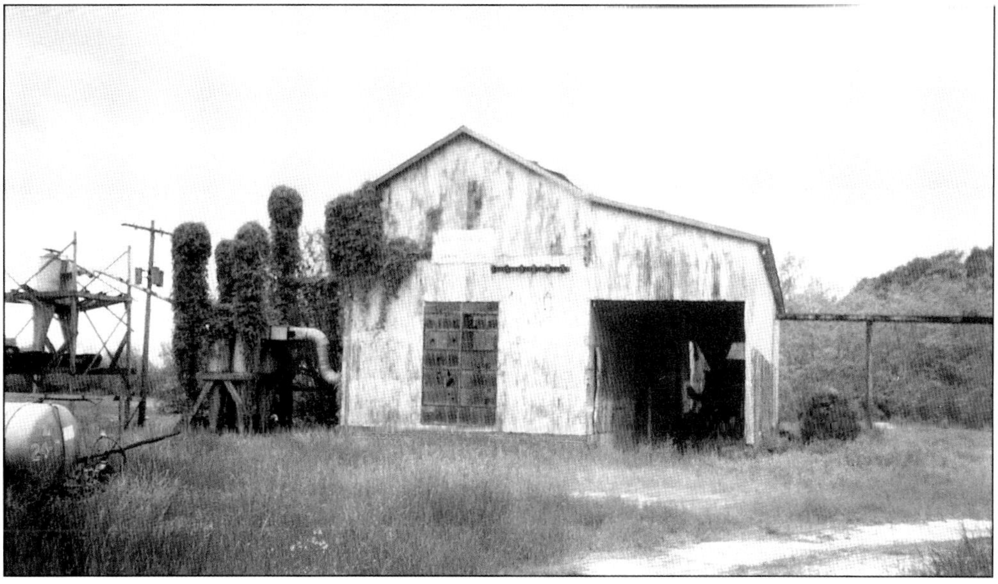

The Antreville Gin, as pictured here, was built by Will Ellis and his son, Cal Ellis, around 1910. The gin was initially operated by Cal Ellis. The Ellis family later sold it to John Farrell, who, after a short while, sold it to George Wilson. Joe Anderson bought it from Mr. Wilson and operated it until his death, from when his son, Perrin Anderson, operated it until 1976, when it was no longer profitable.

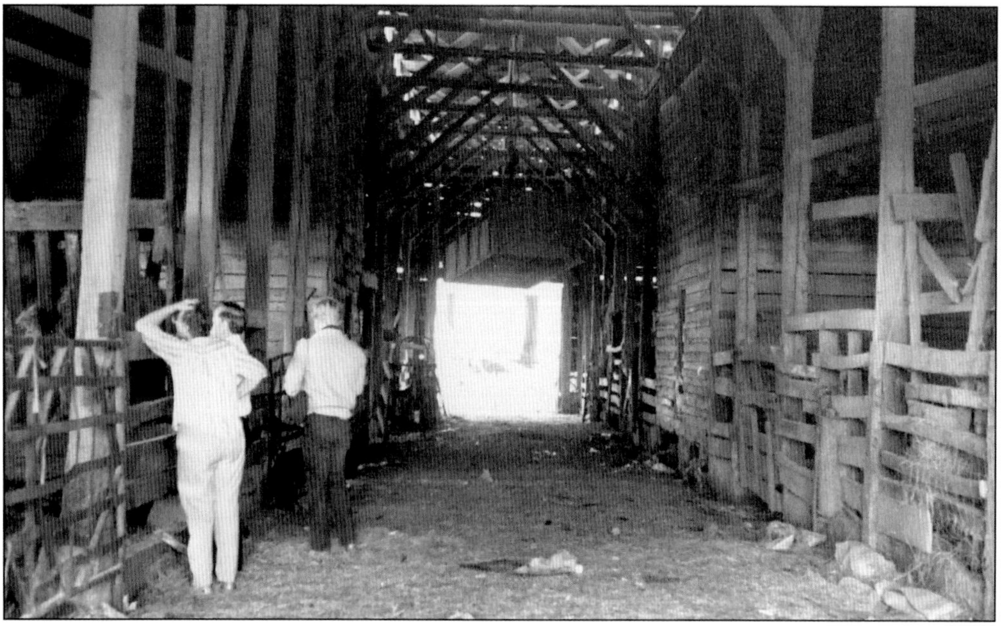

Three brothers, Elias, Willis, and Lawrence McGee, built the McGee Mule Barn on Smith McGee Road in Starr, in 1923. It was here that wild mules were trained and later made available for sale to the local farmers. Some were taken back to the McGee Mule Sales Barn in Anderson to be sold.

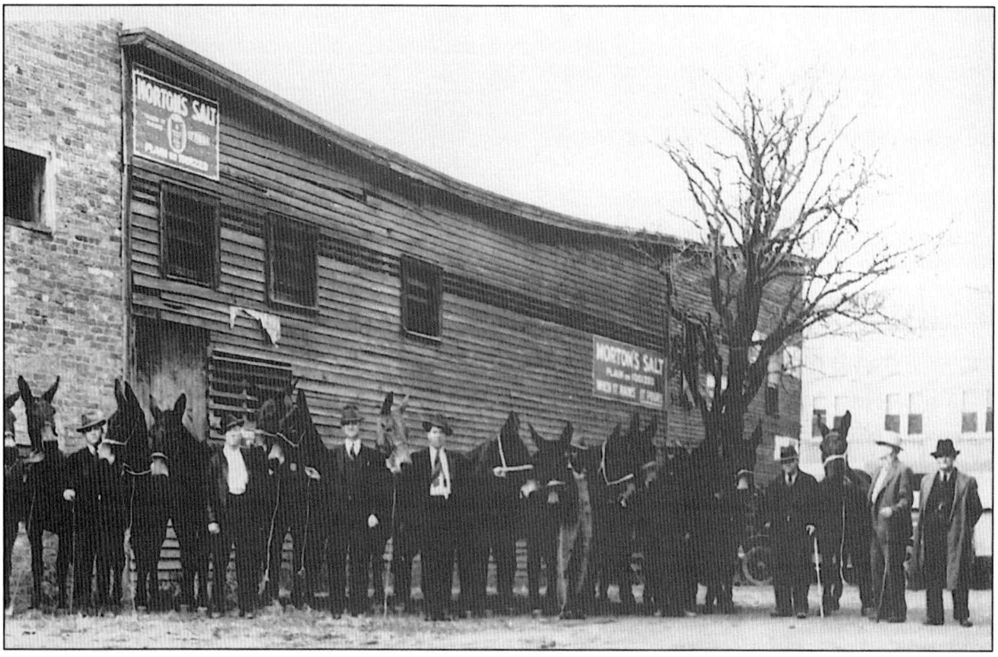

The McGee Mule Sales Barn in Anderson was owned by families from Starr. During the 1920s and 1930s, the owners would go out to Missouri, buy between 50 and 70 wild mules, and bring them back by train to their farms at Starr. The mules were broken to the plow, and then carried to the sales at this barn in Anderson during the fall. Pictured, from left to right, are Willis McGee, Prue Willis McGee, Mr. McNinch, and Elias McGee.

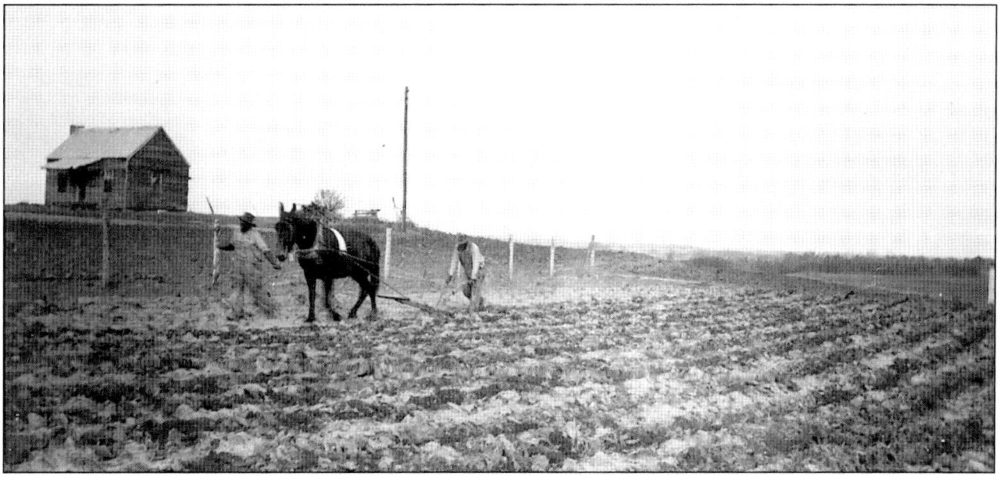

Farmhands are seen here, breaking a mule to the plow during the 1920s and 1930s. After Mr. W.T.A. "Bunk" Sherard's death in January of 1937, Marcus Campbell remembers the most unforgettable sight. Mr. Campbell, as a lad, was on the bank of Parker Bowie and Old Bell Road, and as far as he could see in both directions were mules, wagons, and black farmhands with hoes over their shoulders, coming from Elias McGee's farm to work the Sherard Farm that year.

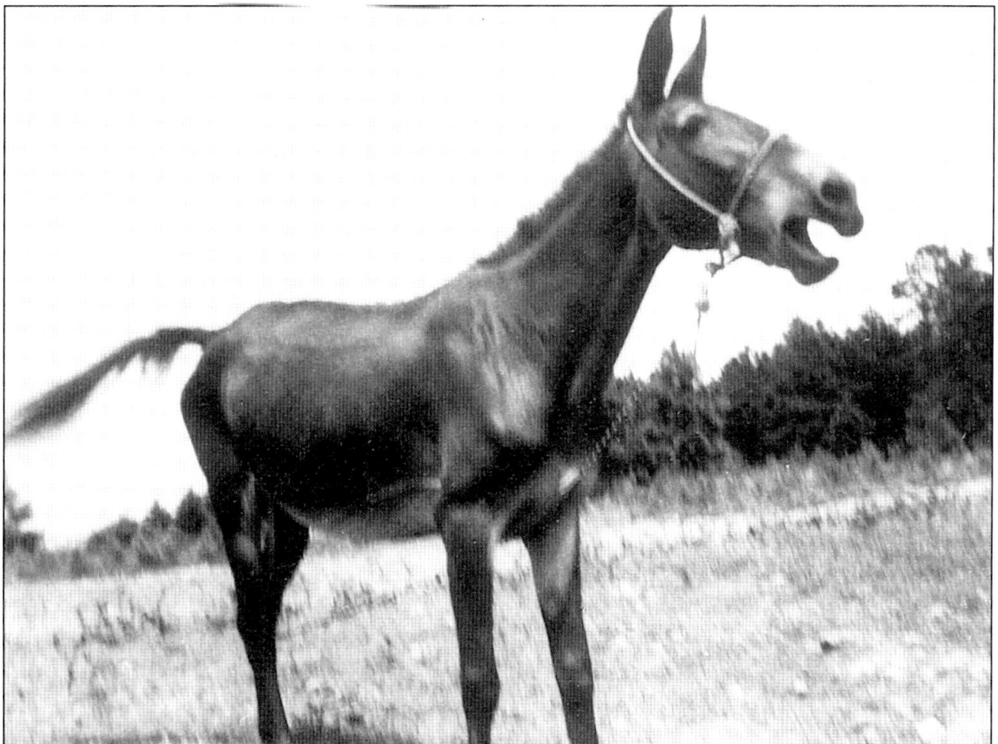

"Old Pete," owned by Rodney Bowman and photographed by Bowman's ten-year-old daughter Jan Bowman, seems to be giving orders to some reluctant mule buddies. He appears to be a real sergeant—look at the stance, the nose, the ears, and the tail. It can truly be said that mules became the "Vanishing American Heroes" after tractors made their appearance.

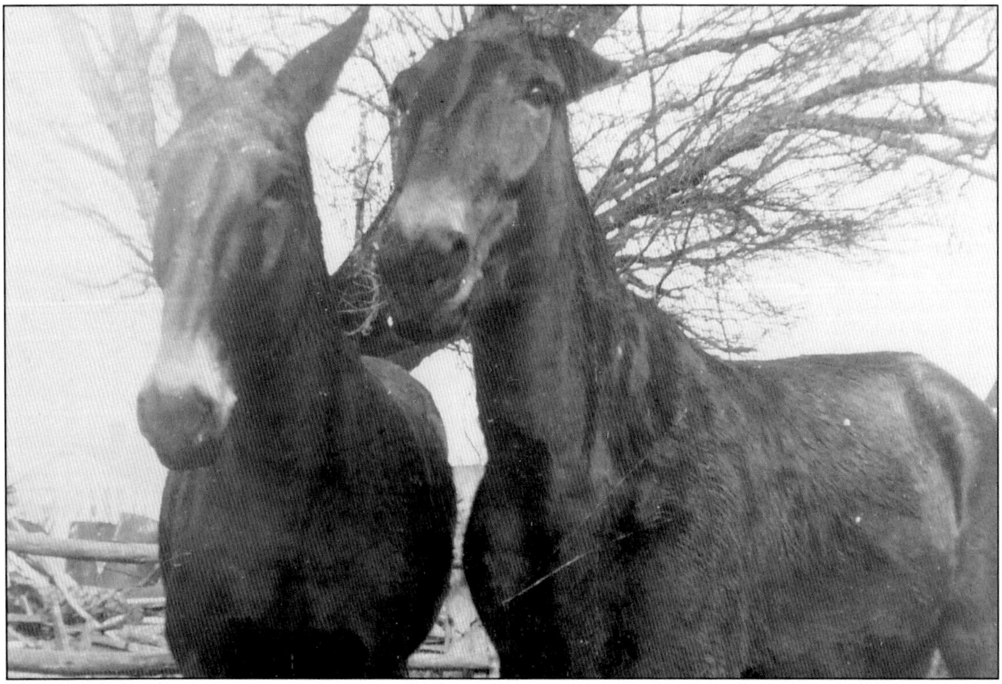

Mules were a vital part of a farmer's livelihood. Before tractors, they were the main source of farmers' labor power. In the "Thursday morning, November 25, 1875 tax assessment of Dark Corner Township," there were 112 mules and asses altogether, and 173 horses. At this time, Moffettsville was known as Dark Corner Township, and there was, as yet, no town of Iva.

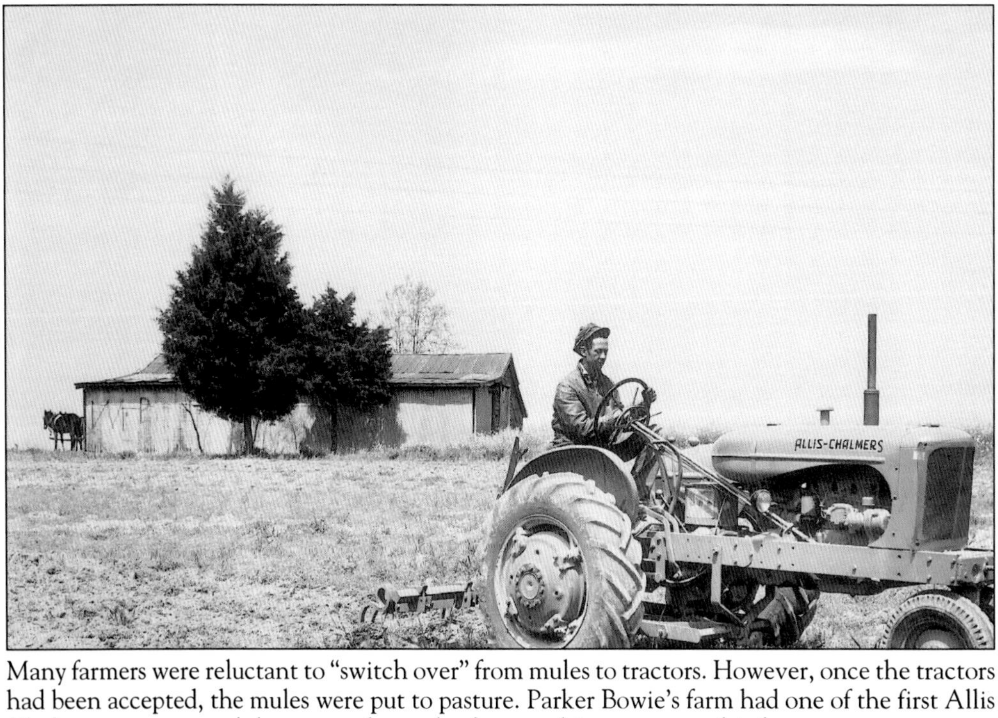

Many farmers were reluctant to "switch over" from mules to tractors. However, once the tractors had been accepted, the mules were put to pasture. Parker Bowie's farm had one of the first Allis Chalmers tractors, and then, years later, the first combine, to use on his farm.

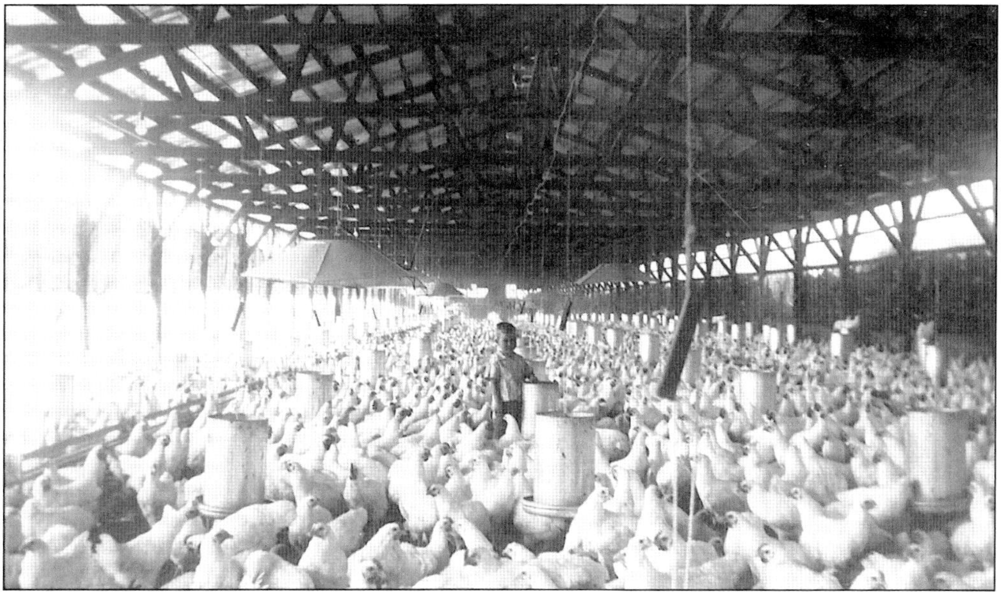

During the early days when Iva and Starr were the "Mule and Cotton Kingdom," Iva was also the "Chicken/Egg Capital." Tony Hanks, pictured here, is helping in the chicken house that was owned and operated by his parents, Gene and Pearl Hanks. As well as grading the eggs and selling them to many local people, the Hanks also sold broiler chickens.

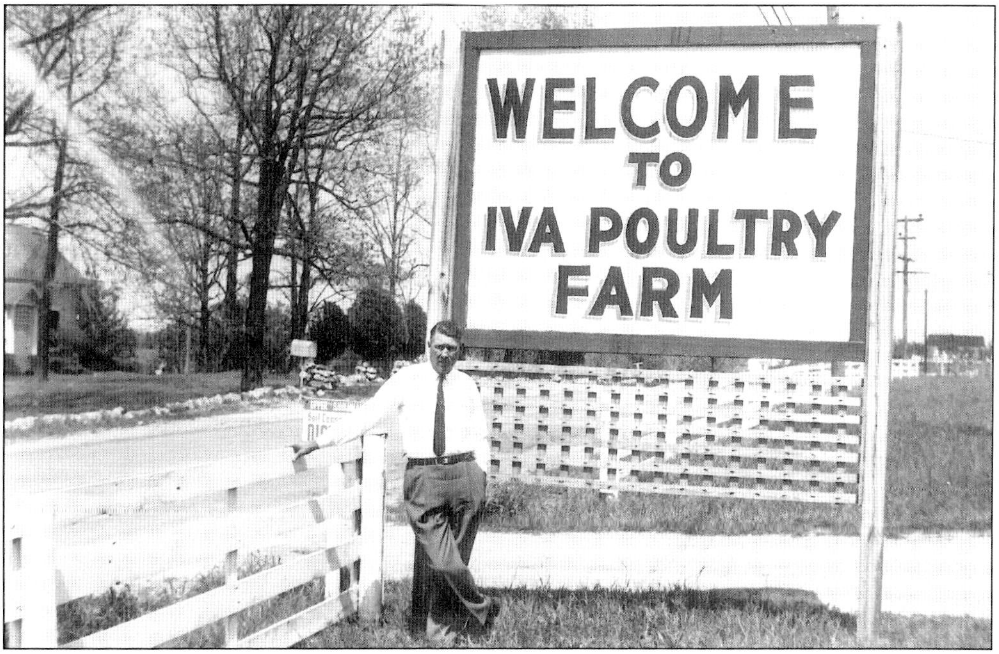

T.C. Gray began his venture with a 4-H Club project in high school. Starting out with 10 hens and 1 rooster, T.C. Gray went on to become the largest breeding and hatchery operation in the Southeast. He and his wife, Thelma Kirkpatrick Gray, developed their own breed from a cross between his white leghorn hens and a much larger rooster from Canada. They named this breed "The Gray Cross," and baby chicks were shipped all over the United States and Canada. Eggs were sold by the tens of thousands.

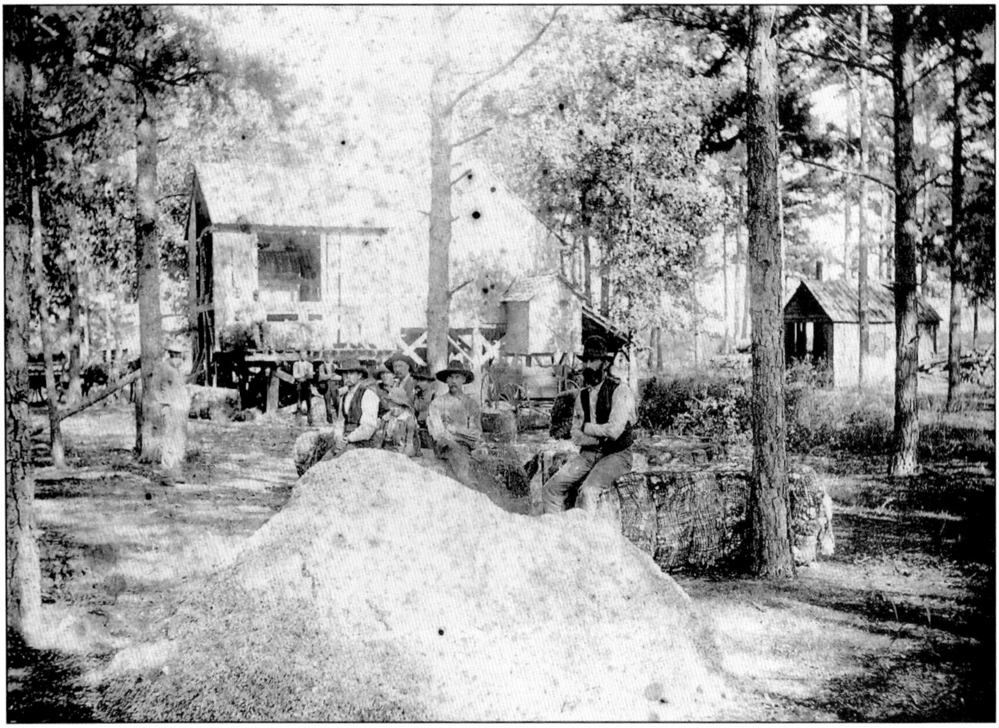

In every community there was at least one cotton gin. When a family picked around 1,200 pounds of cotton, they would haul it to the gin by mule and wagon. After the waste and seeds were taken out, bales would weigh between 500 and 550 pounds.

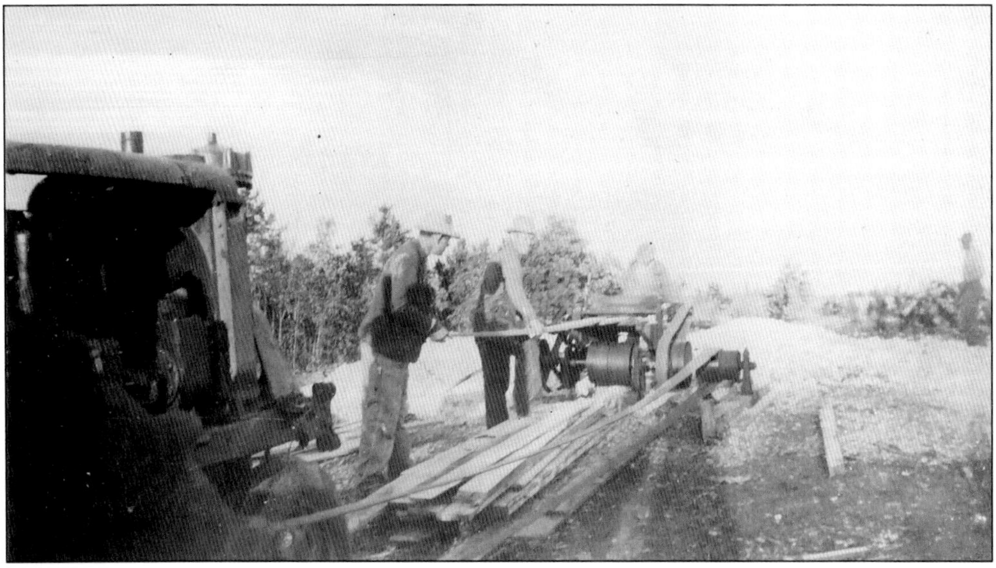

This planer was owned and operated by Dell Cook in the early 1940s. Mr. Cook used an F-20 Farmall tractor to pull this mill. Planer mills were used for sizing and smoothing (or dressing) lumber. At least two workers were needed to operate this machine. Shavings from the lumber were used for various purposes, although Mr. T.C. Gray used the majority for his chicken houses.

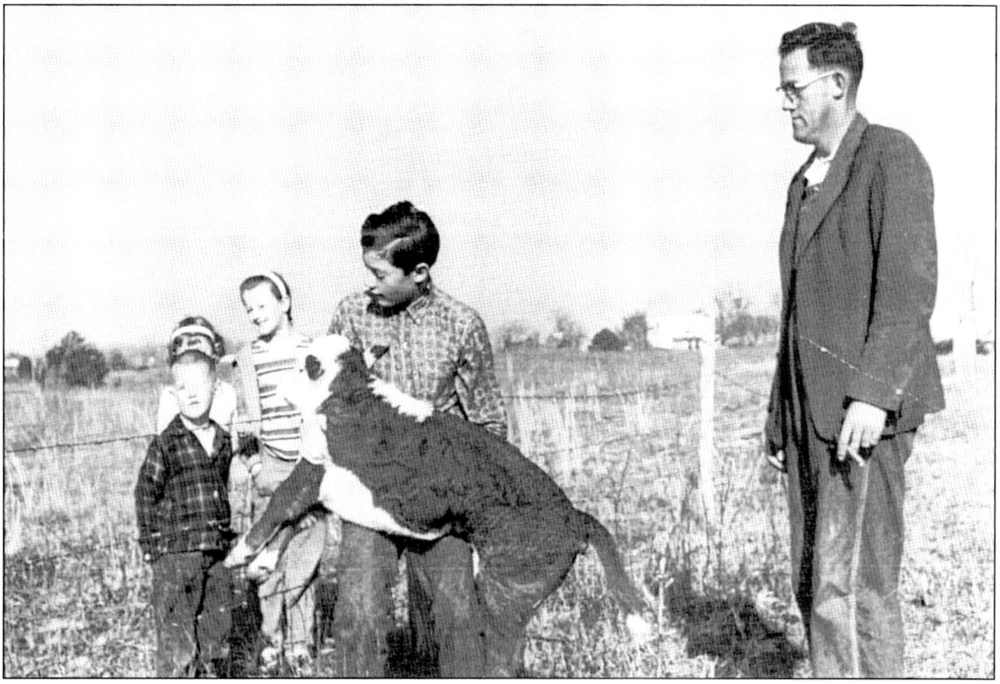

This photograph shows "Pleasant Rural Scenes" of the Campbell family in 1962. There is an old saying that if you lift a calf over the fence every day from the day it was born, you will still be able to lift it when it is grown. Rodney Campbell is pictured here with his father, Marcus Campbell; brother, Wayne Campbell; and sisters Pam and Dale. Rodney is clearly not convinced that the saying is true, and it can be seen that the other family members are all watching with varying degrees of skepticism.

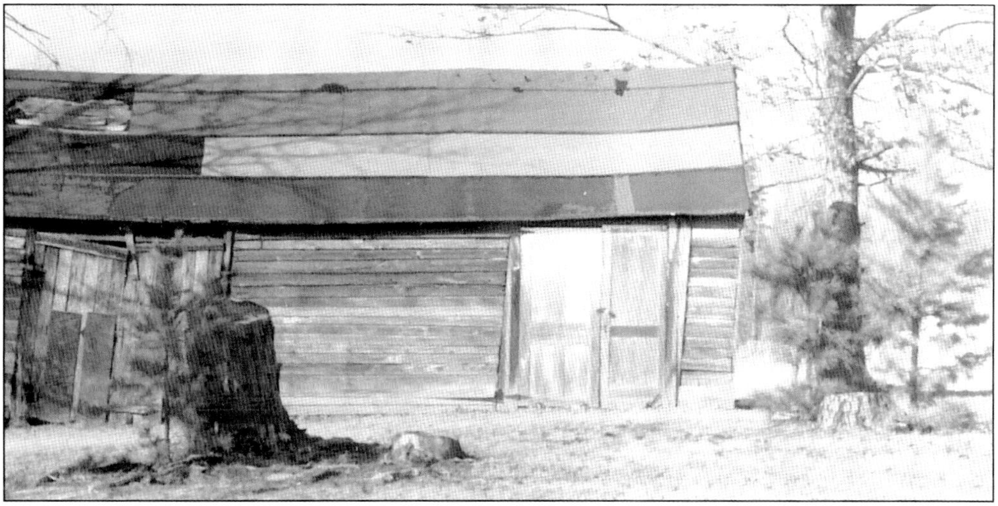

Samuel S. McMahan's Blacksmith Shop operated here for many years, serving all the surrounding communities. His granddaughter, Aileen Alexander, has fond memories of helping her grandfather in the shop by turning the "Big Blower Wheel" to keep the fire going at a very hot temperature. After Samuel McMahan's death, Aileen Alexander's father, Reese McMahan, owned the shop until his death in 1958. The building was approximately 150 years old when this picture was taken.

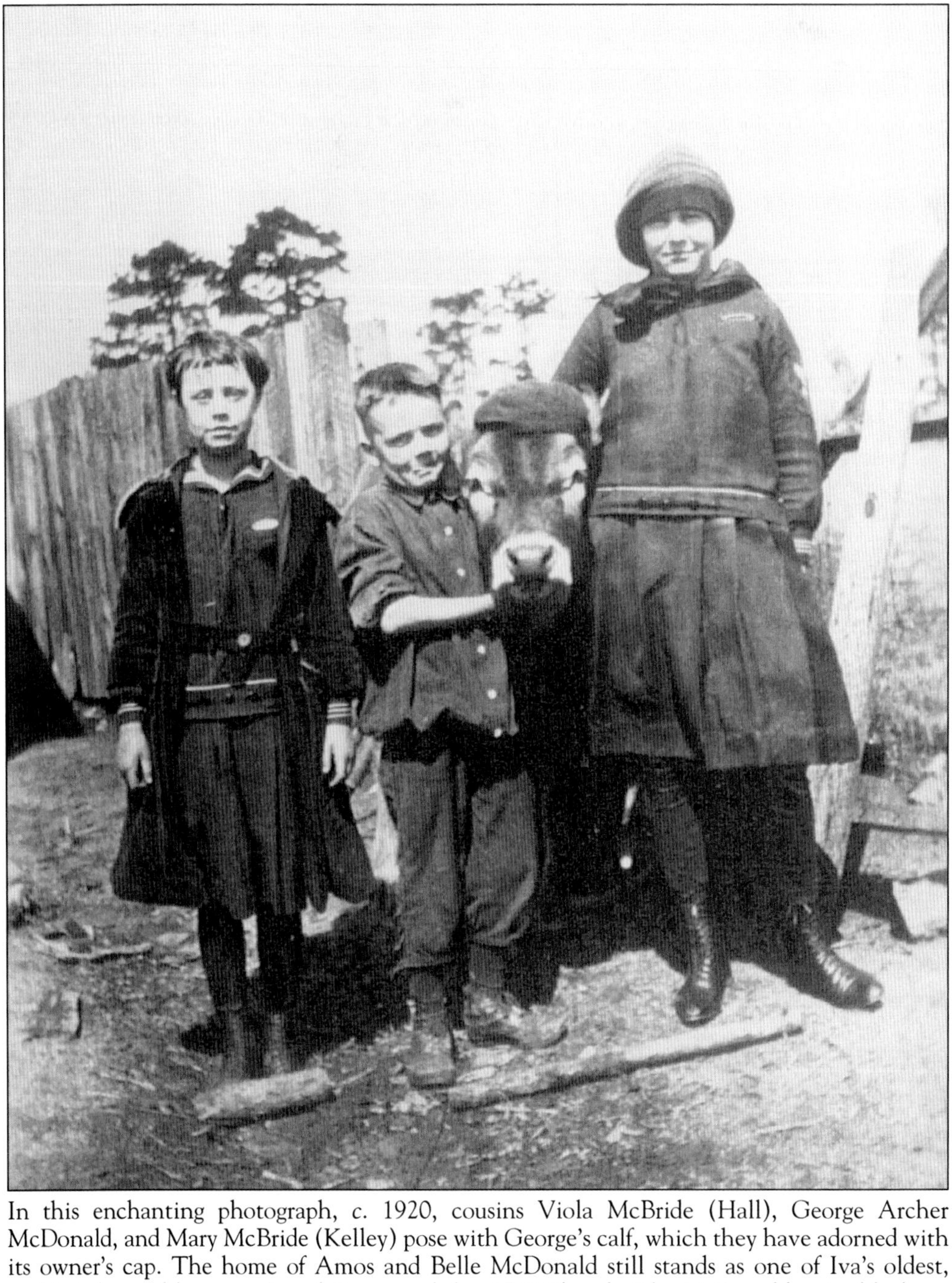

In this enchanting photograph, *c.* 1920, cousins Viola McBride (Hall), George Archer McDonald, and Mary McBride (Kelley) pose with George's calf, which they have adorned with its owner's cap. The home of Amos and Belle McDonald still stands as one of Iva's oldest, and it is located between Broad Street and the ARP Church. The McDonalds raised leghorn chickens for their eggs, which were sold to Anderson Hospital. Cows, pigs, and an occasional horse and mule, all called the McDonalds' Betsy Street mini-farm "home." George and his sister Luva enjoyed many happy days of small town life with their extended family, including their McAlister cousins, whose home was located between the McDonald home and the church. A barn, chicken houses, pigpens, and a fishpond comprised the McDonald compound, which provided ample room for fun and adventure.

Five

Families, Homes, and Youth

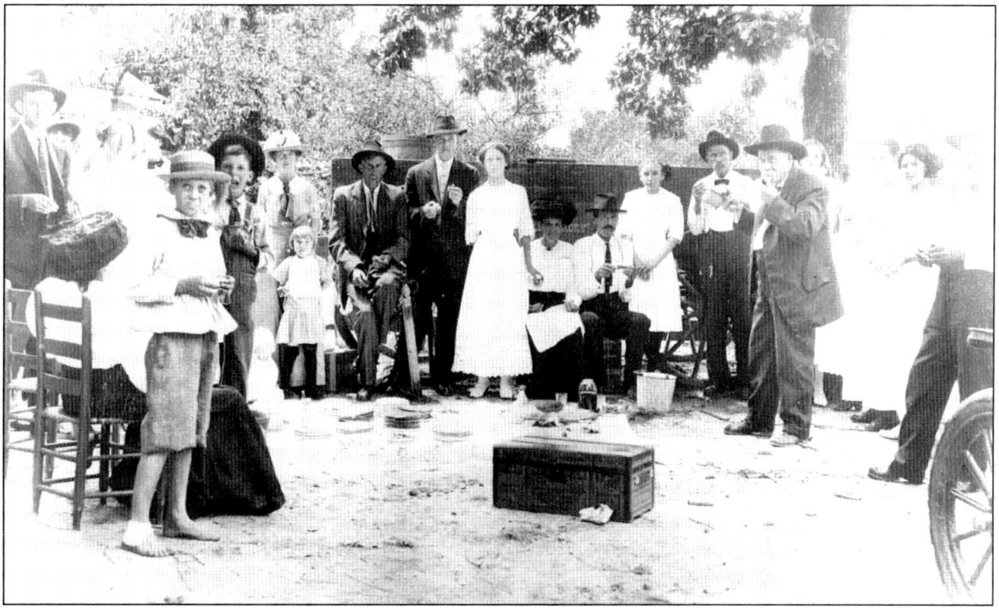

The family of Samuel McMahan celebrated a family get-together every year, and it was always held at Mr. McMahan's home. The "trunk" was used to carry the lunch, which is seen here spread on the ground. It is also interesting to note the fancy trim on the women's dresses and the large hats on the men and the women. The McMahan family continues this reunion tradition each August.

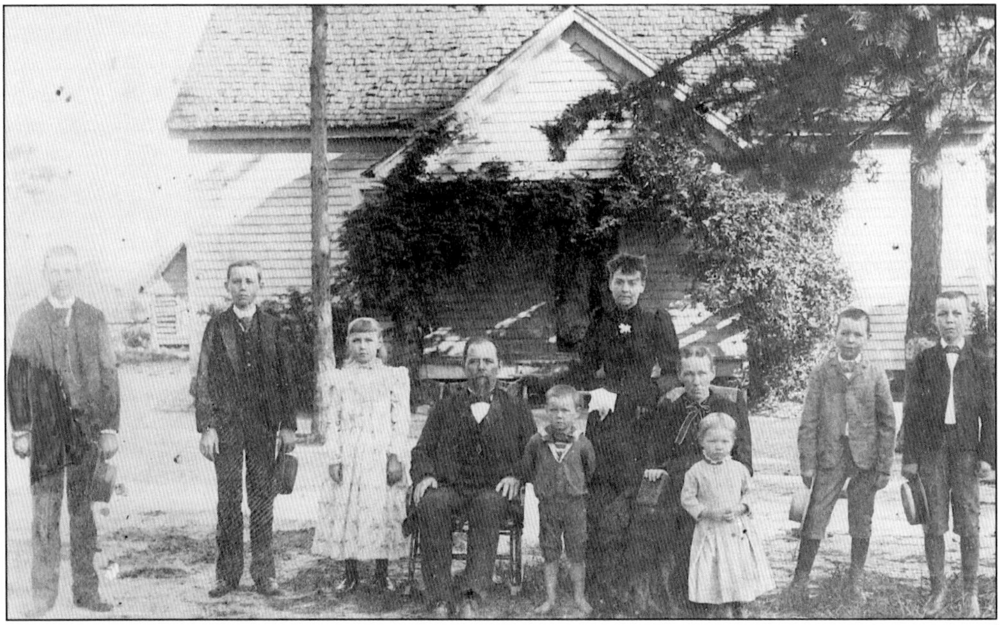

This picture of the Reverend Richard Cater Ligon family was taken in front of the manse of the old Good Hope Presbyterian Church in 1893. Reverend Ligon preached at the church from 1877 until 1902. The old cemetery is located approximately 3 miles west of Iva. Shown here, from left to right, are the following: (standing) George Howe, Joshua Wideman, Louise ?, John Frank, Kate Wideman, Lucy Laurie, Richard Cheves, and Joe Cater; (seated) Reverend Richard Cater Ligon, Mrs. Ligon, and Margaret Sumter Ligon.

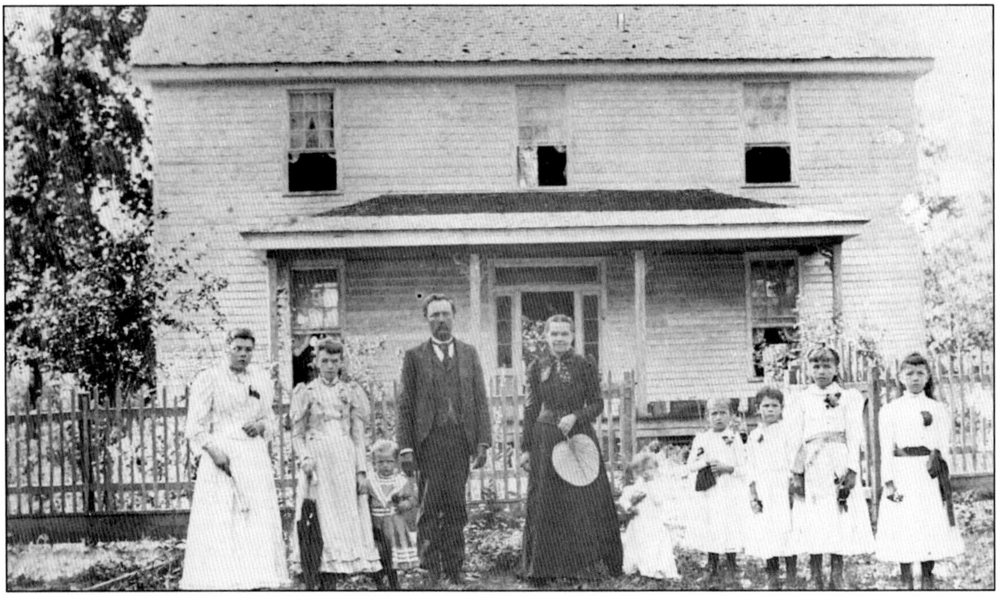

This picture of the Lawrence Sebastian Clinkscales family dates from around 1893. One child, Harold Clinkscales, was born after this photograph was taken. Seen here, from left to right, are Valeria Clinkscales Masters, Florence Clinkscales Wilkins, Grady Clinkscales, Lawrence Clinkscales, Mamie Clinkscales, Rossie Clinkscales Anderson, Winnifred Clinkscales Strom, Essie Clinkscales, Lucy Clinkscales, and Xenia Clinkscales Ligon.

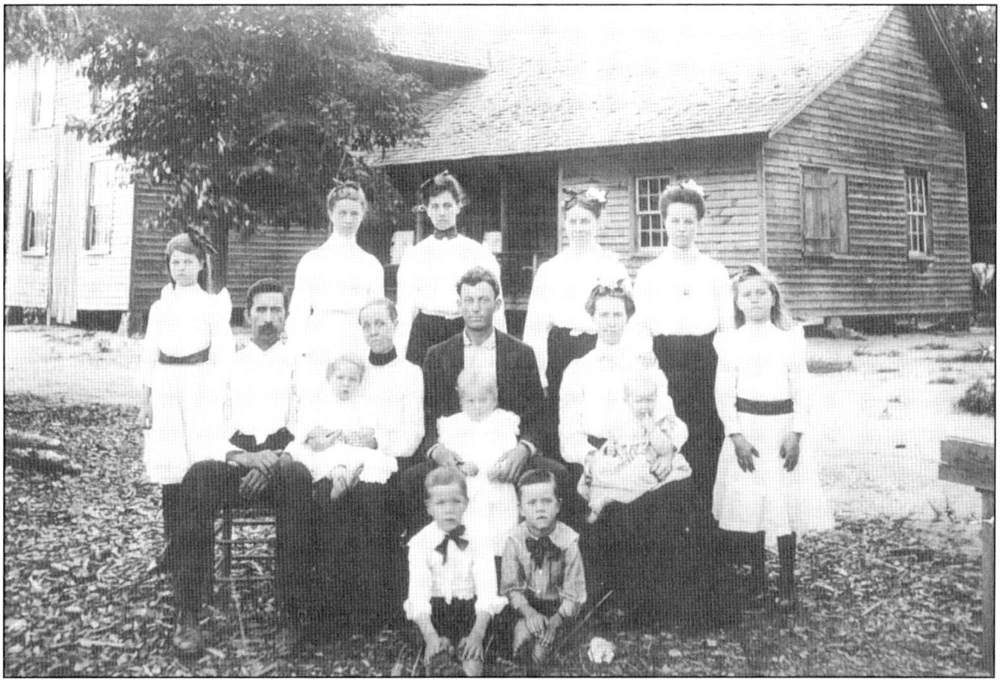

The W.W. Burton family is pictured in 1904. Family members seen here, from left to right, are as follows: (front row) Columbus Burton and Hubbard Burton; (second row) William Walters Burton, Emma Hall Burton holding Goss Burton, Columbus R. Burdette holding Clyde Burdette, Daisy Burton Burdette holding Edgar Burdette, and Marie Burton Kelley; (back row) Selma Burton Manning, Lida Burton Hanks, Willie Burton Wiles, Katherine Burton McCarley, and Lula Burton McBride.

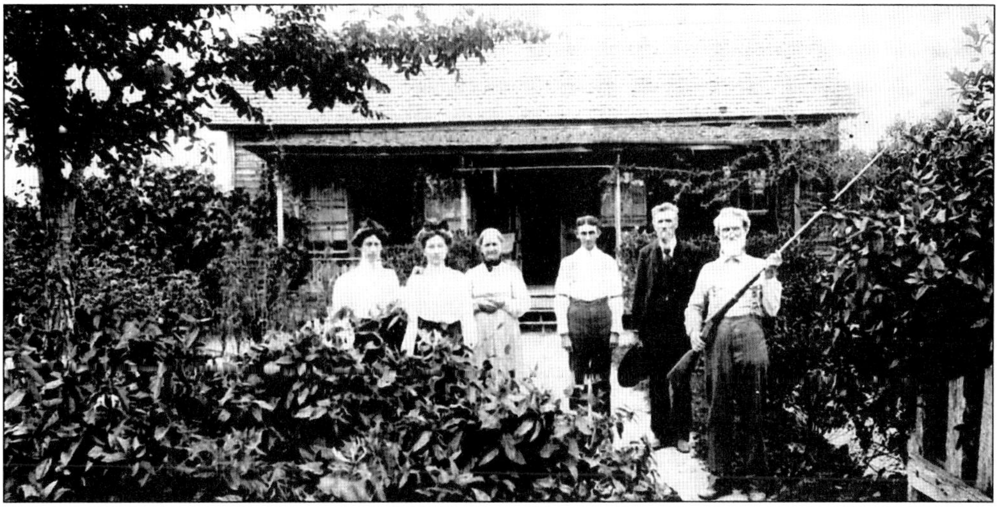

This is the home and family of Mr. Archie McKee. Pictured, from left to right, are as follows: Ora M. Watt and Annie M. Brown, daughters; Emmeline McKee, wife; Lester McKee, son; unidentified; and Mr. McKee. A muzzle-loading gun is held by Mr. McKee. This type of gun, which had to be filled with gunpowder in order to shoot, was common at that time. Mr. McKee was a large landowner, and he also operated a small store. He was the grandfather of Mary Watt, Kathleen Watt, and Sara Ellen W. Hicks.

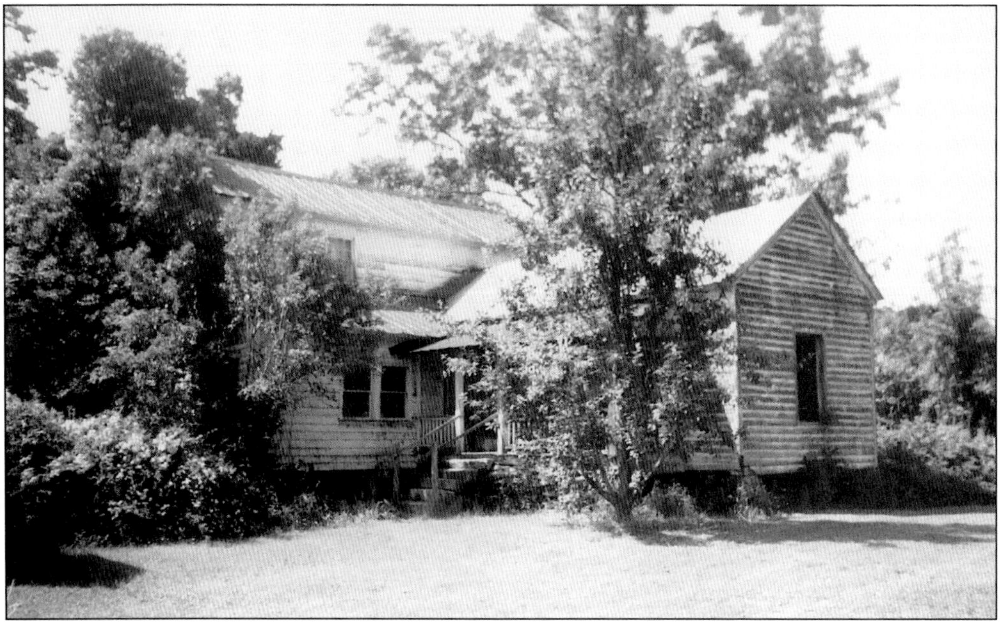

The Enoch McCarter home was built in the 1800s in Antreville. Elizabeth McCarter, daughter of Enoch McCarter, was the last occupant. Miss McCarter taught fifth grade students in Iva for many years. Her siblings' names were Enoch Jr., Lavinia, Lois, and Adella. Mr. Enoch Sr. had twin brothers, Earnest and Eugene, and his other brothers were called Thomas and George. All of Mr. Enoch's brothers had large farms nearby. This house is now owned by Howard Charlesworth.

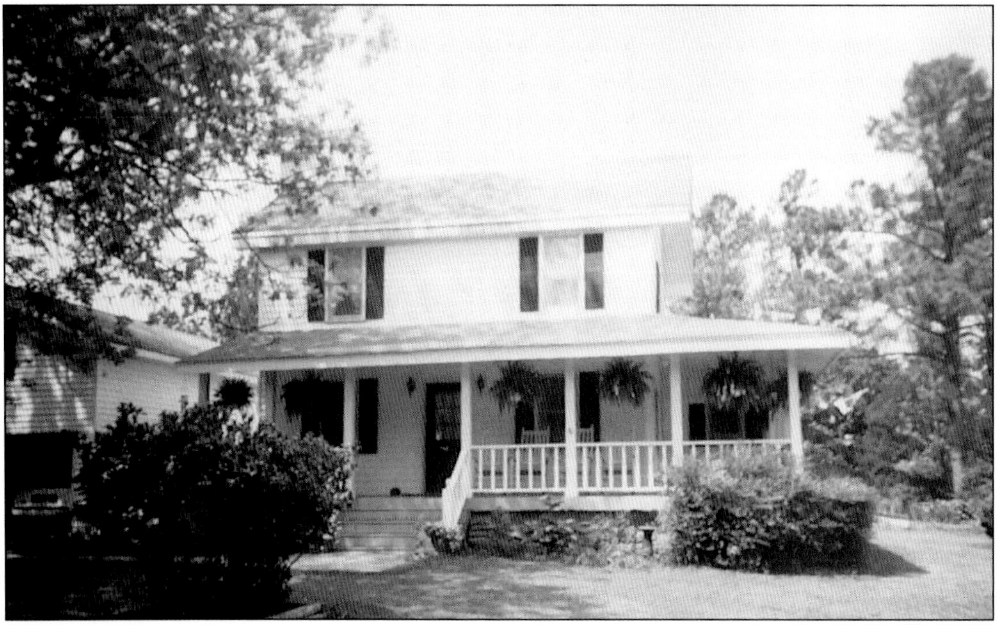

The home of Clyde B. and Carrie B. Ware was built before 1850, and restored in 1990 by its owners, Marshall T. and Betty Jean Ware. This house has always been in the Ware family, and the original log structure is now encased in the present house in Antreville.

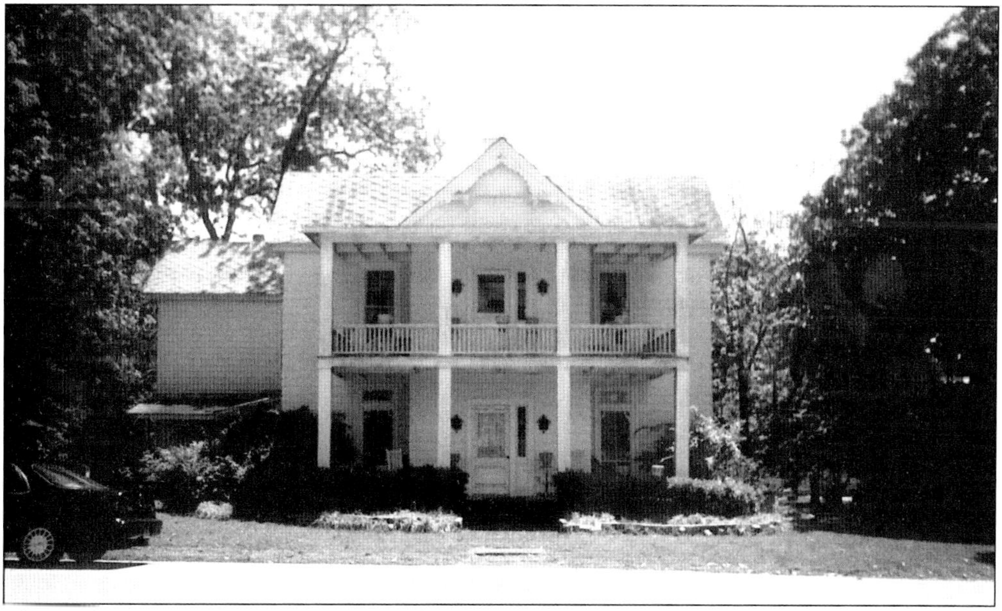

This is the oldest house in Iva. Located on the corner of Cook and Broad Streets, this house was built by Mr. W. Pringle Cook between 1880 and 1890. After the deaths of Mr. Cook and his widow, Mrs. Ella McGee Cook, the house was occupied by their son, Alfred Cook, and his wife, Mary Campbell Cook. It is now owned and occupied by the Pringle Cooks' granddaughter, Marguerite Cook Pruitt.

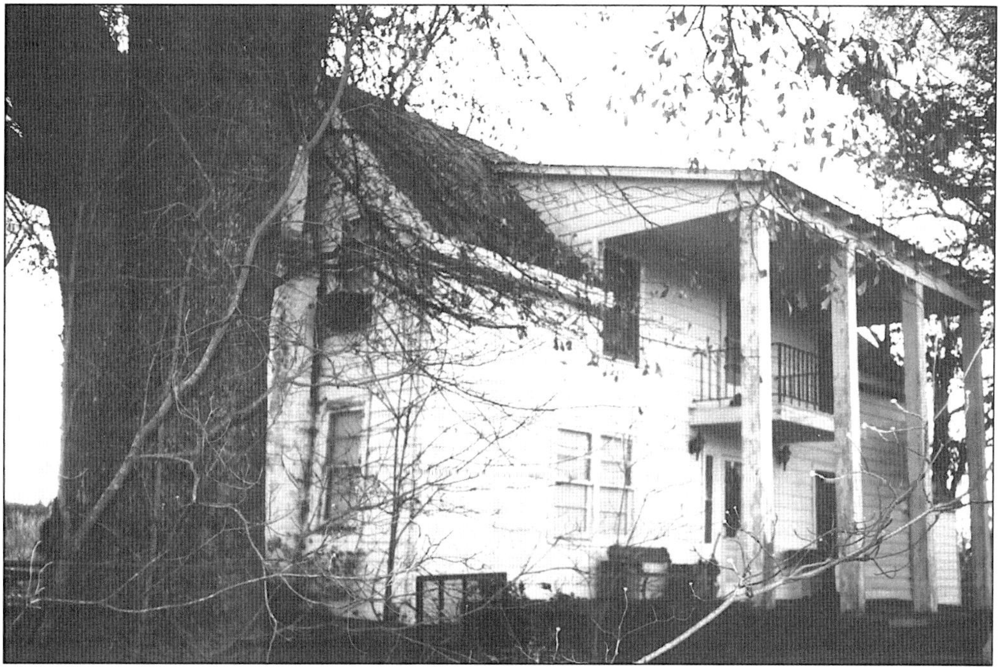

John T. Rainey built this house, in Starr, in 1832. The original house consisted of two rooms, and it was built from hand-sawed logs that can still be seen in the house today. Throughout the years, various members of the Rainey family have owned the home. The house is now owned by Eddie Purcell.

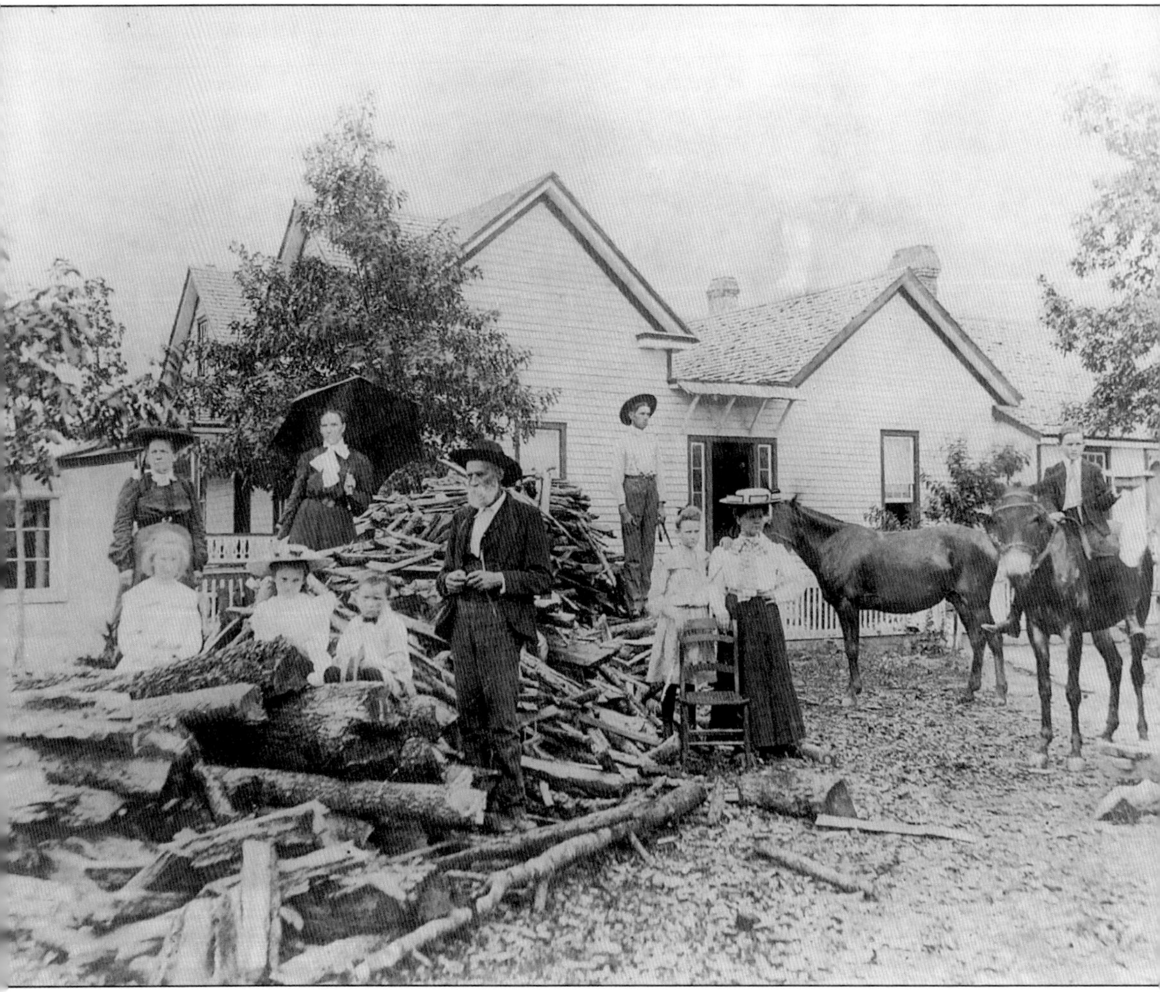

This picture, taken at the home of D.T Simpson Sr., c. 1900, includes members of two prominent Iva families, the Simpsons and the Cooks. The older man with the beard is Dury Thompson Sr., a local farmer and landowner. His wife, Mary Brown Simpson (Molly), is shown holding a parasol. Mr. Simpson's eldest son, Jesse W. Simpson Sr., is standing on the woodpile. His sons D.T. Jr. (sitting on the wood pile) and Hubert (on the mule) can also be seen. Lucy Simpson Hanks, the girl closest to D.T. Sr., and Thermutie Simpson Gailey, the older girl standing behind the chair, are daughters of Mr. Simpson. Mr. W.P. Cook (not pictured) was a longtime merchant and undertaker in Iva. His wife, Ella McGee Cook, is the older lady in the rear. Daughter Clara is directly in front of Mrs. Cook. Miss Essie Cook, who became a schoolteacher at Iva High School, is the younger girl standing behind the chair. The house, now occupied by Roy Glenn and Madell Hanks Glenn (daughter of Lucy), is located on East Broad Street in Iva.

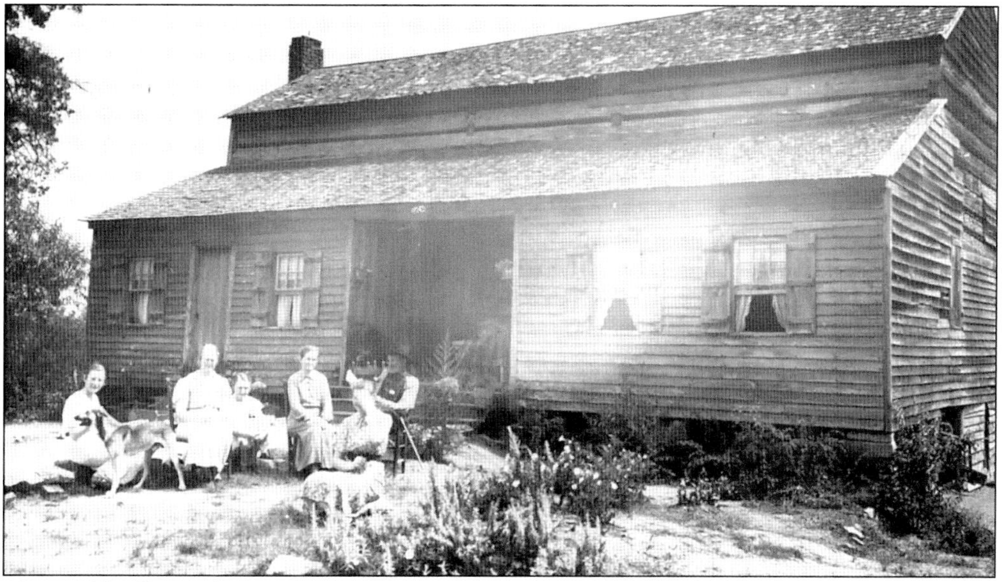

The Caldwell-Hutchinson House was built around 1780 at Lowndesville. Its upper story was made from massive, 49-foot-long, pine timber logs, which had been hand-hewn and squared. The house was purchased, c. 1876, by Barney Hutchinson. The last occupants were Katherine Hutchinson and her brother, Bandon, until 1980, when it was turned over to the Corps of Engineers with plans to make the house part of the McCalla State Park. Pictured here, from left to right, are the following: daughters Ruth H. McCarley, Katherine Hutchinson, Marie Hutchinson, and Frances H. Belcher in front; mother Mary Lou Kelley; and father Mallie B. Hutchinson.

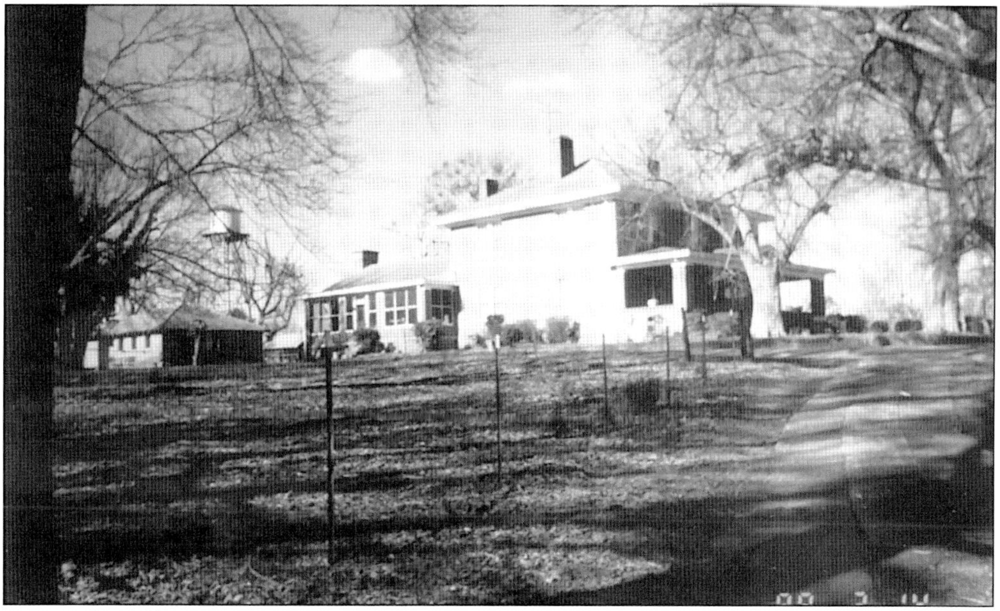

Savannah Valley Farm, in Starr, was owned by the Kenneth McGee family. Built prior to 1850, the building is listed by Pendleton Historical Society as a "Centennial Farm." "The Big House" was built by Willis McGee for his son Jesse (who served in the Civil War and is buried in Starr Baptist Church Cemetery).

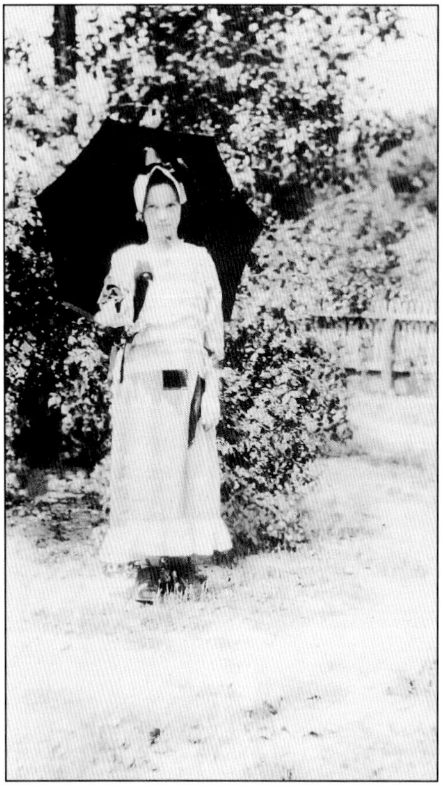

This picture of 15-year-old Madell Hanks Glenn was taken on her way to a "tacky party." The idea of this type of party was to award a prize to the person who looked the tackiest. Boys did not dress "tacky" for these parties. The youngsters played games such as "spin the bottle," "wink," "post office," and "four in the middle." Everybody had a good time.

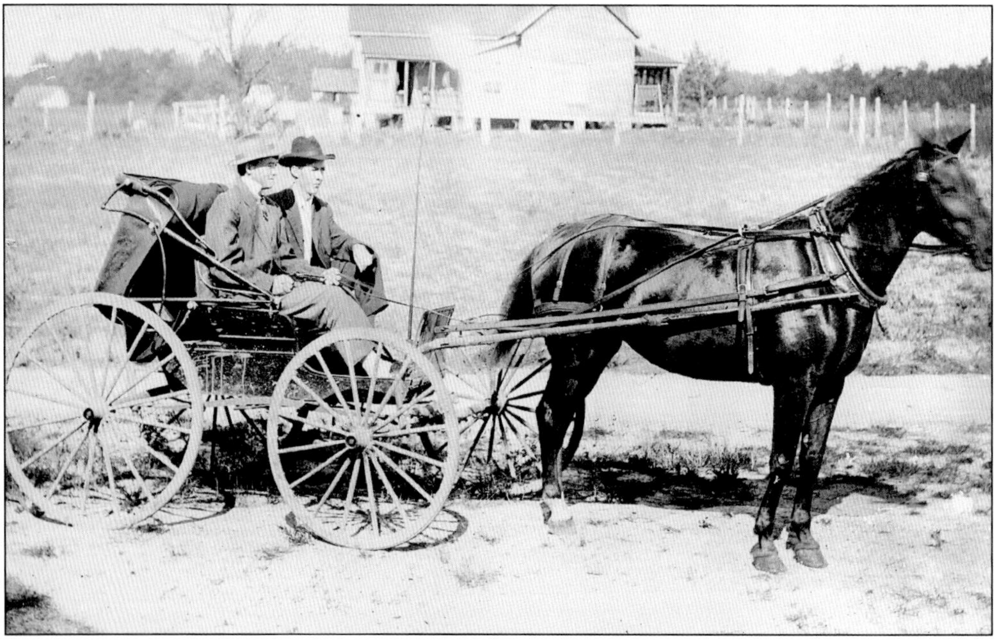

Mr. Hubert Simpson and Mr. Willie Gailey are seen enjoying a buggy ride. This horse and buggy belonged to Hubert's father and Willie Gailey's father-in-law, Mr. Thompson Simpson. These two young men often rode this buggy to Wilson Creek, where they would place spent shells on a board and then use the floating shells as a target to practice their marksmanship.

This unidentified little girl is very unhappy. It appears that she has skinned both her knees and, perhaps, her little hand. It is likely that she would rather not have had her picture taken at this time. Tincture of iodine was the medicine that was most used for cuts and bruises in this era. She probably also could have used a kiss and a hug.

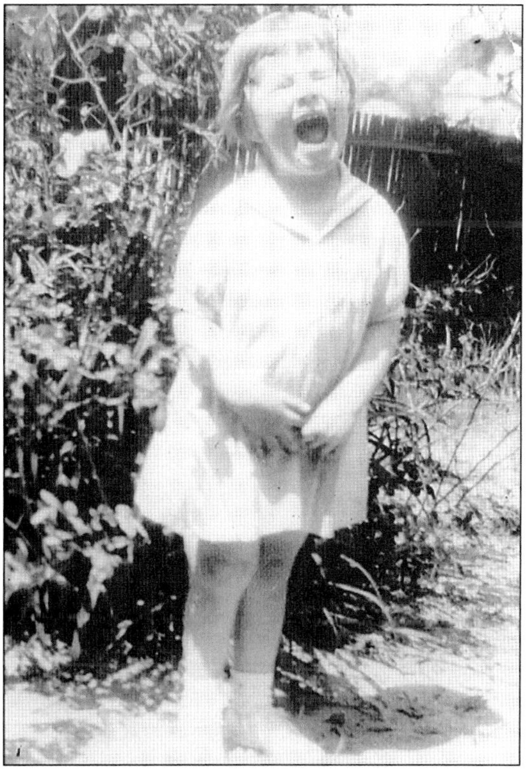

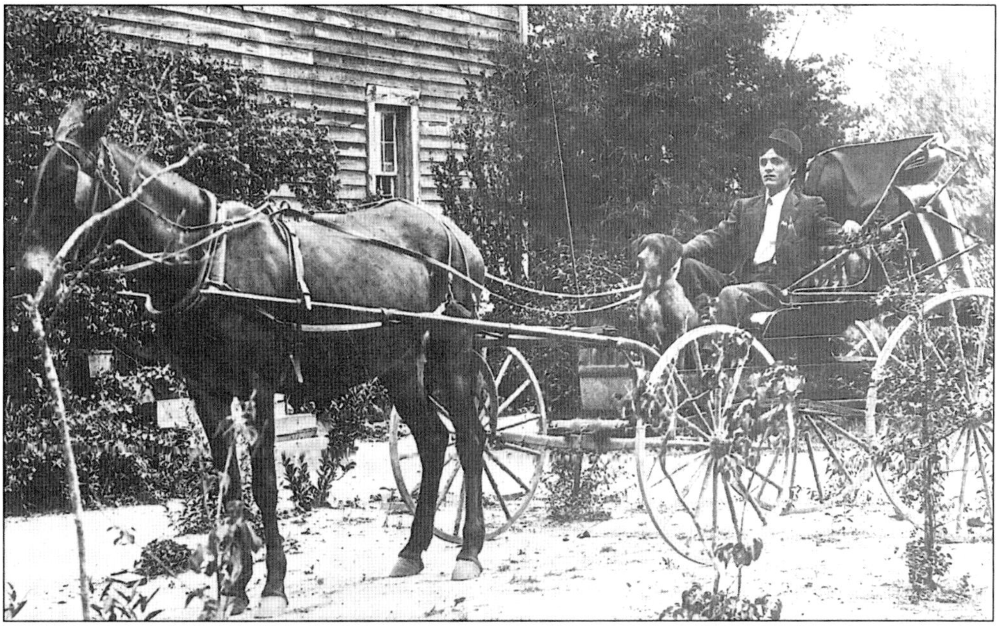

Cleburn Allen (Clebe) Wiles is seen here, in his early twenties, taking a ride in his new buggy with his dog. This picture was taken, in the early 1900s, at the home of his parents, David and Annie McBride Wiles. He worked at Jackson Mill and bought this buggy from S.H. Findley & Company in Iva. He later married Theola Burton, and they had three daughters, Mary Campbell, Mildred Brown, and Edith Williams.

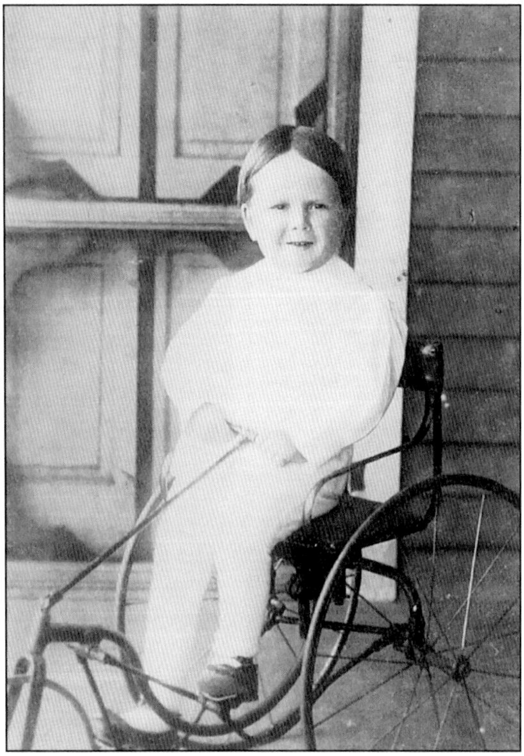

In this photograph, taken around 1916, George McDonald tries out a wonderful new toy on the side veranda of the family home on Betsy Street. Due to the carefully parted hair and "Sunday-go-to-meeting" outfit, it would appear that this was a meticulously posed photograph, rather than a candid, everyday shot.

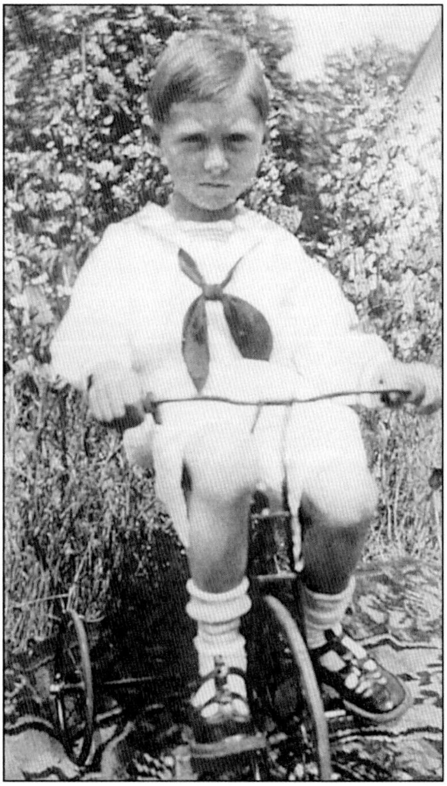

Young Carl Evans is seen in his sailor suit, enjoying a ride on his tricycle in 1928. Carl presently likes to take part in festivals all around Iva, where he entertains groups by performing his clown and magic acts. Carl is an active member of the REVIVA organization.

J.W. Simpson and his younger sister, Mildred Simpson Campbell, appear to be content to have their picture made. They are wearing typical attire for 1921, a time when a photographer would come to Iva with his crude cameras, tripods, and focusing cloths. The children were hurriedly dressed because the cameraman came unannounced. J.W. Simpson later married Dorothy Milford, and Mildred is now married to Jack Campbell. This photograph was taken at the home of Franklin Hayes.

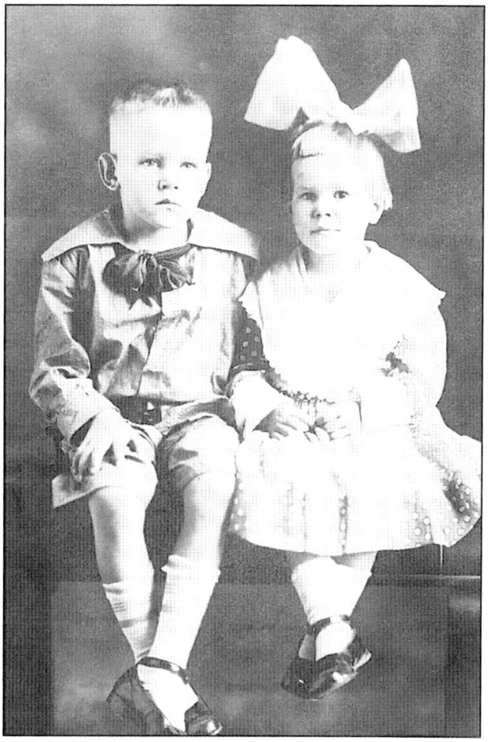

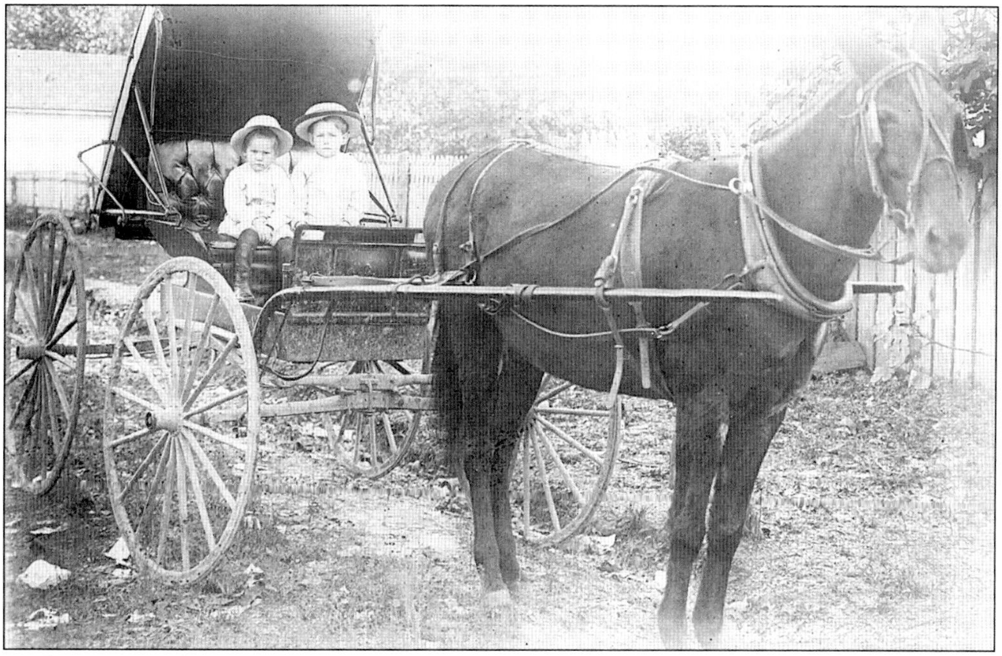

In the 1920s, a horse-and-buggy ride was always fun, if you could get a driver. Marcus and Jerome Simpson of Iva are pictured here, going for a ride. They are the sons of Laurin Simpson and Lois Jones Simpson. Jerome joined the Air Force in 1941 and served in New Guinea. He was killed, while in service, in a jeep accident on December 25, 1942. Marcus, who served in the Korean conflict, lives in Belmont, North Carolina.

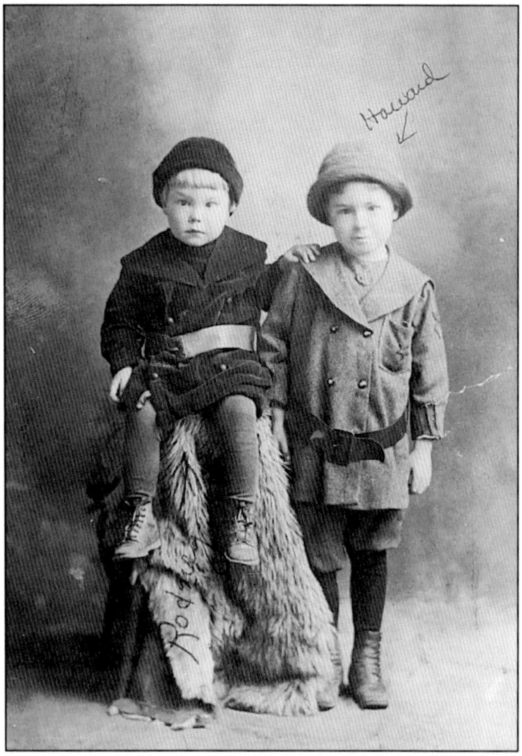

This is the way little boys of Iva used to dress up to get their picture made, or to go to church, *c.* 1914. Rodney Bowman, age three, and his big brother, Howard, appear to be on their best behavior in this photograph. As the children of Zannie and Lula Prince Bowman, Rodney and Howard were the first of what was to become a family of 11 boys and 1 girl. Rodney, an avid REVIVA member, died in 1991.

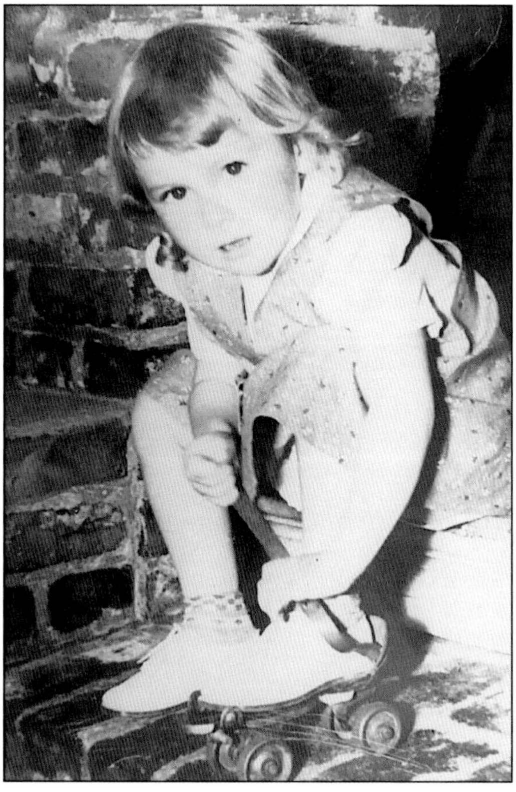

Rodney Bowman's daughter, "Bunny," age three, is pictured putting on her roller skates for an afternoon outing on the sidewalk near her home. Today, children's sports include skateboarding, snow boarding, skiing, and rollerblading, just to name a few. Times do change, but it is all fun!

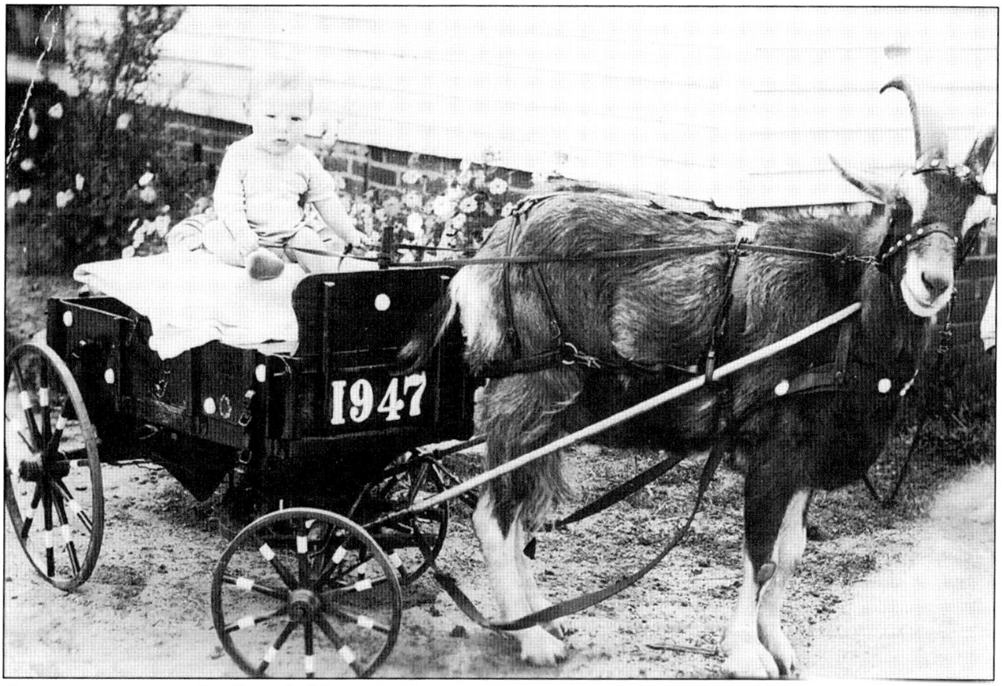

An exciting time for Iva children in the 1940s was when the "goat man" came to town. He made his rounds to Upstate towns every so often. Pictured here is one-year-old Ottman Metz, riding the goat cart at Central Avenue on the "Mill Hill" in Iva. Ottman is the son of Mr. and Mrs. Winston Metz.

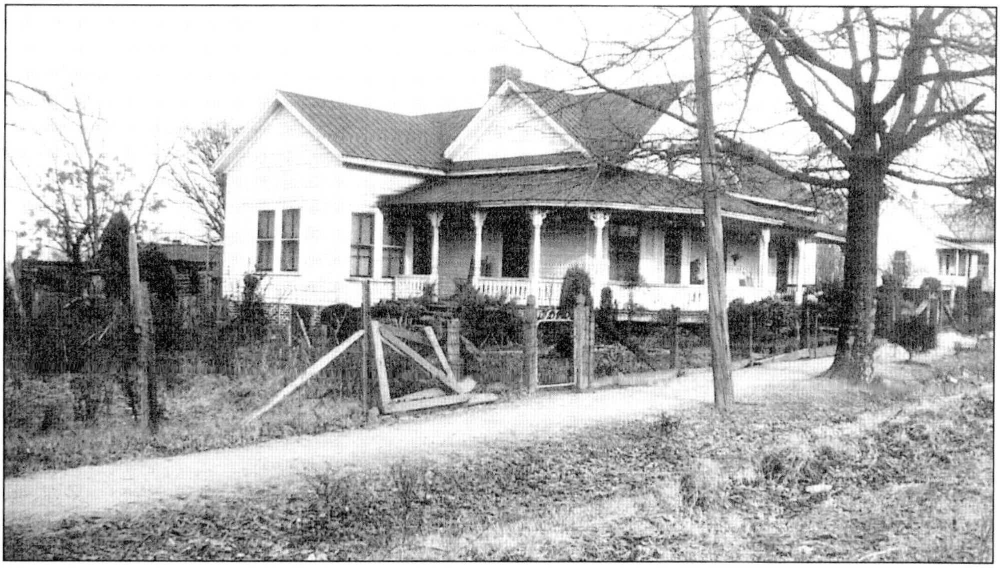

The Thomas Amos and Belle McDonald home on Betsy Street, in Iva, was once a large farm where leghorn chickens were raised. Anderson Hospital was provided with 90-dozen eggs a week from here. Later, in the 1930s and 1940s, this building served as a boardinghouse for teachers at the Iva School, which was located a block away.

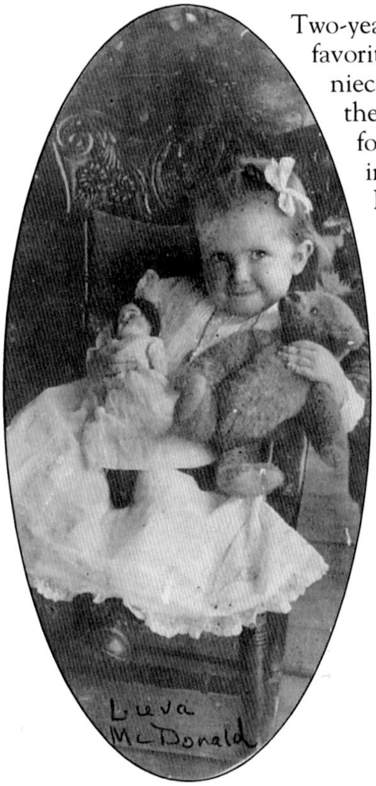

Two-year-old Mary Luva McDonald proudly shows off her two favorite toys in this photograph, which was taken in 1908. Her niece and namesake, Mary Faith McDonald Craft, still has the treasured china doll. Luva grew up to be a music teacher for 45 years, having studied at the Julliard School of Music in New York. Luva was the daughter of Thomas and Belle McDonald.

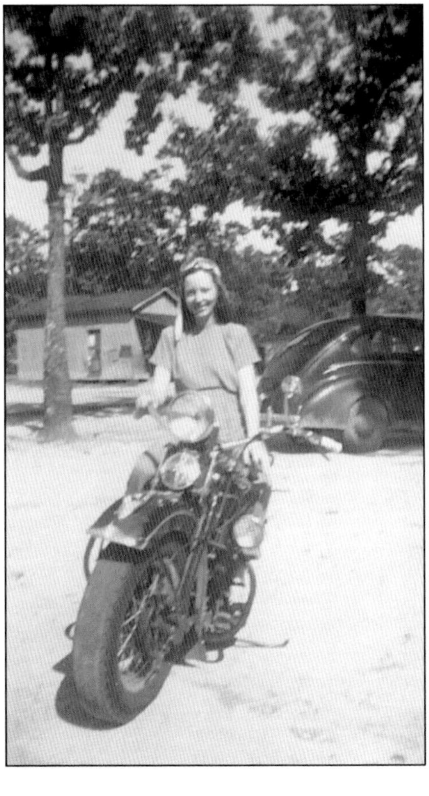

Young people of the Iva area, during the early 1940s, loved to ride motorcycles, and many times they would organize groups to ride to the beaches together. Abalena Hanks Cook, probably on her brother Aaron's Harley Davidson, appears to be ready to go. Abalena and Aaron often rode together with Paul Gray. Abalena later married Dell Cook, and they had one son, Jimmy. She retired from The Peoples Bank of Iva as executive vice-president.

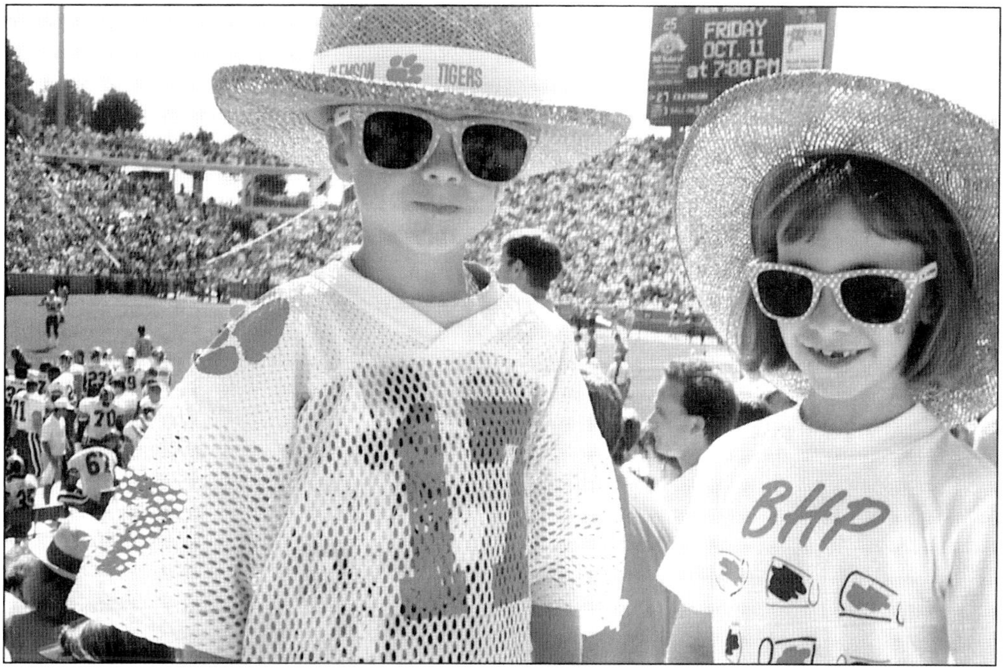

By the 1980s, times had changed, as can be seen from this photograph. These two young children, Reid McGee of Iva and Katie Blume of Belton, were in the crowds to root for their Clemson University football team, which had won the 1981 National Championship.

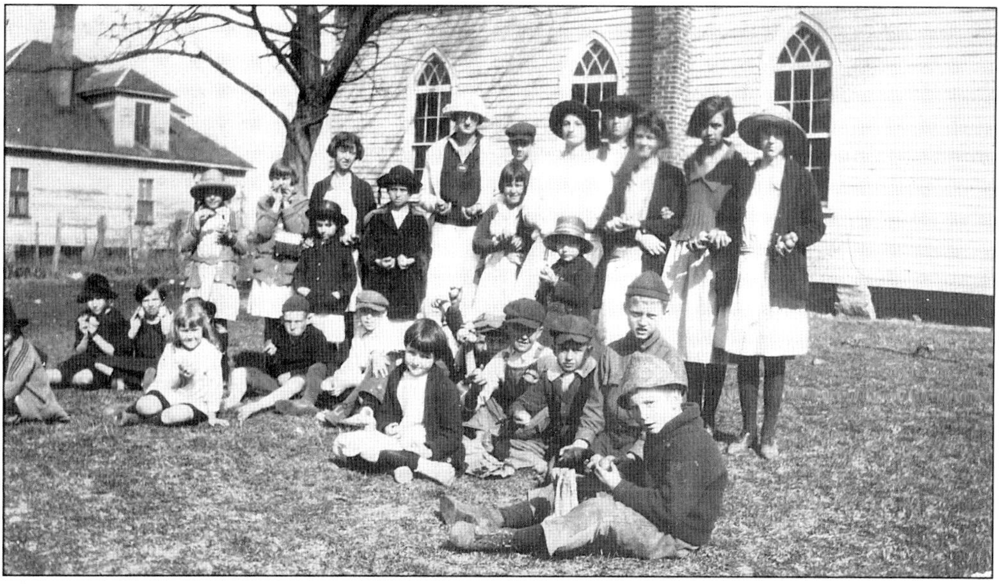

This is an Easter egg hunt, in the mid-'40s, at the Iva Associate Reformed Presbyterian Church. Out of an egg comes new life, and the baby chick coming out of the shell symbolizes Christ coming out of the tomb. The beautifully colored eggs symbolize new life that spring flowers bring.

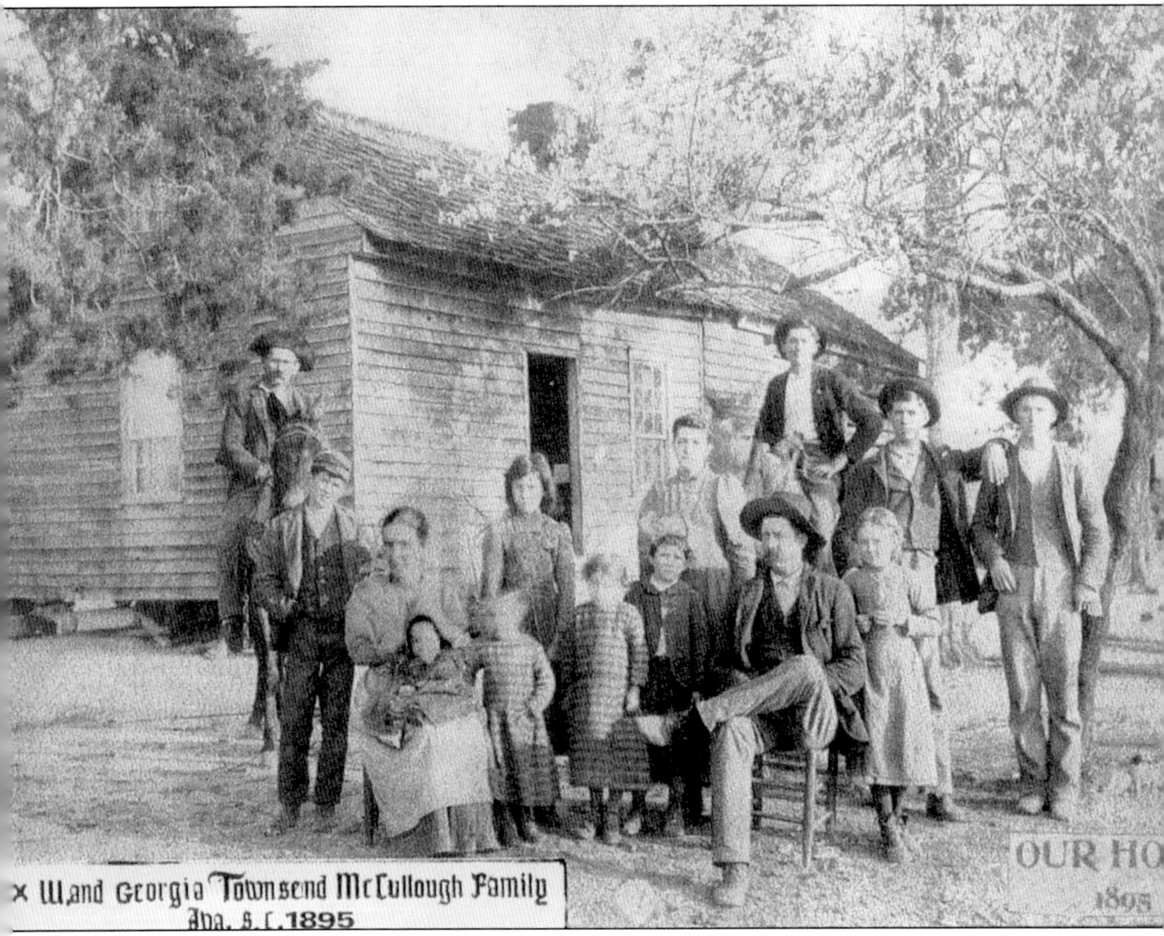

This picture of Alexander and Georgia Townsend McCullough was taken in 1895. Alexander was the son of John and Eliza Wiles McCullough, and his wife was the daughter of W. Thomas and Margaret Townsend of Lowndesville. Their children were Robert D., Alonzo H., Austin A., Samuel D., Bessie L., Rosetta, Ben Tillman, Itta, Floyd W., Netta, Carl E., Nannie, and two other children who died as infants.

Six

Churches and Cemeteries

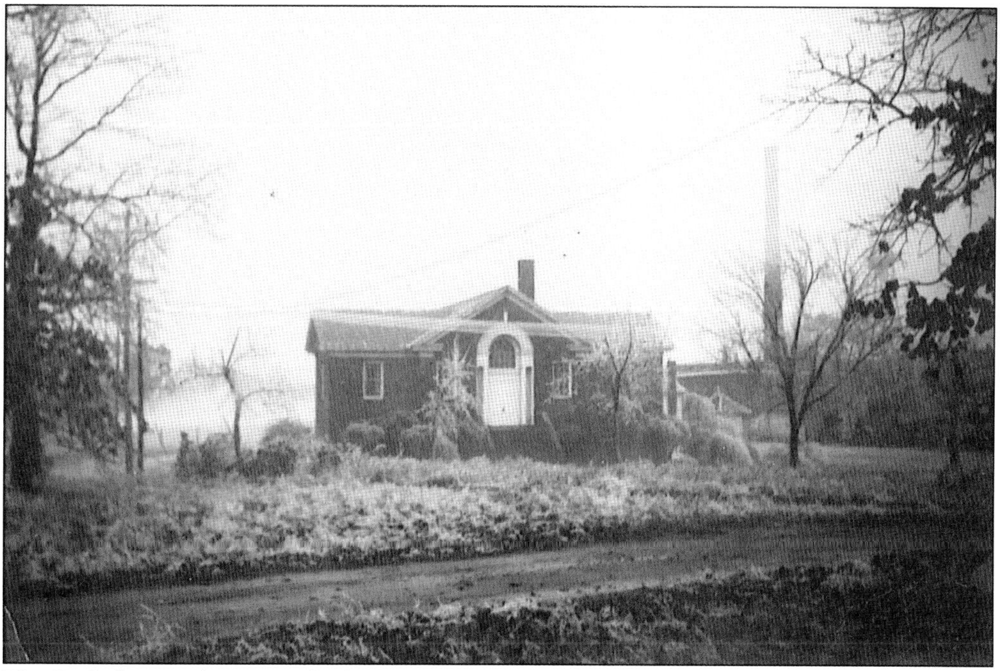

The Bethel United First Methodist Church in Iva was organized in 1889 and located on land donated by Dr. A.G. Cook. The cemetery remains near the site of the old Iva High School. In 1927, a new church, pictured above, was built on land donated by Mr. Alfred Moore, Jackson Mills' president. The first service was held on April 15, 1928. In 1949, a parsonage was built next to the church. In 1974, a new sanctuary and a fellowship hall were added, with the first service taking place on March 27, 1977. The present pastor is Reverend Sam Thomason.

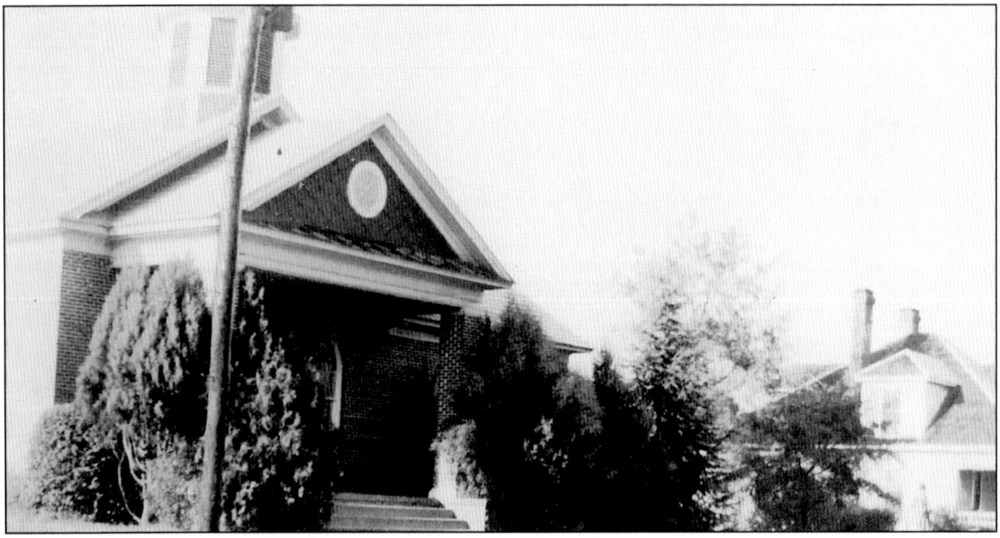

The Iva Associate Reformed Presbyterian (ARP) Church was organized on November 8, 1895, by the second Presbytery, with 21 charter members. The first church building was erected around 1897. The church, as it stands now on Betsy Street, was erected in 1924. The Echols family was the first to live in the first manse, which was a frame building, built in 1907, just a few feet below the present manse site.

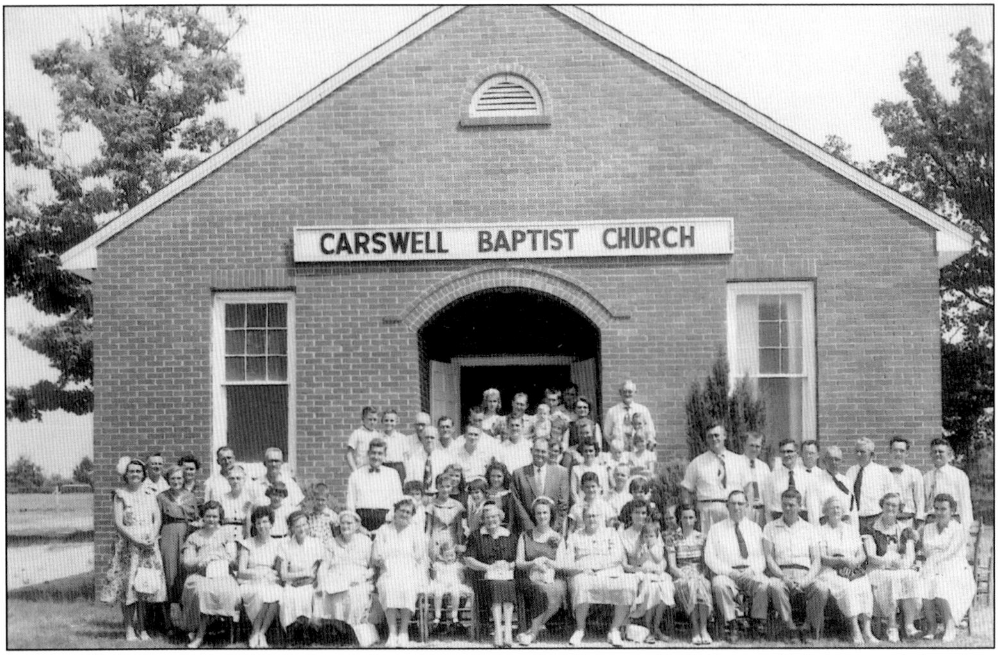

Carswell Baptist Church originated as a two-story building called Carswell Institute. The first story was used as a church and school. The second story was used by the Herman Masonic Lodge. The building was erected in January 1876. It was the first public school in Anderson County. In the late 1800s, it ceased to be a private institution. In 1924, Savannah, Hebron, and Varennes schools were combined to become Bowen school. Across from Carswell Baptist Church is a house of logs pegged together. Now owned by Mrs. Henry Holcombe, it originally belonged to Sam McAdams, a former Iva mayor.

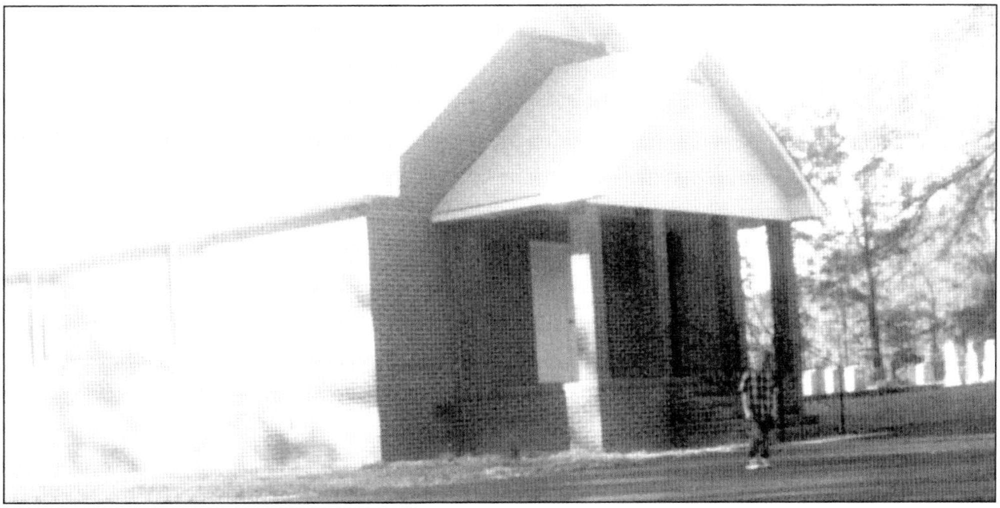

Generostee Associate Reformed Presbyterian Church is the oldest ARP church in Anderson County. It dates from around 1790, when it was founded by people of Scottish descent. The church gets its name from Little Generostee Creek, which was named for the American Indians' expression "Atchinaausdi" (at·cheen·a·oos·di), meaning "little cedar." The white settlers thought that the American Indians were saying "Generostee." The church burned in 1985, and this new brick church was built on Parker Bowie Road, west of Iva.

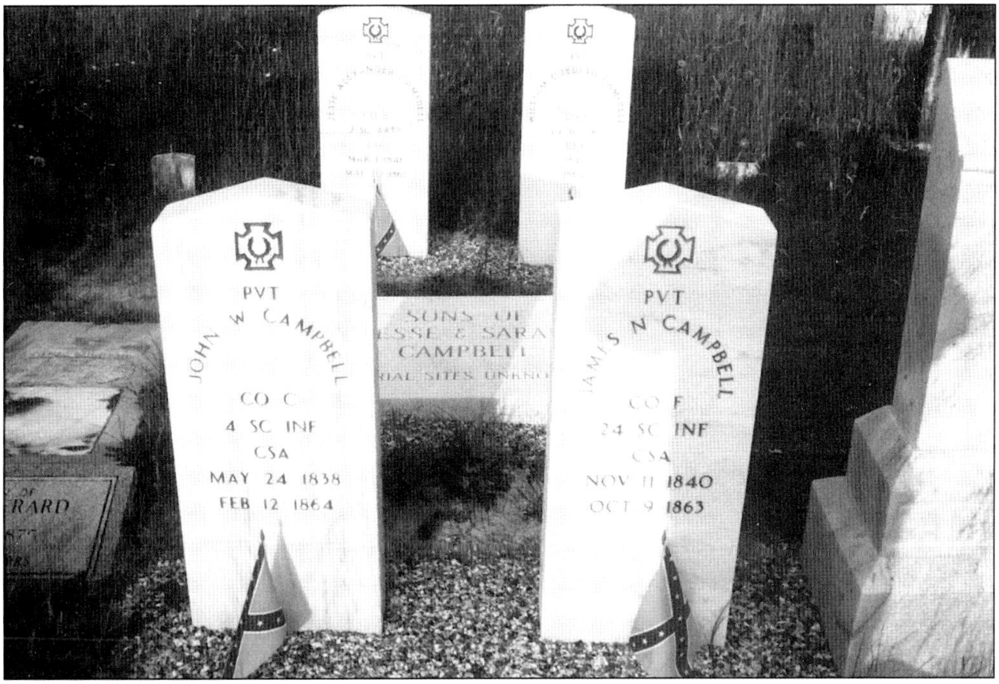

Four Campbell brothers of the Moffettsville community served and died in the Civil War. They were the sons of Jesse and Sarah Campbell, and their names were James N. Campbell, John Wesley Campbell, William Obediah Campbell, and Jesse Alexander Campbell. Burial sites are unknown for these four brothers, and in March of 1998, James N. Campbell's great-grandson, Marcus Campbell, erected four Civil War monuments in their names at the Generostee ARP Church.

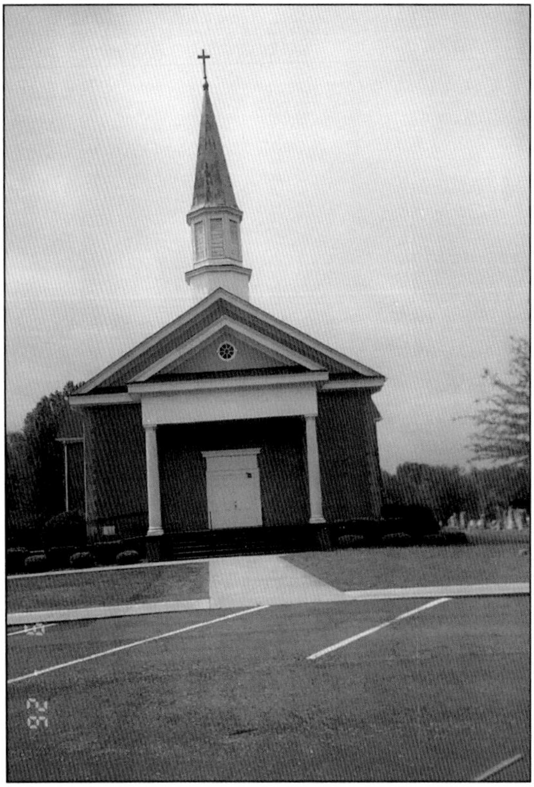

Built in 1858, Starr Baptist Church has been known for generations as the "Cross Roads." Located on Highway 81, it was the first rural brick church in Anderson County, and was established as a mission by the old Shockley's Ferry Church. The bricks were made in the stream below the church. Three of the original bricks are over the front door of the present church. It became Starr Baptist Church on April 19, 1936. Until 1941, the church remained virtually unchanged.

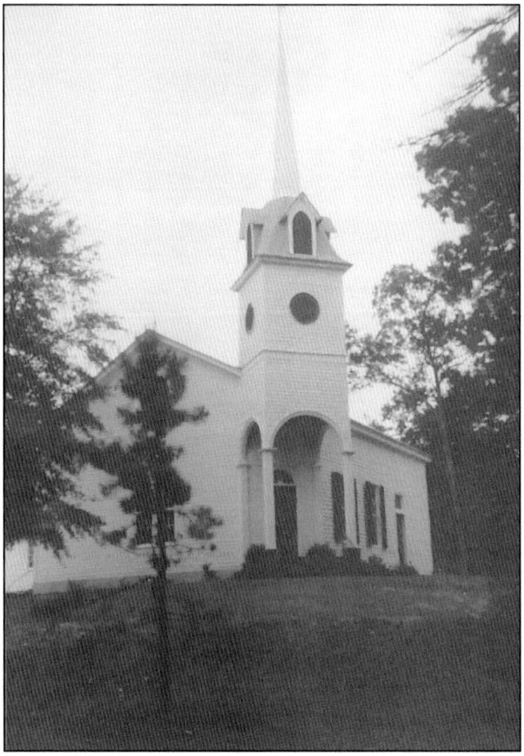

Lowndesville Providence Presbyterian Church is one of Lowndesville's most prominent landmarks. The church dates from 1841, and it continues to hold services today. A popular and picturesque scene for artists, the lovely, white, framed building has its original flooring and walls, which have been well preserved.

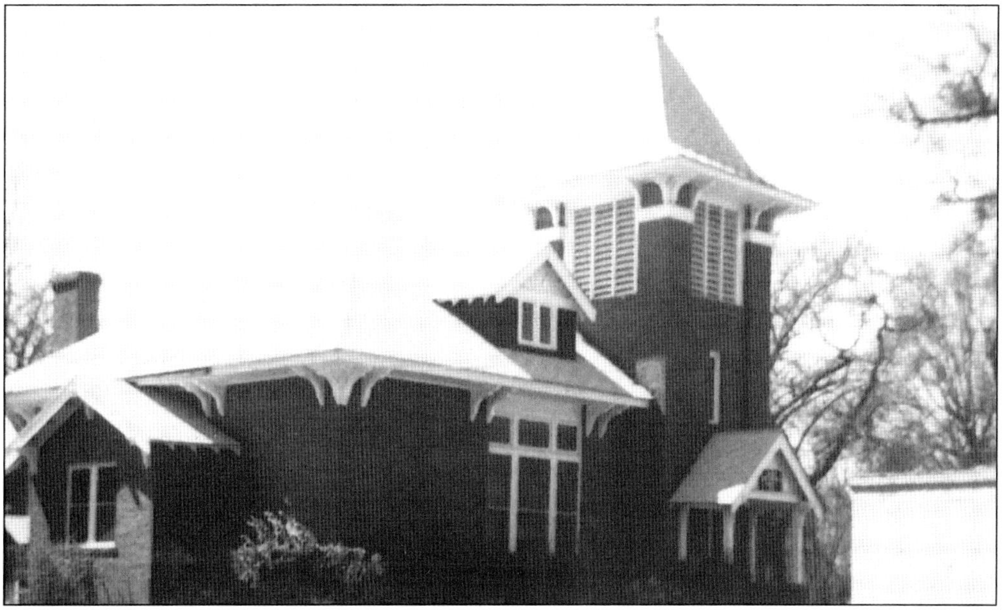

Smyrna Methodist Church was originally called the Bowie Meeting House, and it was organized in 1808. Its name was changed to Smyrna in 1823, and its present location is on the corner of Depot and North Main Streets in the lovely little town of Lowndesville, which is 7 miles south of Iva. The church has been at this location since April 7, 1917.

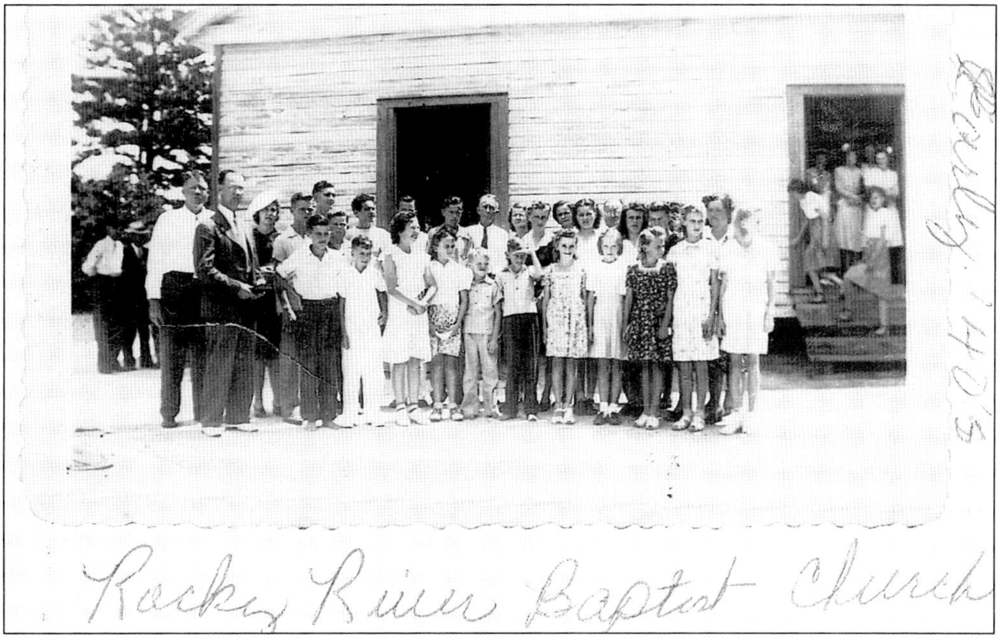

A baptismal group is shown in front of Rocky River Baptist Church in Iva. From left to right are, (front row) the Reverend M.A. Guest, Boyd Smith, Billy Purdy, Virginia Boles, Bobby Campbell, Bobby Smith, Marion Alewine, Joyce Hanks, Sue Thornton, Jeanette Burton, and Doris Alewine; (back row) John Mahaffy, Mrs. M.A. Guest, Howard Simpson, Billy Tacker, Jack Hall, Lamar Smith, Cooley Campbell Sr., Zilly Campbell, Bernice Compton, Sadie Smith, Lucia Gurley, Jess Smith, Faye Smith, Juanita Smith, Lulee Bell Busby, and Roxy Compton.

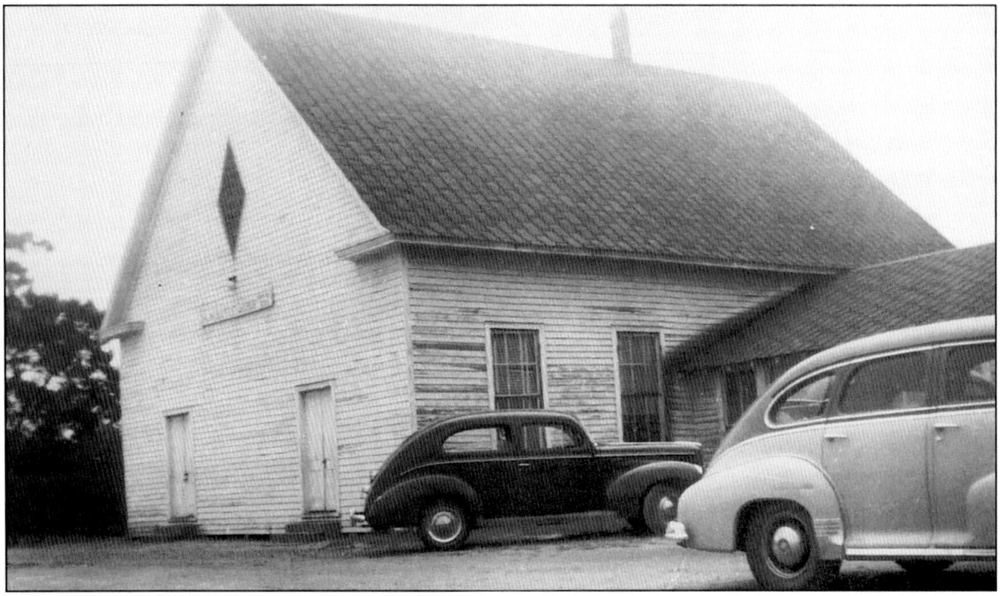

Union Baptist Church, formerly the Fellowship and Liberty Church, was organized in 1834. The original church was located two miles below Craft's Ferry on the Savannah River, near Alexander's Mill. In 1858, the church fellowship united with Liberty, and it was then located at Barnes Station.

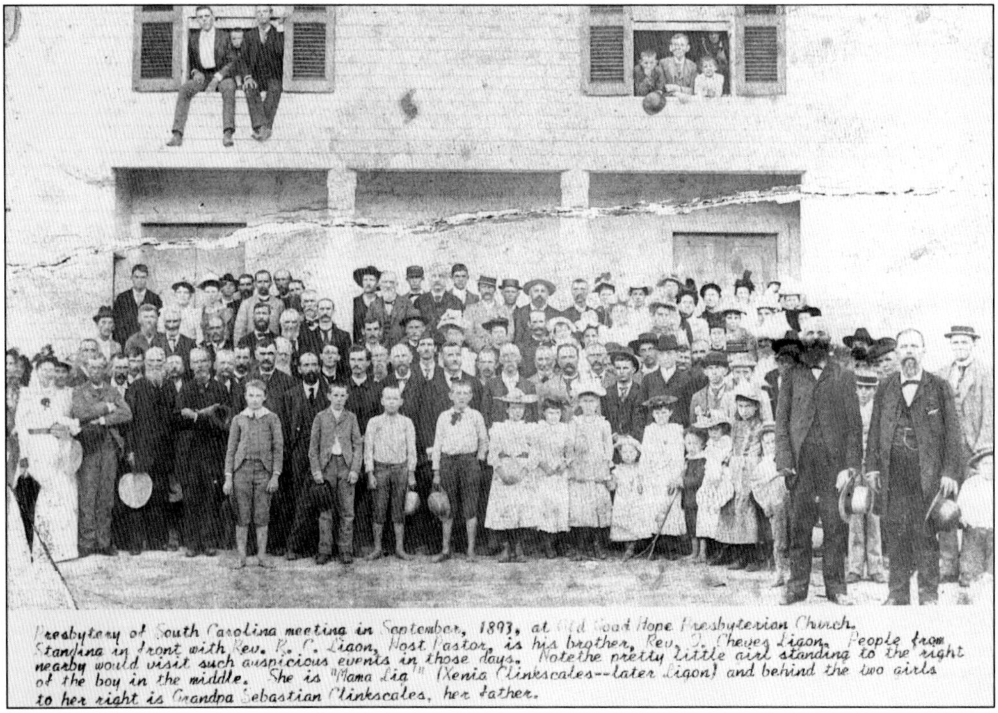

Standing in the yard are members of old Good Hope Presbyterian Church, including two sons of Reverend R.C. Ligon. This was the third structure of Good Hope Presbyterian Church. In 1909, a beautiful brick edifice was erected in the town of Iva, after being moved from the country.

The Reverend Richard Cater Ligon was minister of Good Hope Presbyterian Church for 25 years from 1877 until 1902. Prior to his coming to Iva, Reverend Ligon served as pastor at Providence Presbyterian Church in Lowndesville.

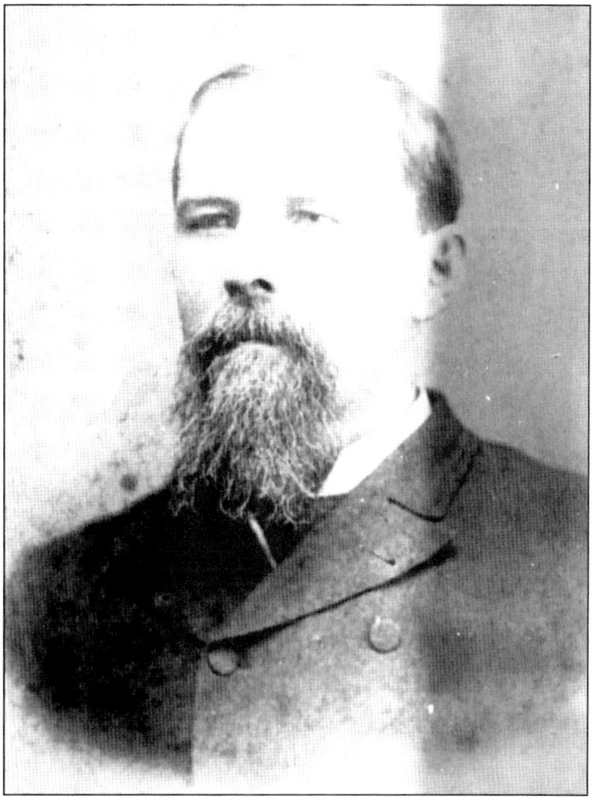

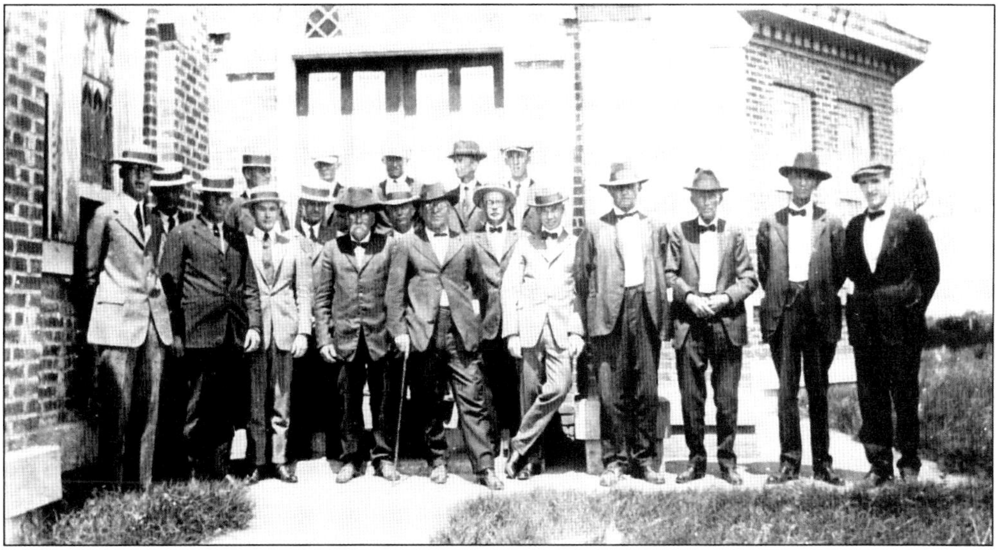

The group posing for this picture comprises members of the men's Bible class at Good Hope Presbyterian Church in Iva. This church was organized in 1789, one month before George Washington was inaugurated as the first president of our country. The church moved from the country to Iva in 1909. It is the oldest church in Anderson County in continuous existence since its organization.

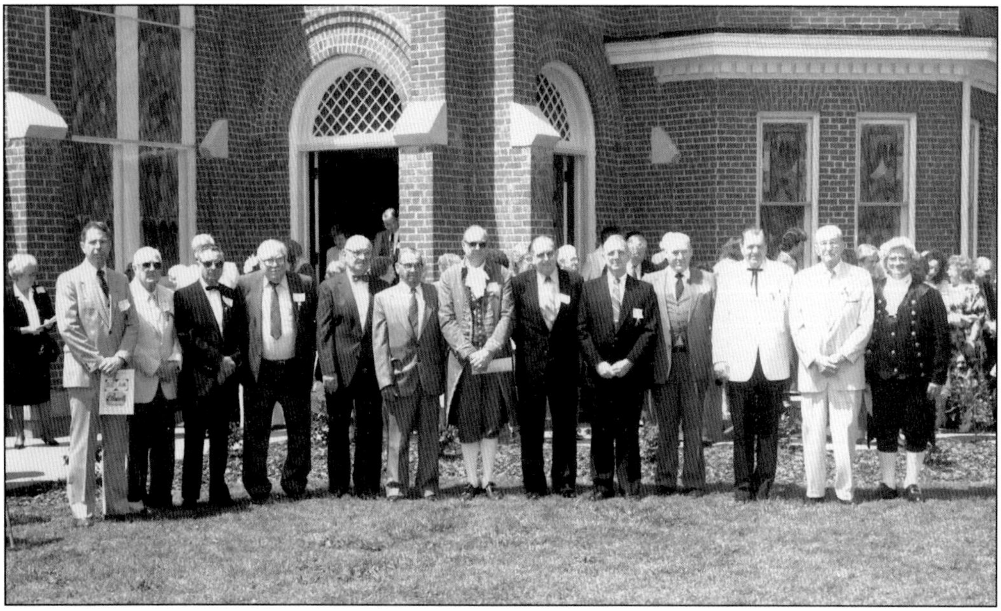

Elders of Good Hope Presbyterian Church are pictured on the occasion of Good Hope's hosting the quarterly meeting of Foothills Presbytery. From left to right are as follows: Lindsey Funchess, Carroll Erwin, Duane Gailey, Olin Helms, Broadus Bryant, Charles Beatty, Herman Hughes, Broadus Holbrook, David Newby, Gaines Mathis, Bruce Tarleton, Everett Parks, and Ernest Evans.

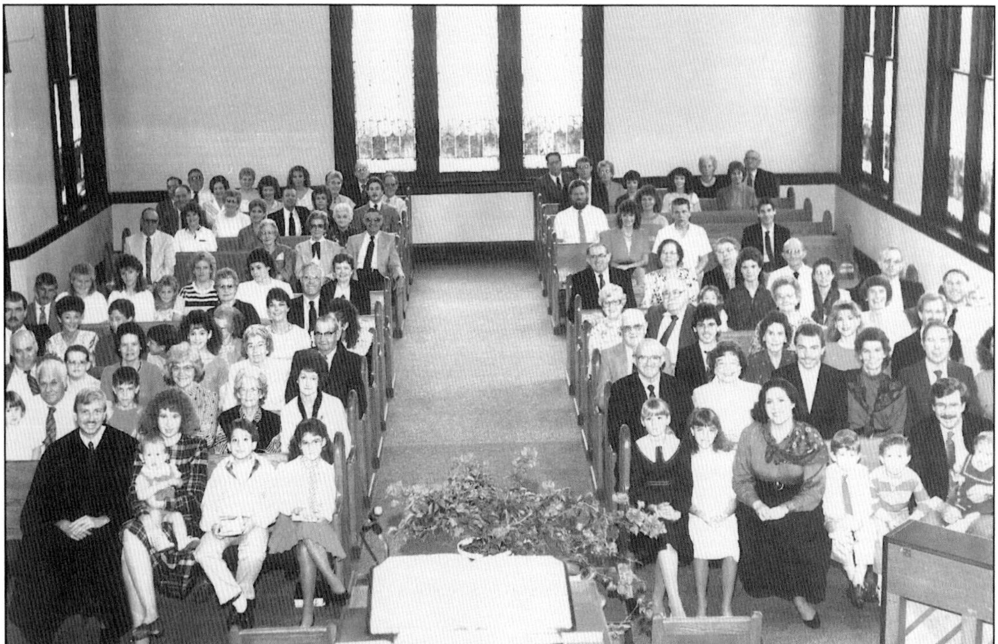

This picture of Good Hope Presbyterian Church was taken during the bicentennial celebration, held in 1989. Members pose with big smiles for the camera. The church's beautiful stained-glass windows are pictured in the background. This is one of the oldest Presbyterian churches in South Carolina.

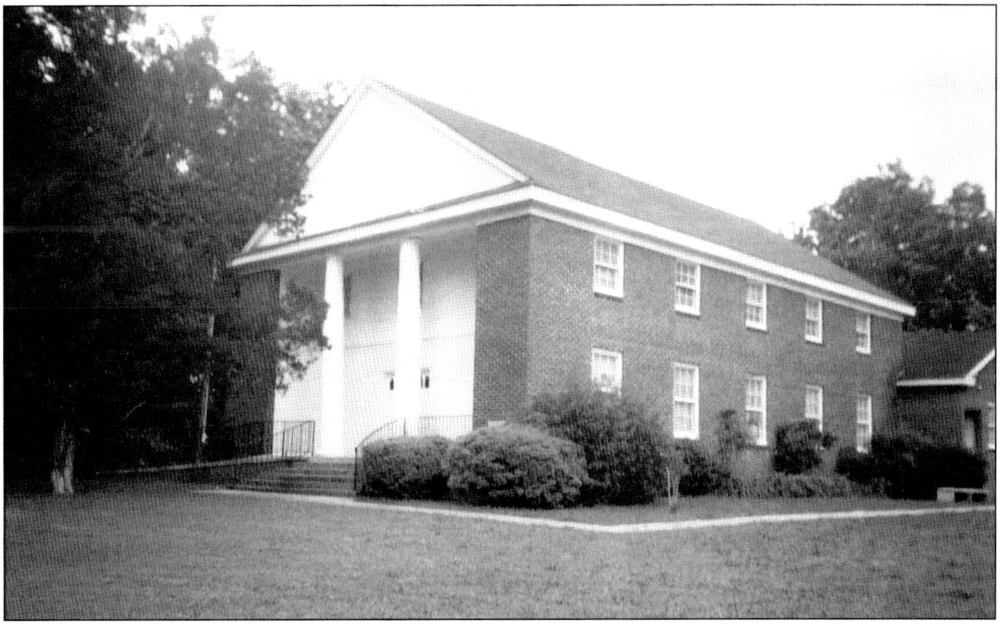

Shiloh Methodist Church is located in Antreville. This church was organized in 1828, and the pictured building was constructed in 1858. It was remodeled in 1958 for its centennial celebration. The slave balconies were enclosed for Sunday school rooms during remodeling, and the outside stairway leading to the balconies was removed. The columns, in front, are original.

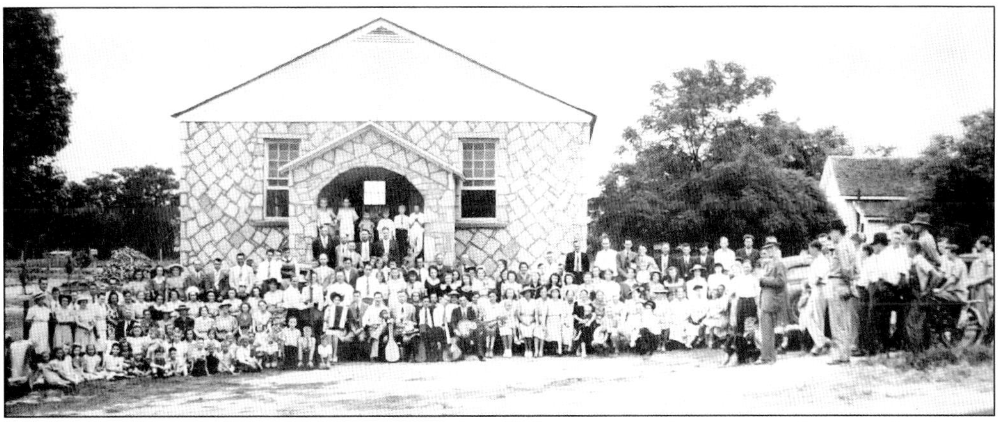

Members of the Church of God, in Iva, are seen here posing for a group photograph. A new sanctuary was built in the 1970s, adjacent to the original rock structure. The church's current pastor is Reverend Lollis.

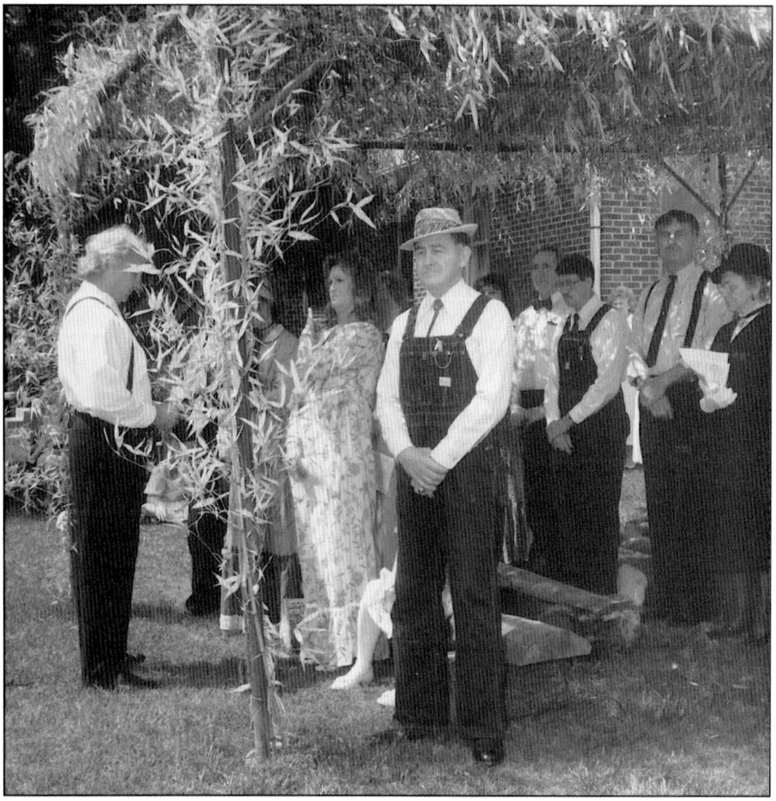

The Iva First Baptist Church celebrated its centennial in 1990 with a Brush Arbor service and ceremony. A descendant of the Reverend Seigler, one of the first ministers of the church, took part in the ceremony.

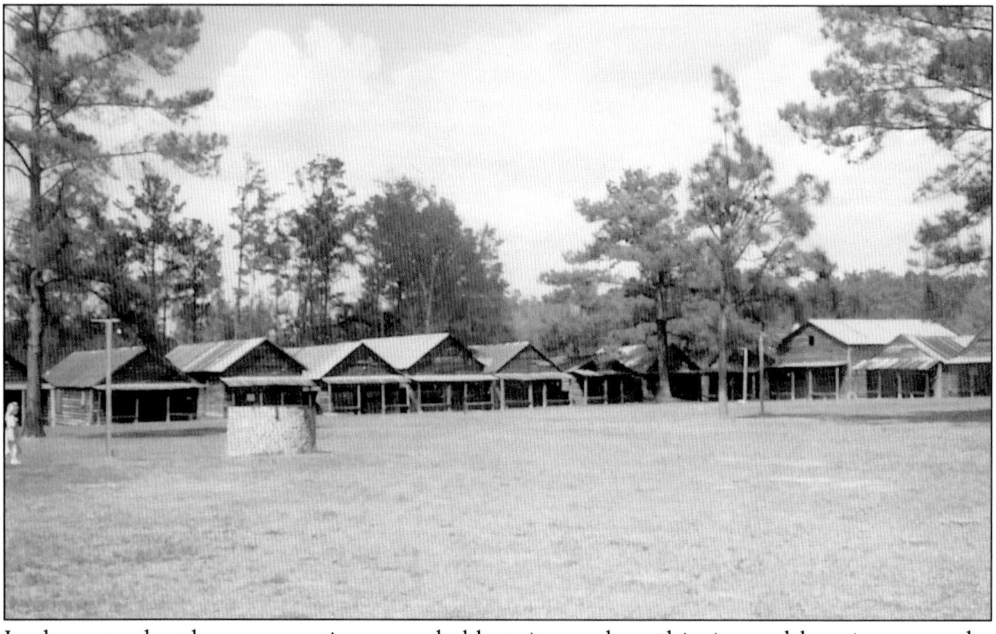

In the past, church camp meetings were held at sites such as this, in rural locations over the state. It was a time for family fellowship and worship. Families came and stayed for days at a time, bringing all the supplies they needed. Several churches joined together for these events of Bible study and fellowship.

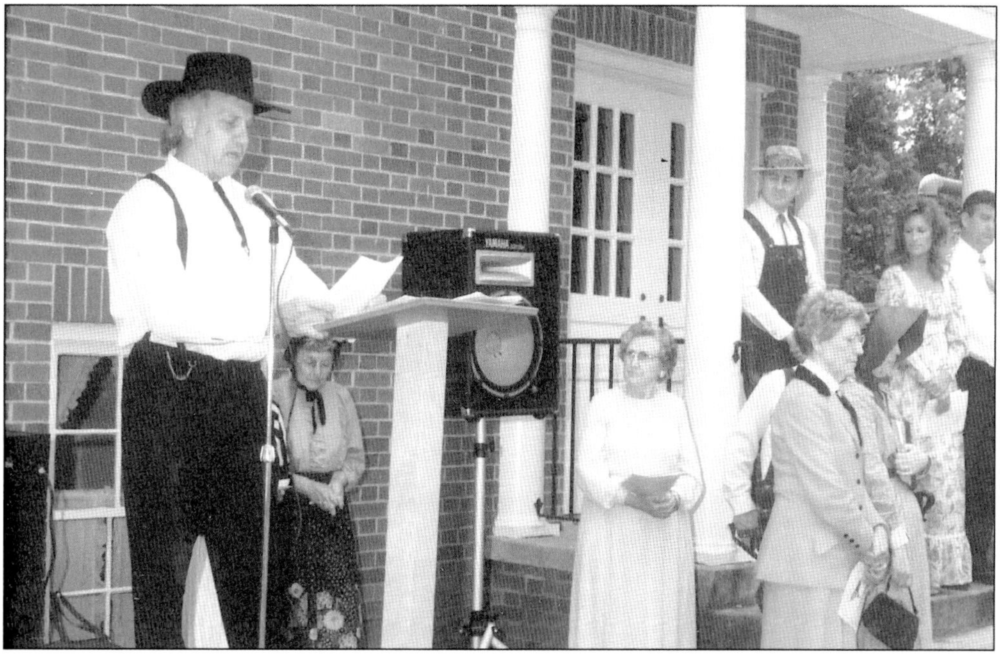

Tommy Seigler, a descendant of one of the first pastors of Iva First Baptist Church, shares history, during the centennial program, with church members Polly Compton, Emma Gailey, Ethyl Hall, Raymond Butler, Sharon Davis, and J.R. McGee, pictured above from left to right.

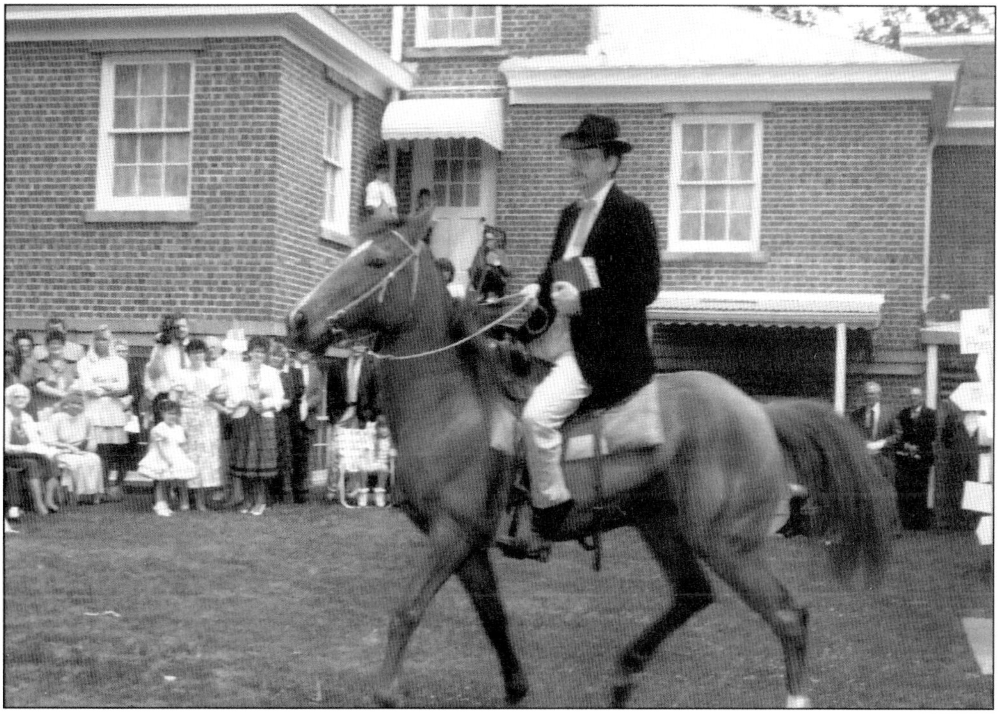

Johnny Wiles was portraying a "Circuit Rider Preacher" during Iva First Baptist Church's centennial celebration (1890–1990) at its Brush Arbor event. A circuit rider preacher was a preacher who traveled from church to church on a regular circuit route.

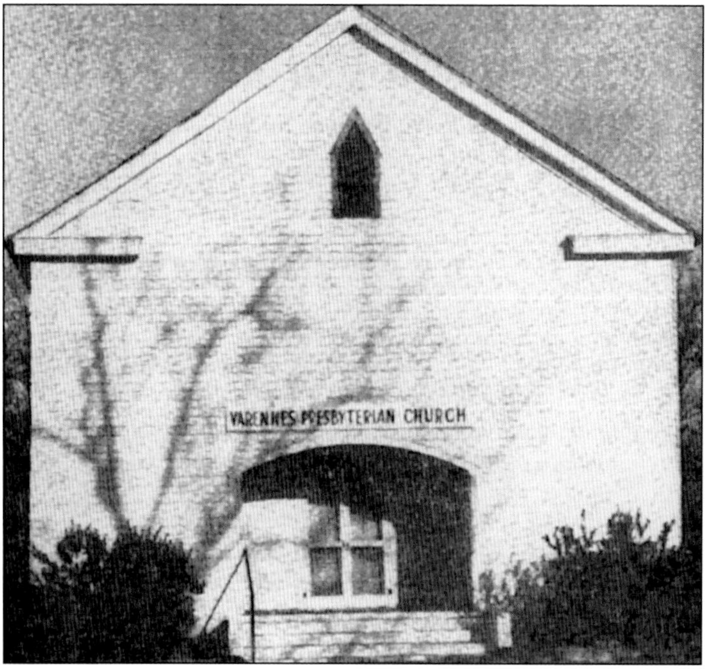

Varennes Presbyterian Church, founded in 1813, was housed in three different locations. It moved, in 1837, 3 miles away, near the home of Jesse P. McGee. The first location was near the old Anderson place. The present building, near Iva, was constructed in 1887, removing the old slave gallery but leaving parts of the bell-shaped sounding board.

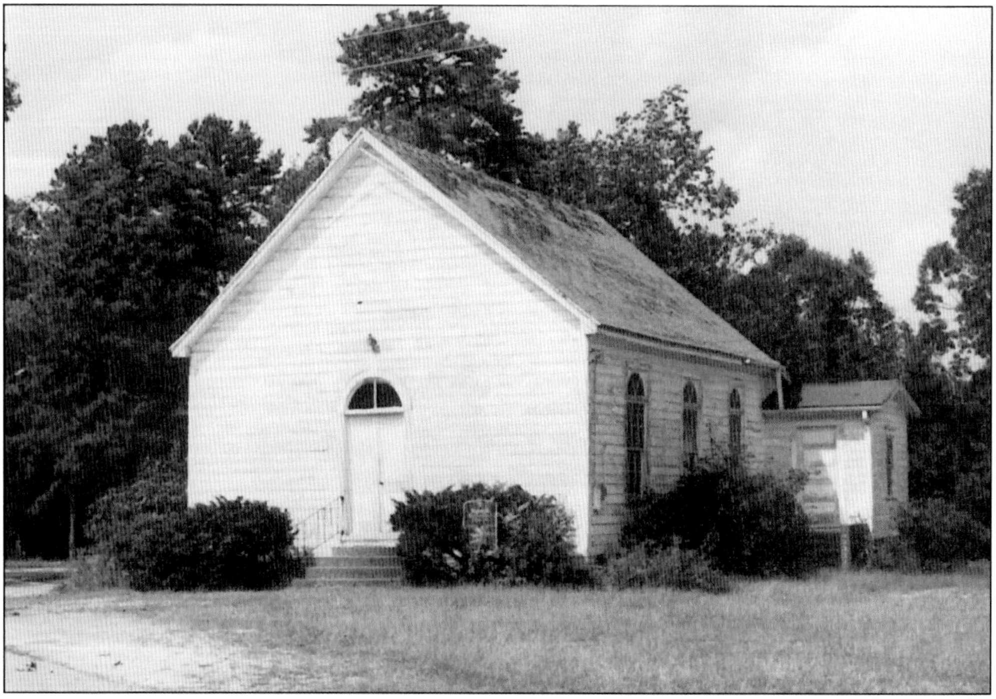

Ruhamah Methodist Church was organized in 1822 and dedicated to God in 1836. It was given the name from Hosea in the Bible. Camp meetings were held here between 1830 and 1848. The present church, built in 1977 near Starr, off of 29 South, is presently on a charge with Hebron and Starr United Methodist Church.

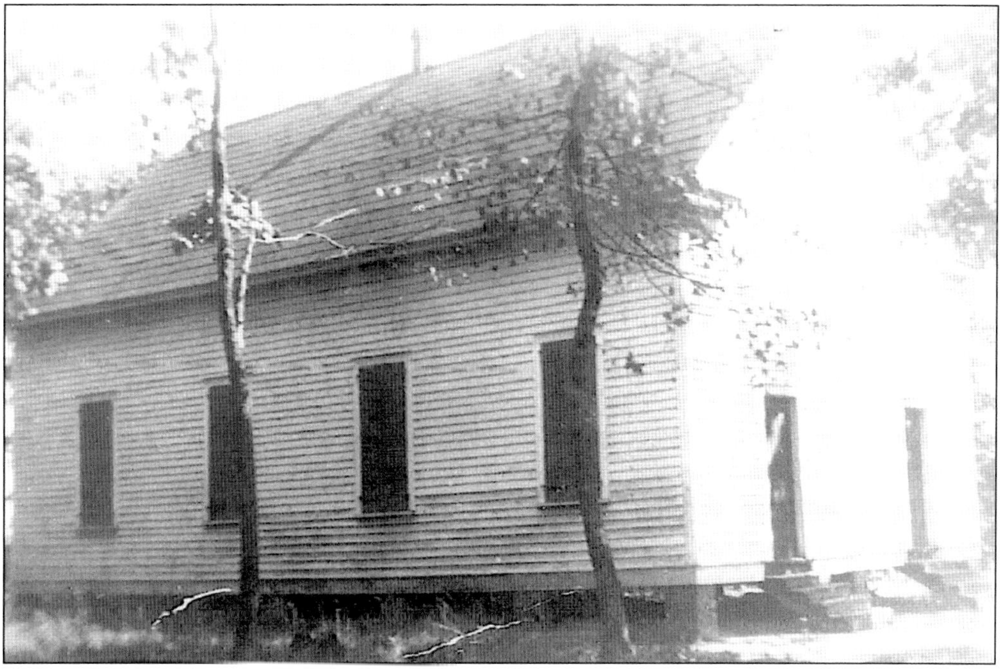

Flat Rock Presbyterian Church, pictured above, traces its beginning to 1832, when the Baptists and Presbyterians used to worship together under a grove of trees, with a board as a pulpit. In 1855, a church was constructed; although the two groups shared the building, they worshiped at separate times. In 1888 and 1906, respectively, the Baptists and Presbyterians each built their own churches. This church is near Starr.

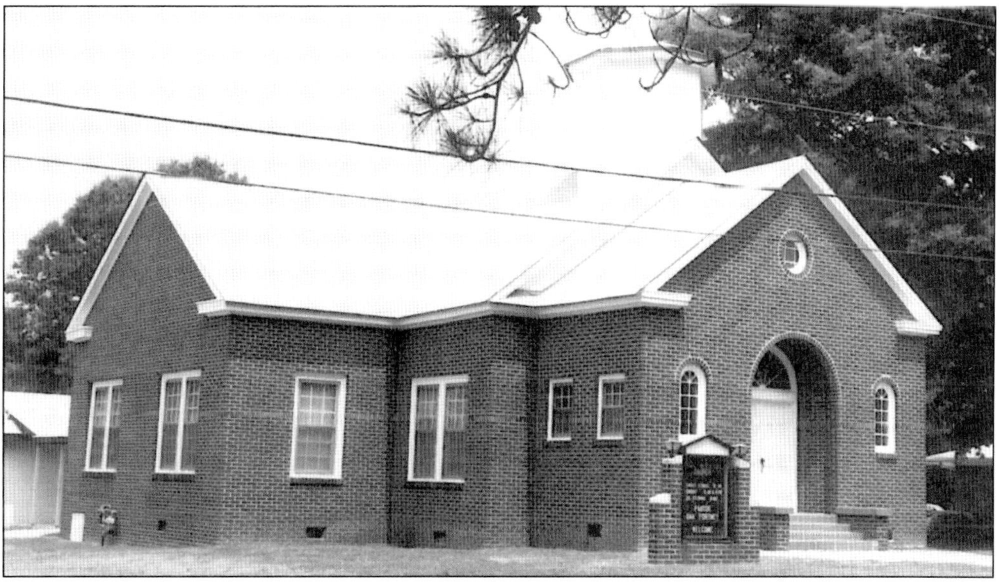

First Wesleyan Methodist Church was organized following a tent revival that was led by Reverend J.M. Hames in the spring of 1917. Reverend Hames became the first pastor of the church, located on Poplar Street in Iva. Charter members were J.V. Ozmint, Zora Ozmint, Daisy Buffington, Lizzie McCoy, Carrie Gibson, Susie West, John Bryant, Georgia Bryant, Will Phillips, Anora Phillips, Corine Bannister, and Roy Martin.

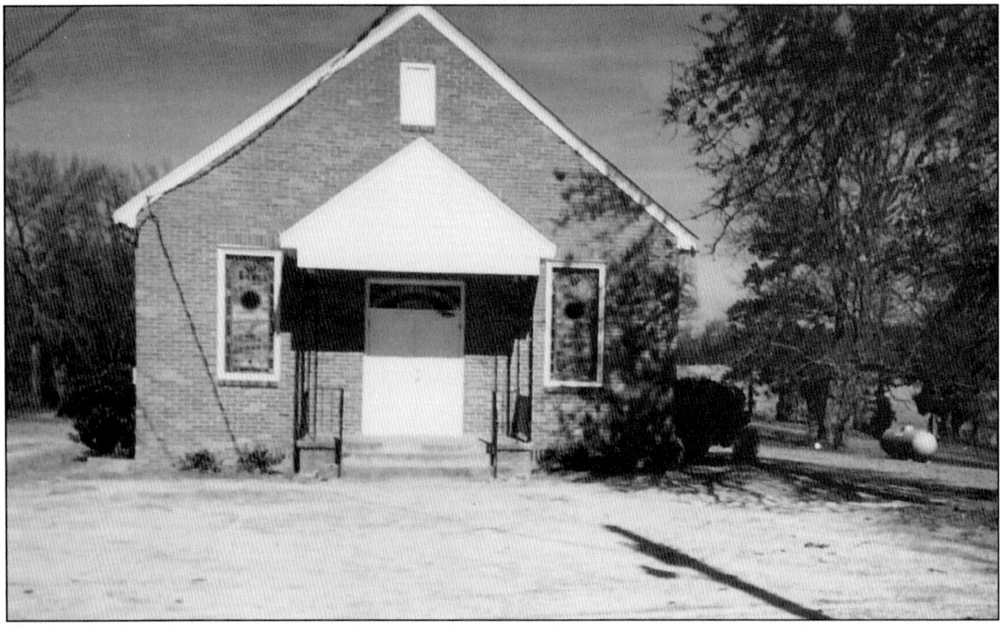

Hebron Methodist Church was organized under a brush arbor in 1876 as Pleasant Grove Church. In 1890, a wooden frame building served as a church and school, until a tornado destroyed it on May 10, 1945. The present building was completed in 1948. This church is near Pleasant Grove Baptist Church, and they are both on the outskirts of Iva.

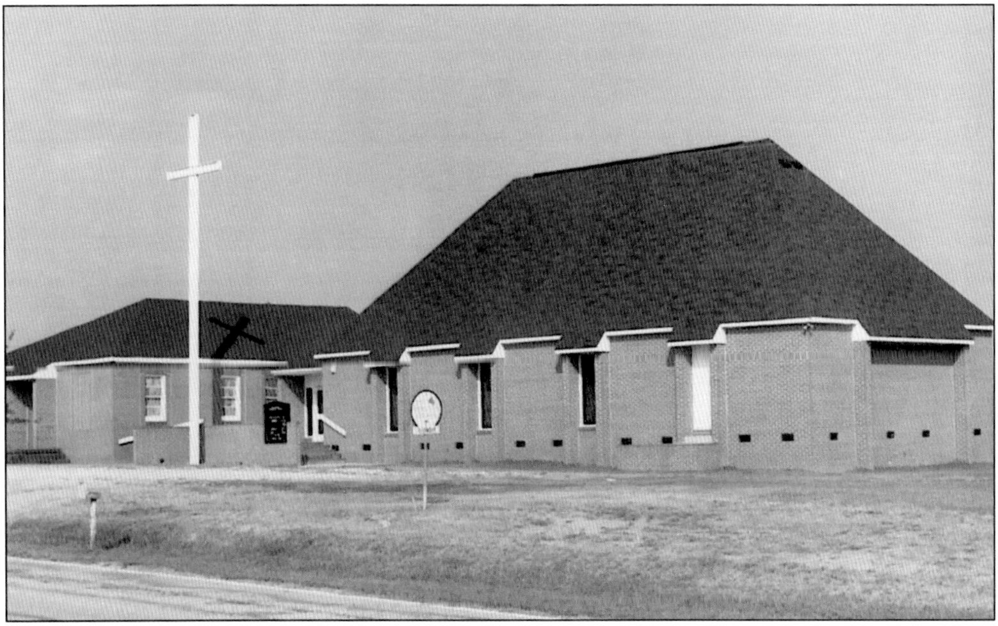

Fellowship Wesleyan Methodist Church was organized in 1894 during a tent meeting held by Reverend I.B. Abbott and his wife. The first church burned in 1936. The second church was built on the same site in 1953, and until construction was completed, the congregation worshiped in a nearby school. The church then moved in 1974, to a site where the parsonage had already been built in 1965. A new sanctuary was added to the church in 1982, and it is now known as the Fellowship Wesleyan Church.

Seven

SCHOOLS

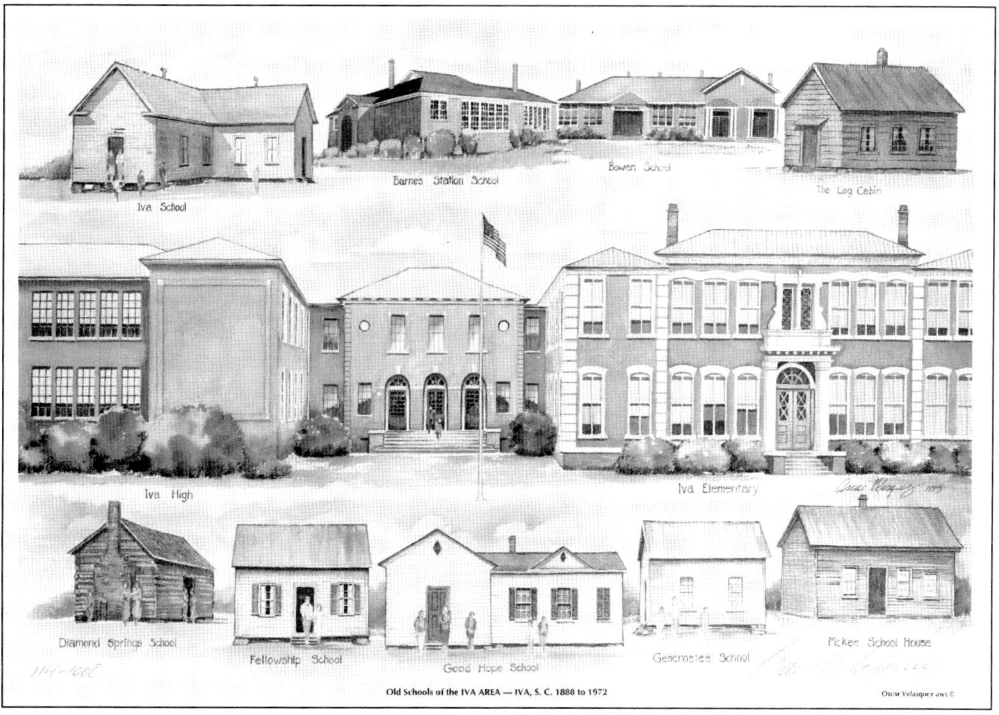

In the Iva area, many of the rural schoolhouses of the early days are clustered around the schools shown in this painting. Pictured, from left to right are, the High School, the old Iva School, and the Elementary School. This picture was painted for REVIVA by the nationally known watercolor artist Oscar Velasquez. Mr. Velasquez also painted the mural on Brown's 5 & 10¢ of the old Iva Depot, the watercolor prints of the Iva Gazebo, the fountain, and other Iva landmarks.

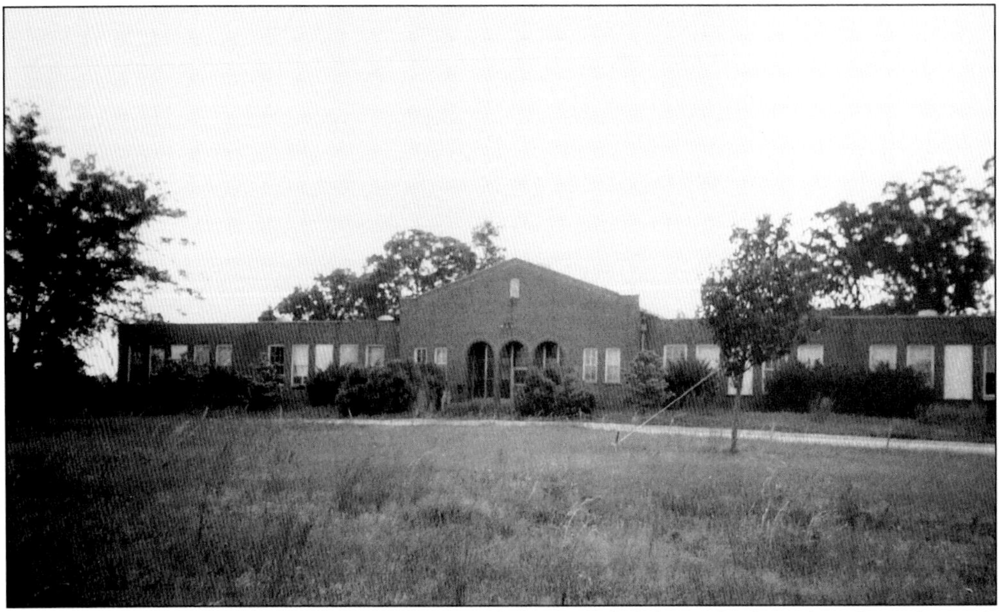

Antreville School started as a three-room building near Shiloh Methodist Church in the mid-1980s. Between 1912 and 1913, a two-story building was erected on the present site, for both elementary and high school students. This building burned in 1925, and for the two years it took to rebuild, classes were held in Shiloh Church. The last class to graduate was in 1953, after which all high school students were moved to Dixie High. Antreville School was closed as an elementary school in 1995.

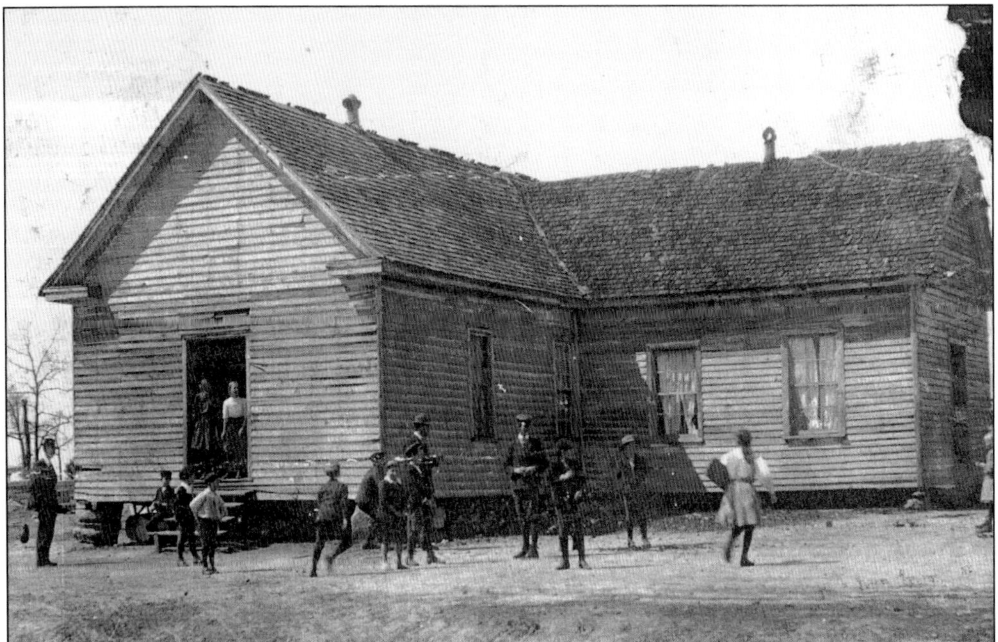

Children are pictured enjoying recess at the old Iva School in the 1900s. This school was torn down when the new brick school was built. The old school stood between the Methodist church and the new school building. Professor J.W. Ligon was the principal of this old school.

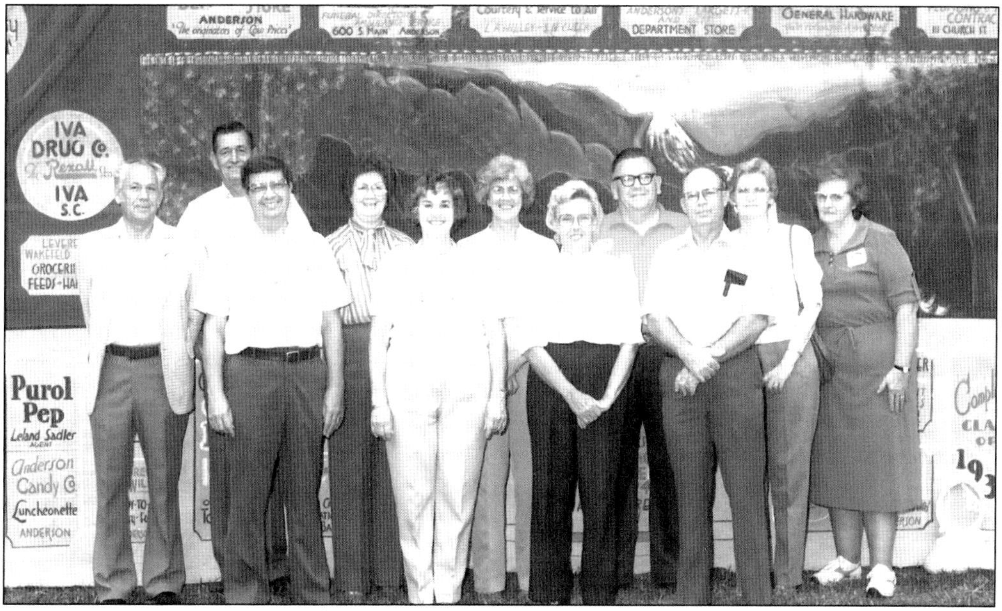

Some members of the Class of 1944 pose for this picture at a reunion held in the 1980s. It is interesting to note the scenic backdrop curtain, dated 1935–1936, complete with names of advertisers. This curtain once hung in the Iva School auditorium.

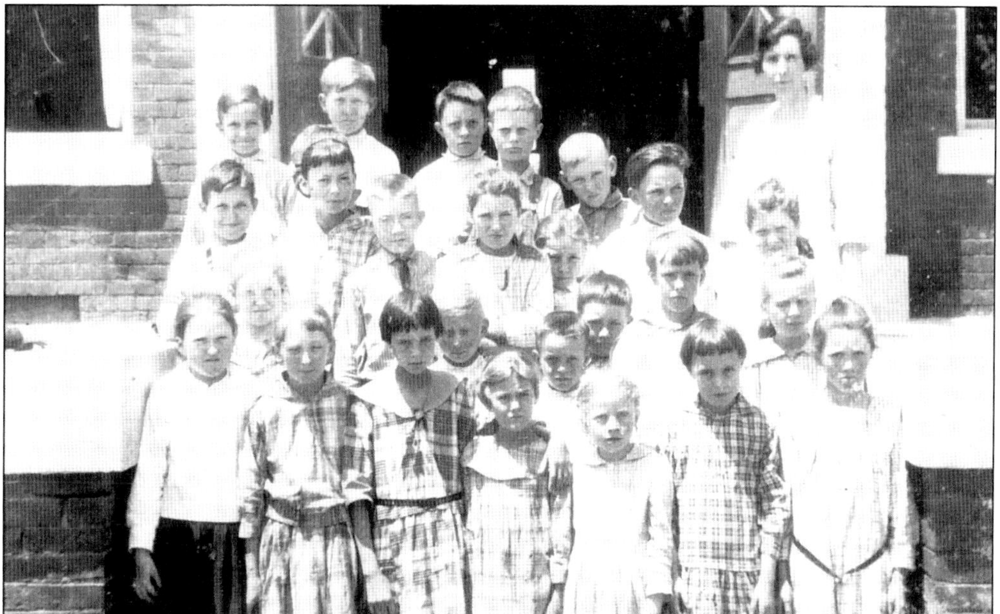

The third grade class of Iva School is pictured here in 1921. They are, from left to right, as follows: (front row) Mary McKee, Lucille Davis, unidentified, Mable Stokes, Lizzie Mae Charping, Viola McBride, and Louise McCullough; (second row) Marie Burdette, Wilson McCarley, Clinton Sanders, Albert Wiles, Sara Sutherland, and Fannie Yeargin; (third row) Louis Belcher, Viola Hanks, Graham Darrell, Ethell Partridge, Henry Leverette, Melvin Deanheart, and Sara Willingham; (back row) Abelle Blackwell, Ebb Hicks, Everett Willis, Otis Mobley, Thurman Mobley, and teacher Mrs. J.B. Hall.

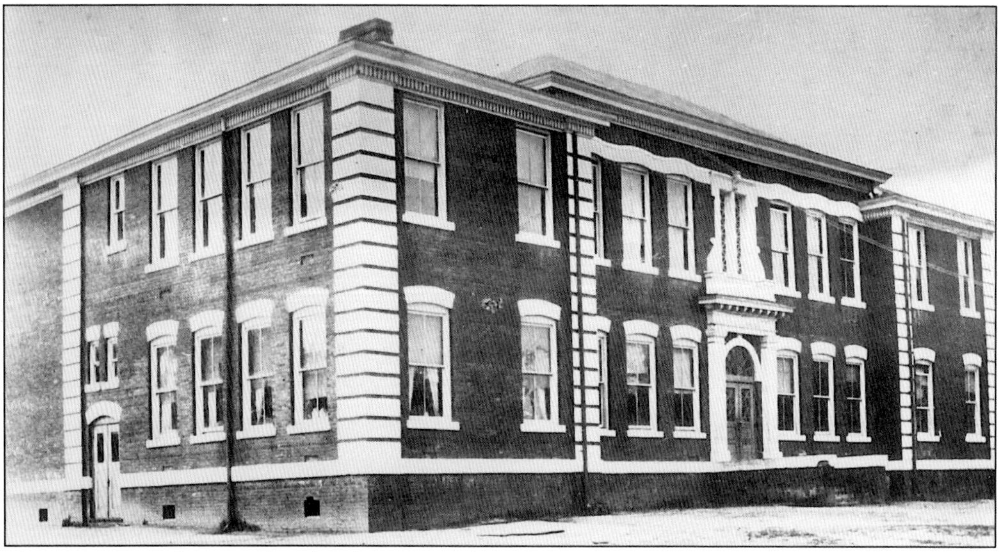

This picture is of Iva High School, as it stood for many years. Many students of the community attended this school, which housed grades 1 through 11. In later years, an additional building was erected onto this one. The school building, which no longer stands today, used to also serve as Iva Elementary School.

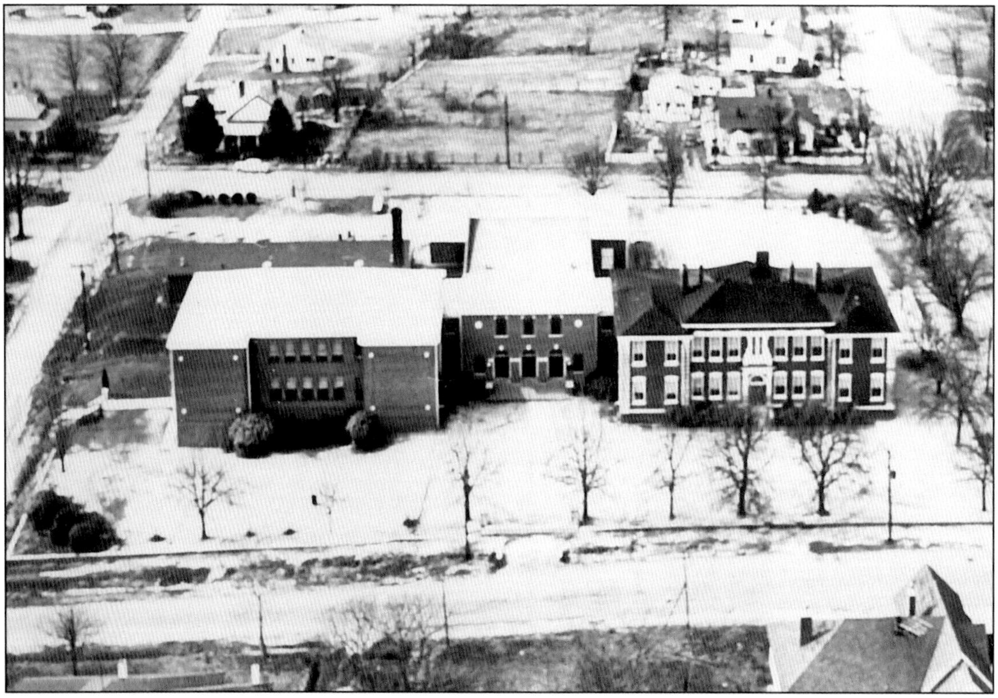

This is an aerial view of the complex, located on Betsy Street, comprising Iva High School (left) and Iva Elementary (right). The auditorium can be seen in the center of the picture, the gym is visible in the back center, and the lunchroom, which is still being used as a Senior Adult Center, is in the back left of the image. The section of building to the right is the original structure (it is the same as the picture at the top of the page). At the time this picture was made, this section housed grades one through six.

This hand-drawn map of the Iva School complex shows the surrounding streets and homes.

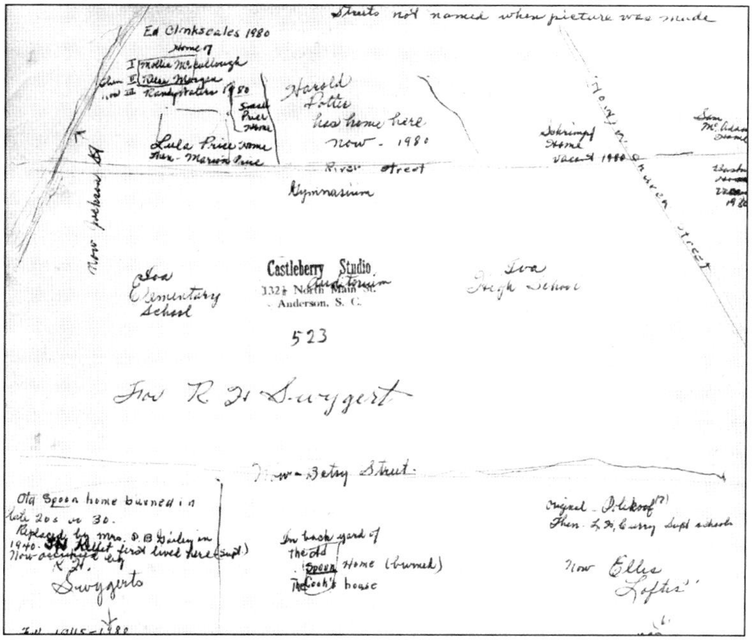

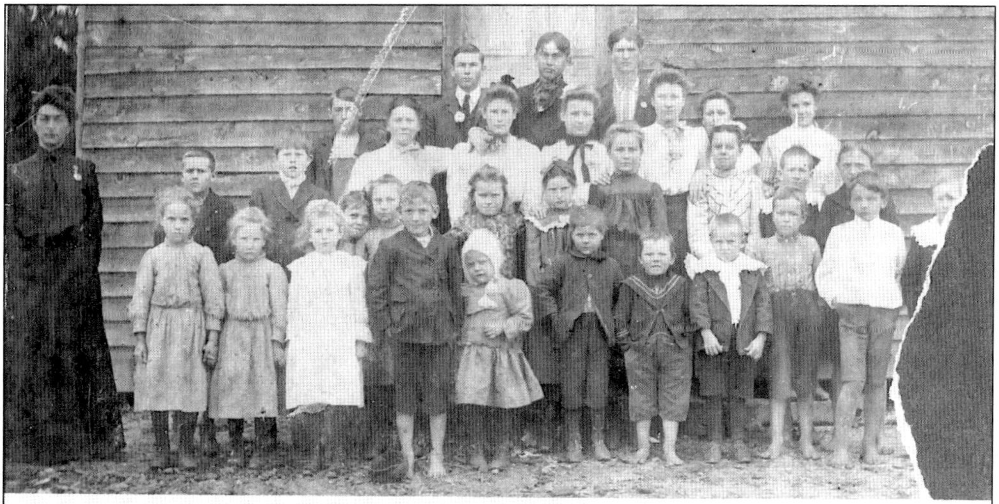

Fellowship School, 1 room

Back Row:	Berry Kelley, Richard Terry, Jim Terry
2nd Row:	Roy Bruce, Lillian Rice, Eva Kelley Rice, Bessie Manning, Emma Kelley, Sally Manning, Carrie Bruce
3rd Row:	Lester Burdette, Charlie Terry, Annie Bruce, Essie Manning, Lola Rice, Roxie Terry, Daisy Manning, Nerva Rice, Austin Kelley, Will Bruce
Bottom Row:	~~Joe~~ Delmis Pilgrim, Ida Pilgrim, Zeola Kelley, Scud Bruce, Hattie Bruce, John Frank Burriss, Unknown, Unknown, Unknown, Robert Hale, Edward Kelley
Teacher:	Miss Nora Parris

Fellowship, a one-room schoolhouse, *c.* 1905, is located on Mills Creek Road, approximately 5 miles southwest of Iva, in the Fellowship community. The teacher was Miss Nora Parris, and the students' names are listed under the picture.

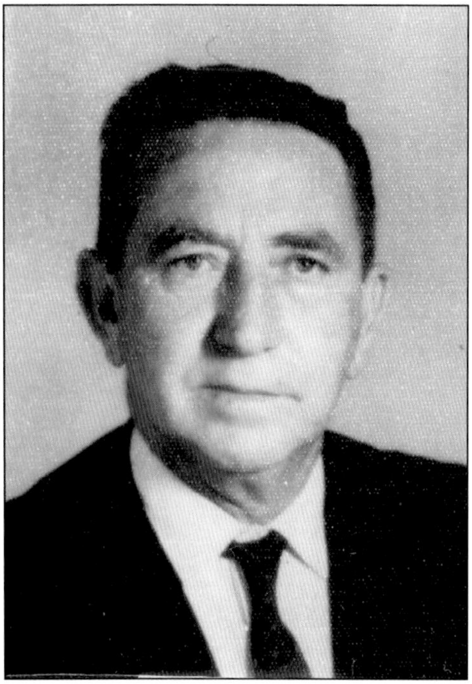

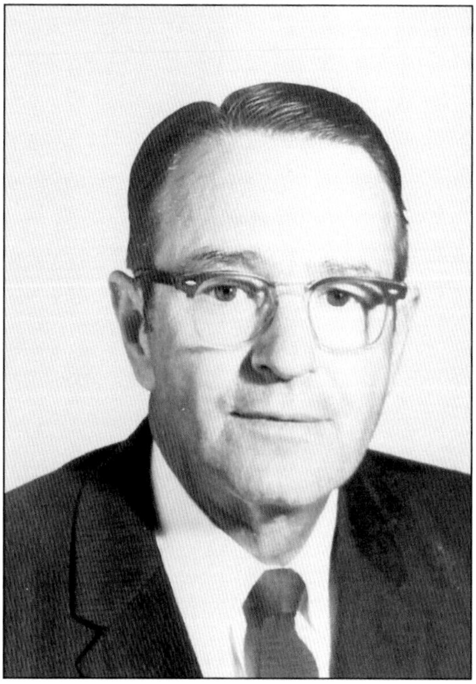

Left: Ed Cook was the principal of Barnes Station School and Iva Elementary School for many years. He was the son of Pringle Cook, and he was married to Vivian Pruitt. They had two children, Marguerite Cook Pruitt and Iva Bryson Shore. *Right*: R.H. Swygert was superintendent of District No. 3 when Crescent High School was built. He was previously the superintendent and coach at Lowndesville, Starr, and Iva. He was married to Clara Louise Emerson, and they had two sons, Herman and Jacob.

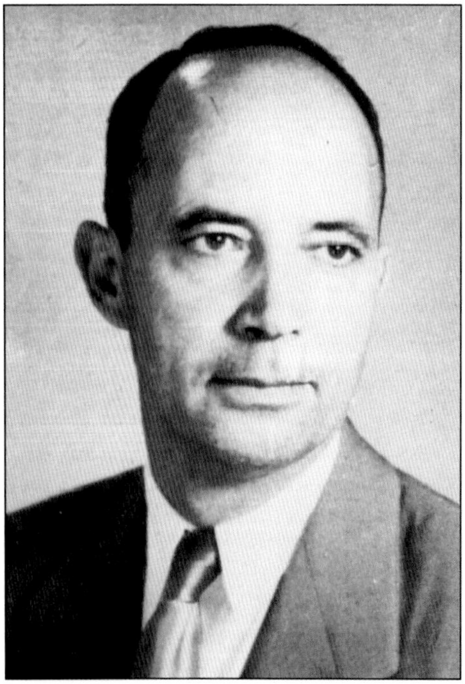

R.M. Stone was the first principal of Crescent High School. During his 43-year teaching career, he coached many girls' basketball championship teams. He served three years in the Navy in World War II. He married Bess Jones, and they had two children, R.M. Jr. and Samantha Jo.

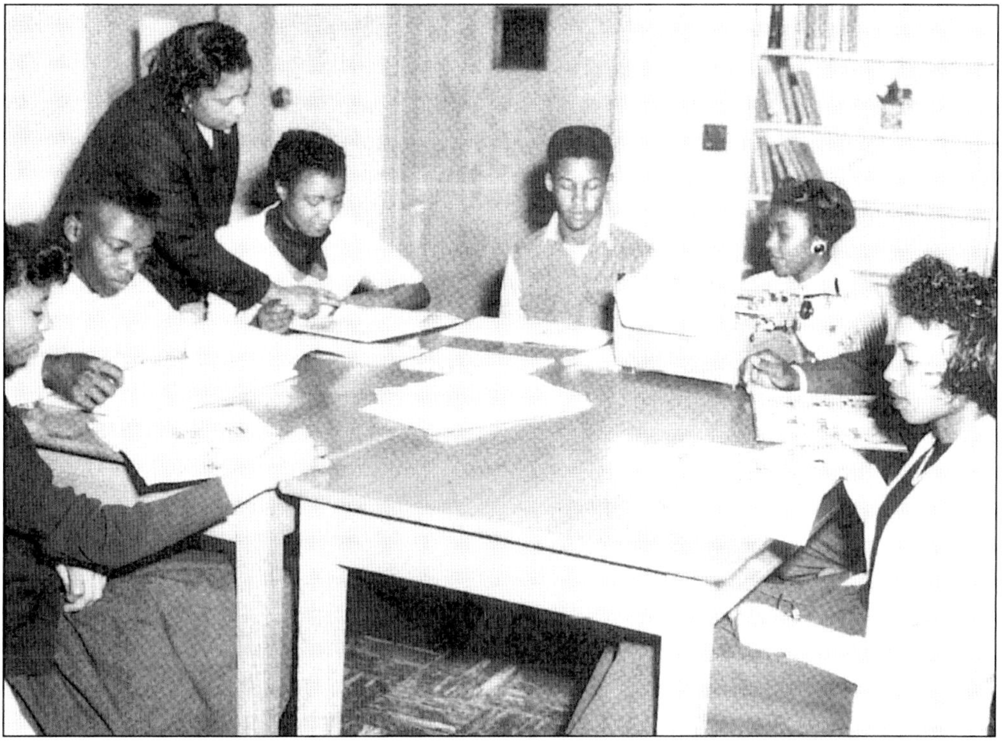

The photograph above shows the 1956 annual staff of New Deal High School: editor Ruby Witcher, advisors Mrs. Bennette C. Williford and Mrs. Virginia D. Boyd, sports editor Levi Leverette, assistant editor Ed. Clarissa Sherard, club editor Vera Pickens, advertising manager Belvin Dubose, and business manager Charles Hunter. This is just one of the student organizations of New Deal. Mrs. Williford later became the counselor at Starr and Iva middle schools. The lady standing is Mrs. Williford.

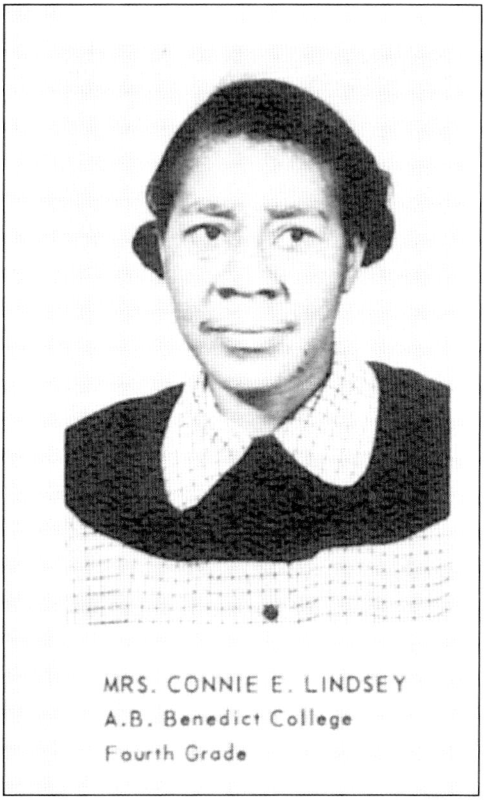

Connie B. Lindsay was a dedicated and well-loved teacher for many years. She was instrumental in the building and naming of New Deal Elementary School for blacks, following President Franklin D. Roosevelt's "New Deal" plan. She also served as the principal of the elementary school. A magnolia tree, planted by Mrs. E.H. Agnew in Mrs. Lindsay's honor, is still standing on the campus today.

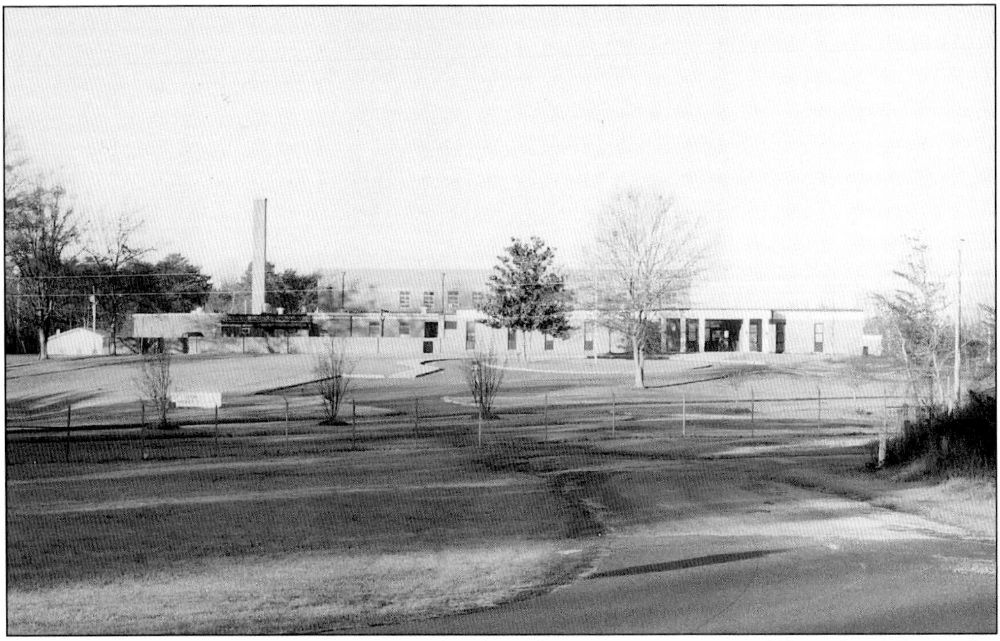

Following integration in 1970, New Deal School became Starr-Iva Middle School for grades six, seven, and eight. Pictured here is the school, as it looks today, after several additions and a renovation project called "operation facelift," which included student involvement in landscaping and beautification. The school is located on Rainey Road in Starr.

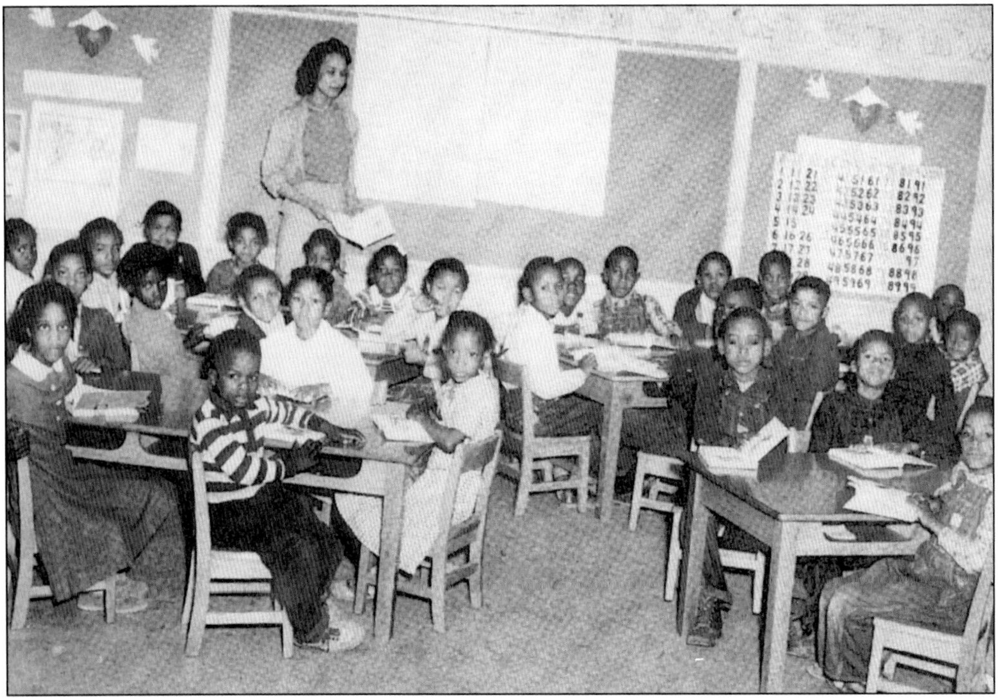

This picture, taken in 1956, shows the first grade C class of Starr's New Deal School, with the class teacher, Mrs. E.O. Woolridge. None of these students have been identified. There were several first grade classes at the school, although this class is of a typical size, for the time.

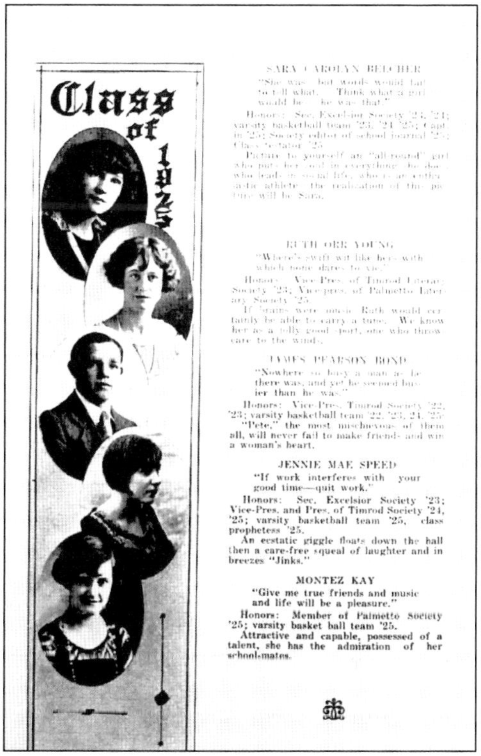

Class of 1925

SARA CAROLYN BELCHER

"She was—but words would fail to tell what. Think what a girl would be—she was that."

Honors: Sec. Excelsior Society '23, '24; varsity basketball team '23, '24 '25; Capt. in '25; Society editor of school journal '25; Class testator '25.

Picture to yourself an "all-round" girl who puts her soul in everything she does, who leads in social life, who is an enthusiastic athlete—the realization of this picture will be Sara.

RUTH ORR YOUNG

"Where's swift wit like hers with which none dares to vie."

Honors: Vice-Pres. of Timrod Literary Society '23; Vice-pres. of Palmetto Literary Society '25.

If brains were music Ruth would certainly be able to carry a tune. We know her as a jolly good sport, one who throws care to the winds.

JAMES PEARSON BOND

"Nowhere so busy a man as he there was, and yet he seemed busier than he was."

Honors: Vice-Pres. Timrod Society '22, '23; varsity basketball team '22, '23, 24, '25.

"Pete," the most mischievous of them all, will never fail to make friends and win a woman's heart.

JENNIE MAE SPEED

"If work interferes with your good time—quit work."

Honors: Sec. Excelsior Society '23; Vice-Pres. and Pres. of Timrod Society '24, '25; varsity basketball team '25, class prophetess '25.

An ecstatic giggle floats down the hall then a care-free squeal of laughter and in breezes "Jinks."

MONTEZ KAY

"Give me true friends and music and life will be a pleasure."

Honors: Member of Palmetto Society '25; varsity basket ball team '25.

Attractive and capable, possessed of a talent, she has the admiration of her school-mates.

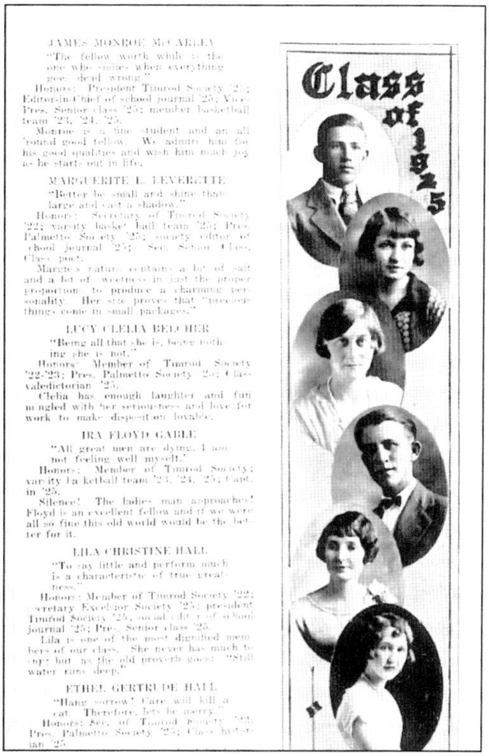

JAMES MONROE McCARLEY

"The fellow worth while is the one who smiles when everything goes dead wrong."

Honors: President Timrod Society '25; Editor-in-Chief of school journal '25; Vice-Pres. Senior class '25; member basketball team '23, '24, '25.

Monroe is a fine student and an all 'round good fellow. We admire him for his good qualities and wish him much joy as he starts out in life.

MARGUERITE L. LEVERETTE

"Better be small and shine than large and cast a shadow."

Honors: Secretary of Timrod Society '22; varsity basket ball team '25; Pres. Palmetto Society '25; society editor of school journal '25; Sec. Senior Class, Class poet.

Margie's nature contains a bit of salt and a bit of sweetness in just the proper proportion to produce a charming personality. Her size proves that "precious things come in small packages."

LUCY CLELIA BELCHER

"Being all that she is, being nothing she is not."

Honors: Member of Timrod Society '22-'23; Pres. Palmetto Society '25; Class valedictorian '25.

Clelia has enough laughter and fun mingled with her seriousness and love for work to make disposition lovable.

IRA FLOYD GABLE

"All great men are dying. I am not feeling well myself."

Honors: Member of Timrod Society; varsity basketball team '23, '24, '25; Capt. in '25.

Silence! The ladies man approaches! Floyd is an excellent fellow and if we were all so fine this old world would be the better for it.

LILA CHRISTINE HALL

"To say little and perform much is a characteristic of true greatness."

Honors: Member of Timrod Society '22; secretary Excelsior Society '25; president Timrod Society '25, social editor of school journal '25; Pres. Senior class '25.

Lila is one of the most dignified members of our class. She never has much to say; but as the old proverb goes: "Still water runs deep."

ETHEL GERTRUDE HALL

"Hang sorrow! Care will kill a cat. Therefore, lets be merry."

Honors: Sec. of Timrod Society '23; Pres. Palmetto Society '25; Class historian '25.

Class of 1925

The Class of 1925 is pictured, along with a quote on their accomplishments and their ideals in life.

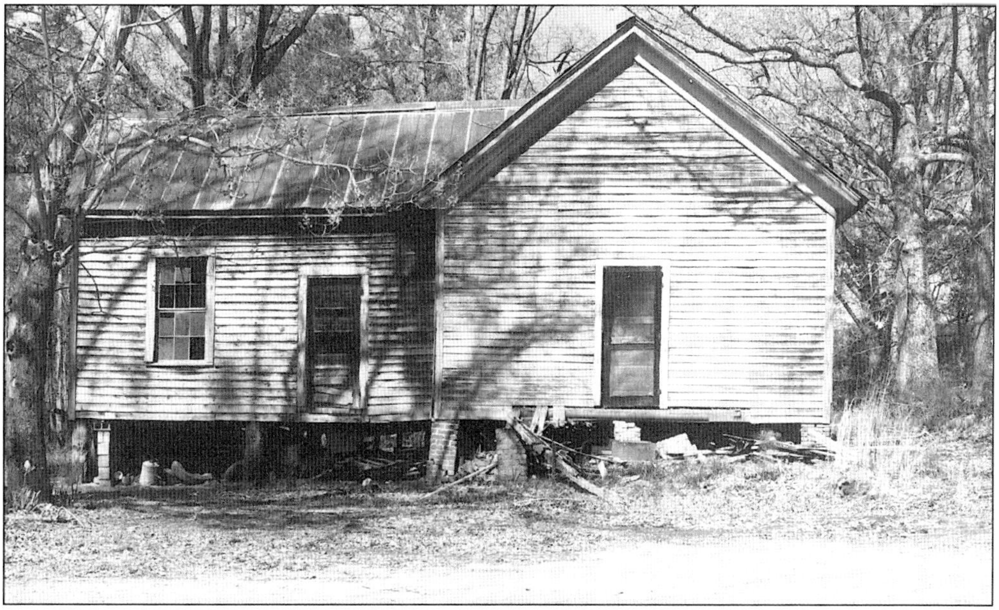

This is the second building of the Generostee School. The first building was within several hundred feet below this one. The third building was within several hundred feet above it. The building in the picture is the only one still standing today. It is located approximately 3 miles west of Iva, in the Moffetsville area.

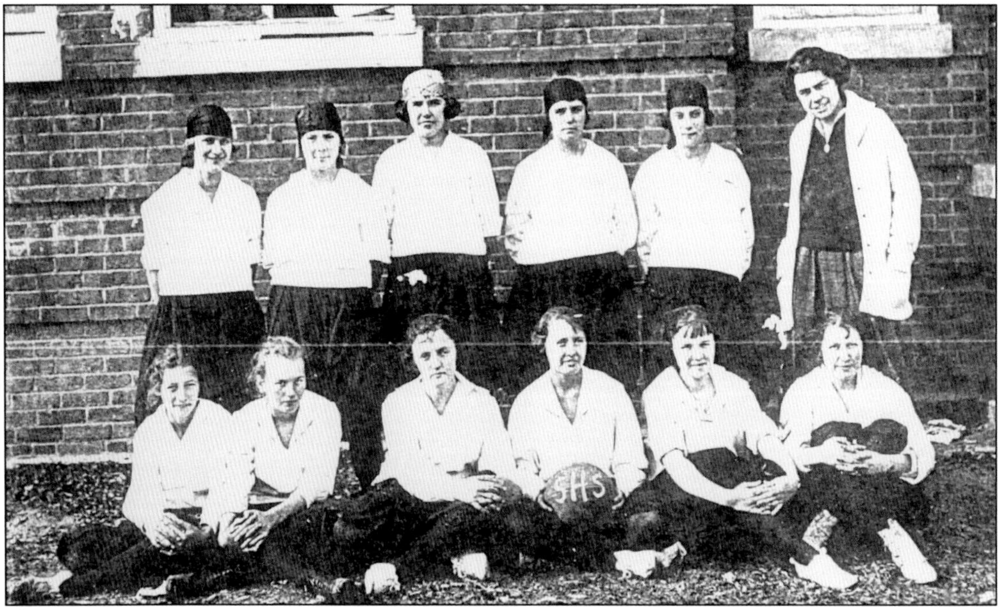

Starr High School girls' basketball team is pictured in the early 1900s. The coach, Miss Mabel Jones, is seen on the right, at the back. Members of the team are, from left to right, as follows: (front row) Margaret Hawkins, Mary Gentry, Clayton Harris, Elvira Jackson, Louise Chapman, and Louise Thompson; (back row) Kathryn Hodges, Marian Herron, Ruby Stuart, Gracie Pearman, and Elizabeth Davis.

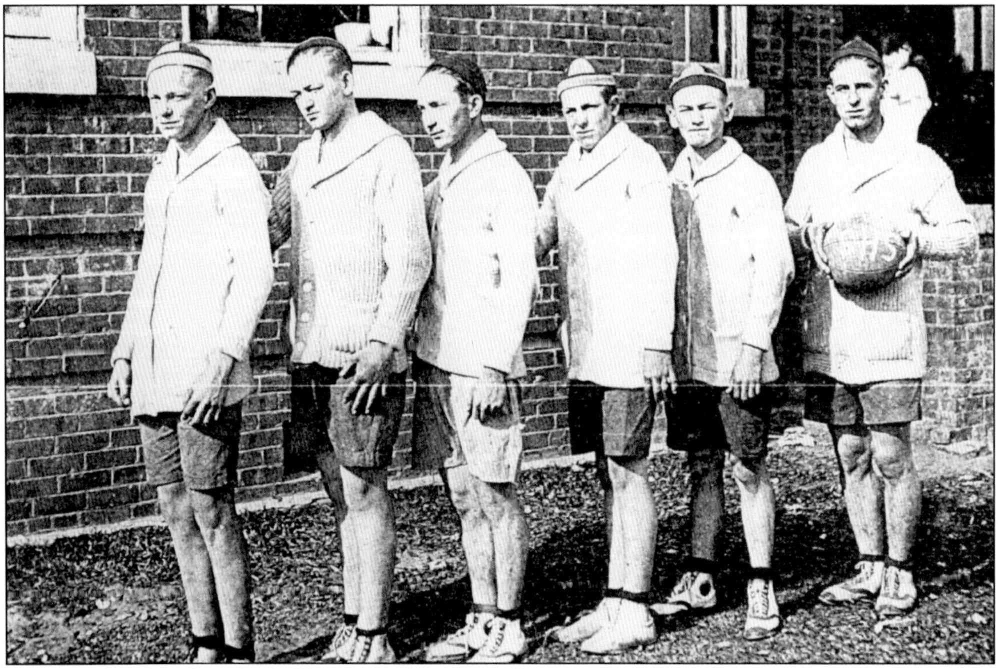

Starr High School basketball team is shown in the early 1900s. Starr and Iva were once rival teams, until 1957 when they became a team at Crescent High School. Seen here, from left to right, are Paul Jones, Fred Jones, Anglie Coggins, Leland Jackson, George Gentry, and Ralph Jackson.

"Tom Thumb Weddings" were very popular in elementary school. Steve Alexander and Elaine Evans were bride and groom for this Tom Thumb Wedding at Iva Elementary School c. 1955. Functions, such as this, were important to students and their families, because, at that time, schools and churches were the focal points of entertainment for the people.

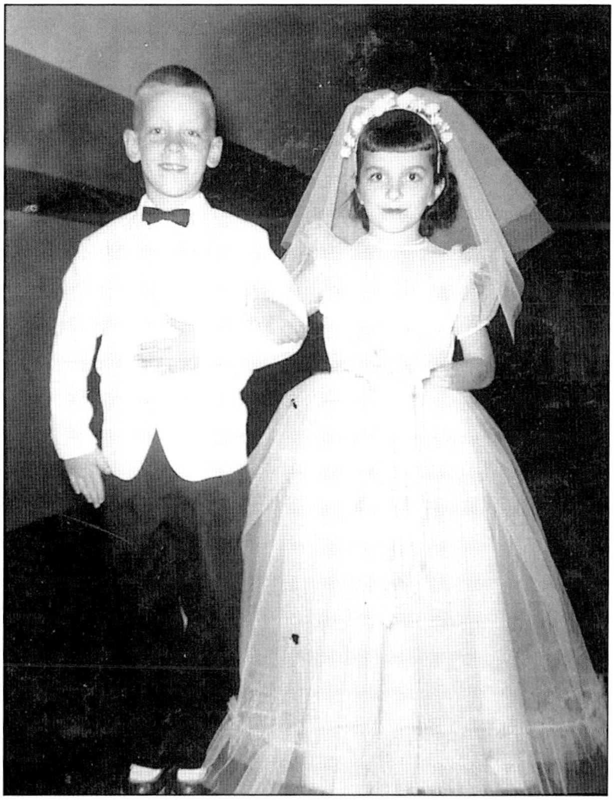

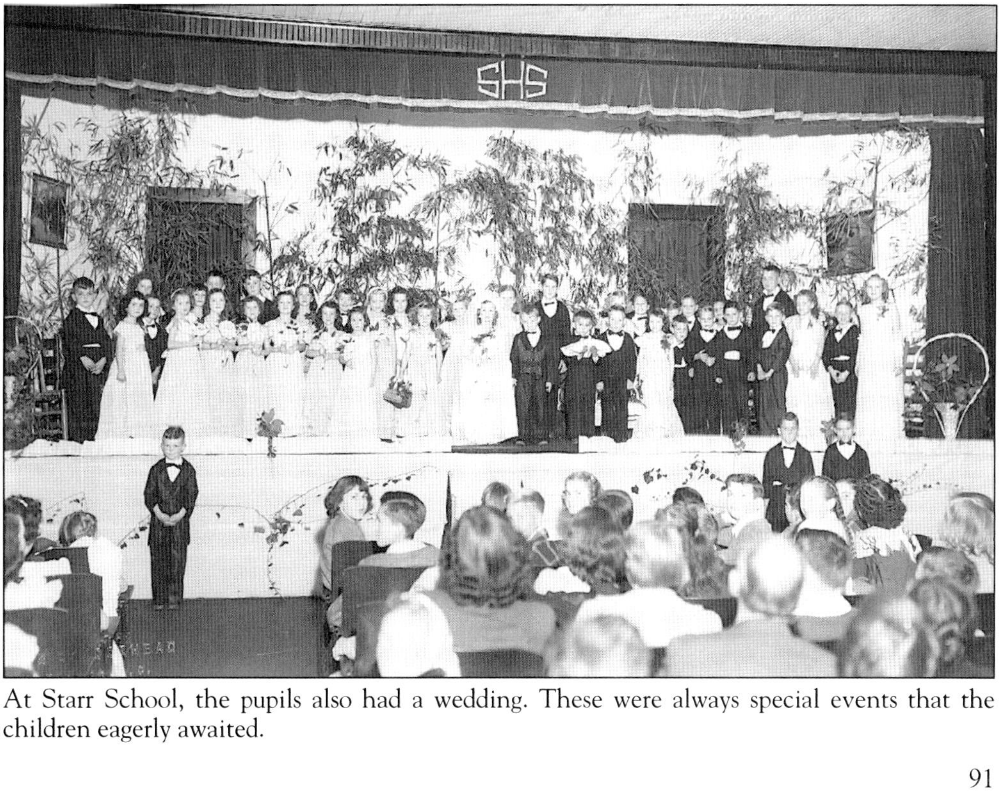

At Starr School, the pupils also had a wedding. These were always special events that the children eagerly awaited.

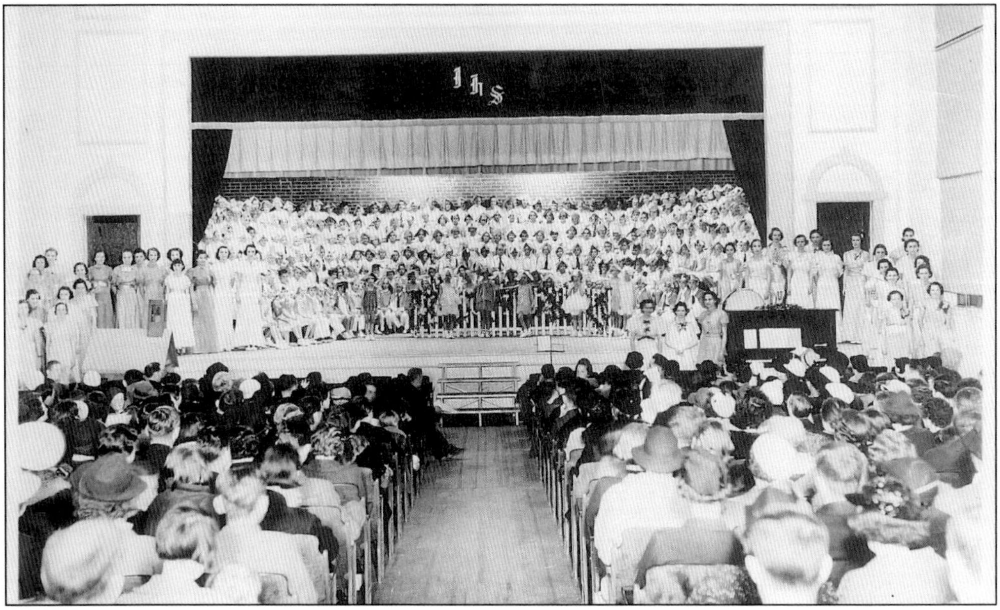

This photograph shows the 1938 May Day Pageant. The students of the Iva Elementary School and Iva High School are seen participating in the event, with skits, music, and dance around the Maypole.

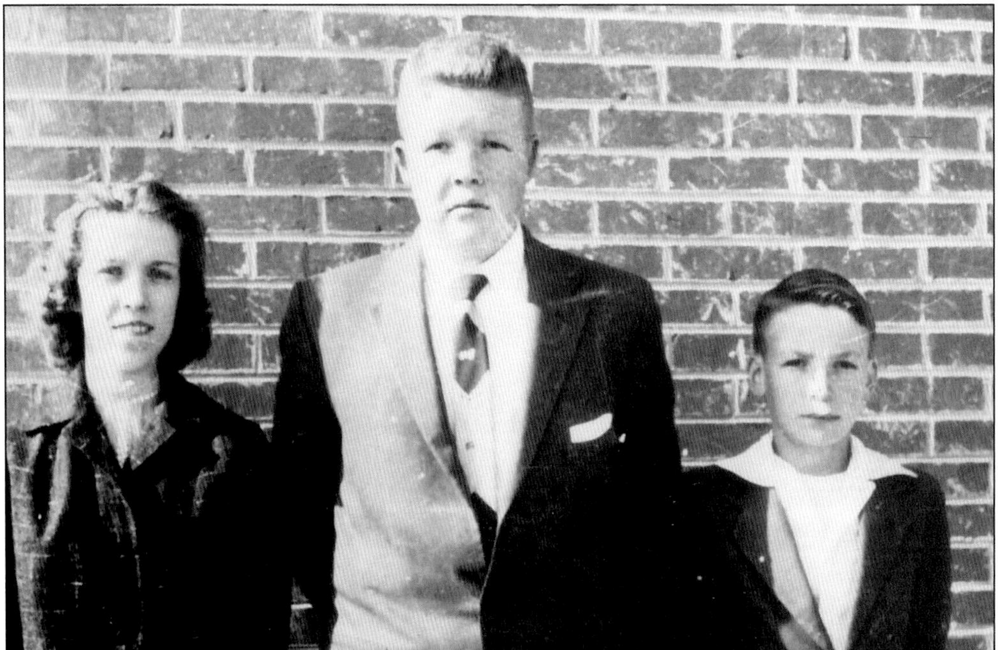

Students of the Starr and Iva communities named the new high school. The name of "Crescent High School" was suggested by three students, Alice Stuart (Lawton), Billy Pike, and Joseph McGee Jr. It was an appropriate choice, because the school was located on a mile-long crescent curve, and a crescent is part of the state flag. Crescent High School opened its doors for the first time in the 1956–57 school year.

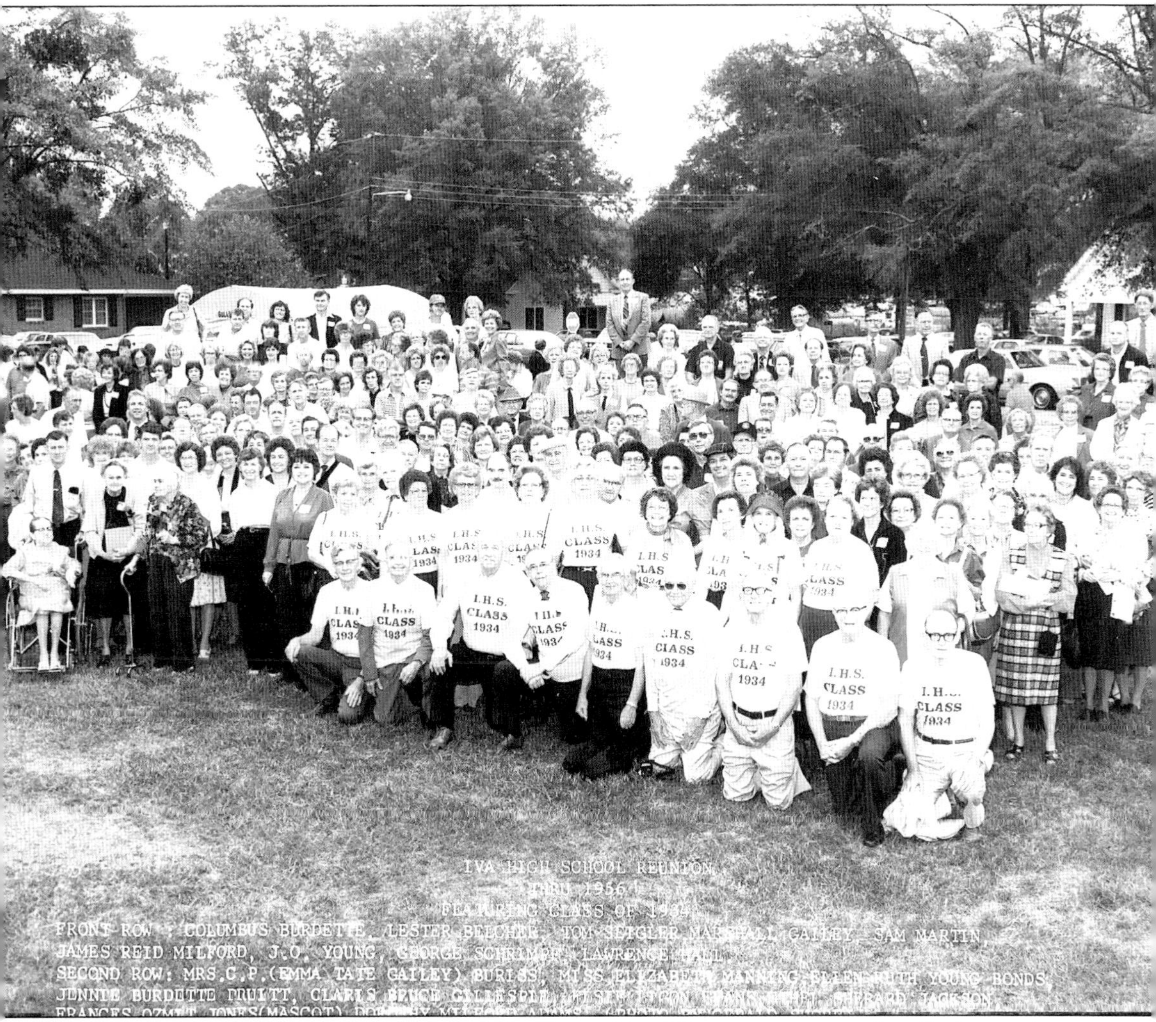

The first Iva High School reunion was held in 1984. The occasion was for all those who attended and graduated Iva High School through the year 1956. It was the 50th reunion of the Class of 1934. Iva Simpson Hayes and Mrs. Selma Simpson represented the Class of 1911, and Selma Burton Manning represented the Class of 1912. REVIVA sponsors the "School Days–Reunion Daze" event every five years. REVIVA will observe its fourth such event in October 1999. Hundreds of former students "come home" from all over the country for this big celebration. Everyone at this event enjoyed activities such as a fashion show put on by Iva Manufacturing Co. and a Charleston dancing demonstration by Elsie Evans, from the Class of 1934. W.S. Simpson Jr., a former principal, served as Master of Ceremony. Articles of interest were on display in the old cafeteria, and pictures were taken in front of the stage backdrop. The entertainment was performed on a lavishly decorated platform, which was the bed of a trailer truck.

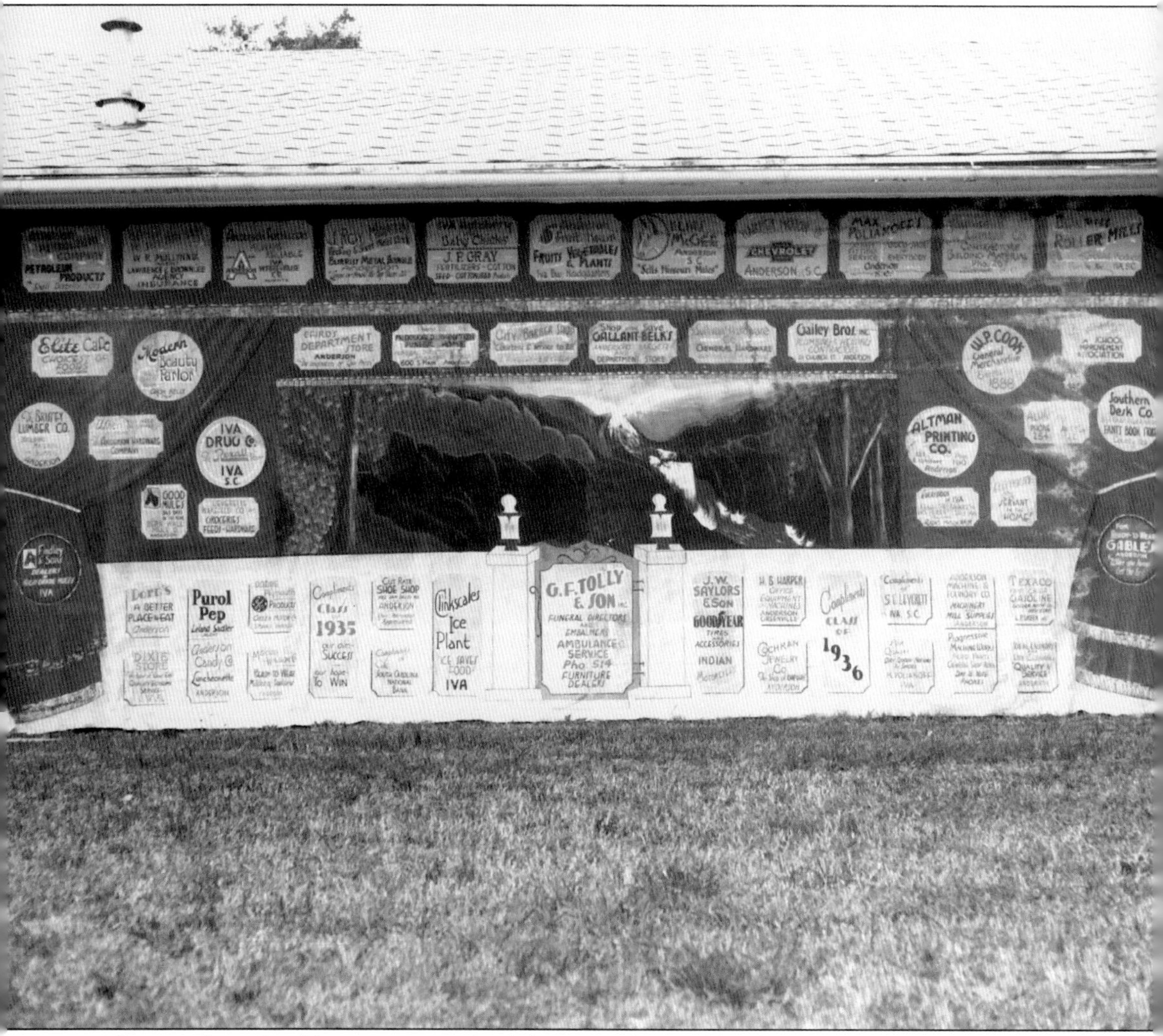

This purple and gold stage-curtain backdrop was donated by the Senior Class of 1935–1936, when Iva High School's new auditorium was built. The curtain enhanced the appearance of the new auditorium, which was already a favorite gathering place, due to its elevated floor and balconies. Today, the curtain is on display at the Iva Museum. The money for the curtain was raised by the presentation of a play, which was put on by the senior class and opened to the public. The curtain was hand-painted on canvas, with a waterfall and mountain scene in the middle, and the names of businesses and advertisements all along the border. Several of these businesses are still in operation today. During those days, the mules were the hottest sale items being advertised.

Eight

Community Events

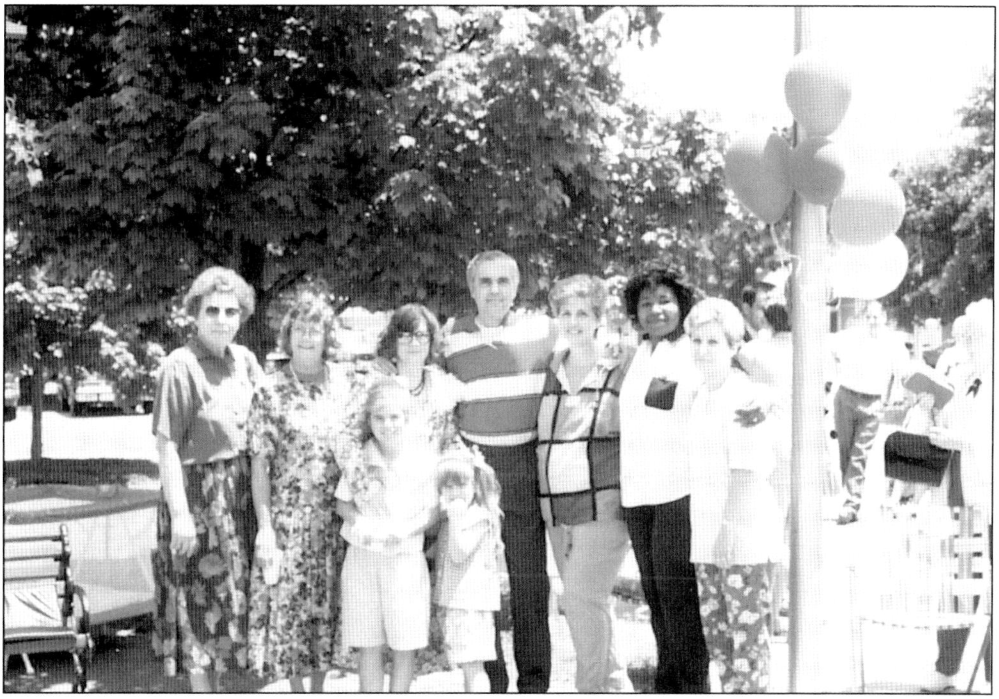

The Dr. Baird Appreciation Day was a special time. Dr. Greg Baird is pictured here with his wife, daughters, and the staff of Iva Medical Center. On this day, the community rallied around their beloved doctor, who had cancer and later died in June 1996.

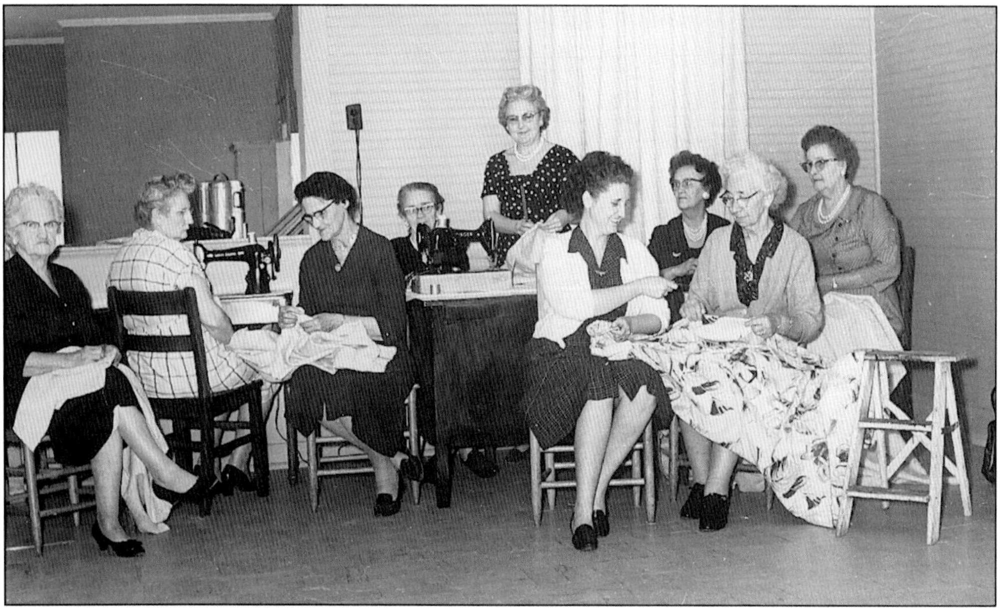

These ladies, at the Jackson Mills community clubhouse, are in the process of making curtains and remodeling the building as it gets a "facelift." This facility was furnished by volunteers from Jackson Mill. Pictured, from left to right, are the following: Delma Atkins, Ida Cann, Mary Dixon, Xenia Brown, Laurie Bowman, Maude Payton, Theola Wilson, Allie Scott, and Yancey Sutherland, as they help with charitable work throughout the community of Iva.

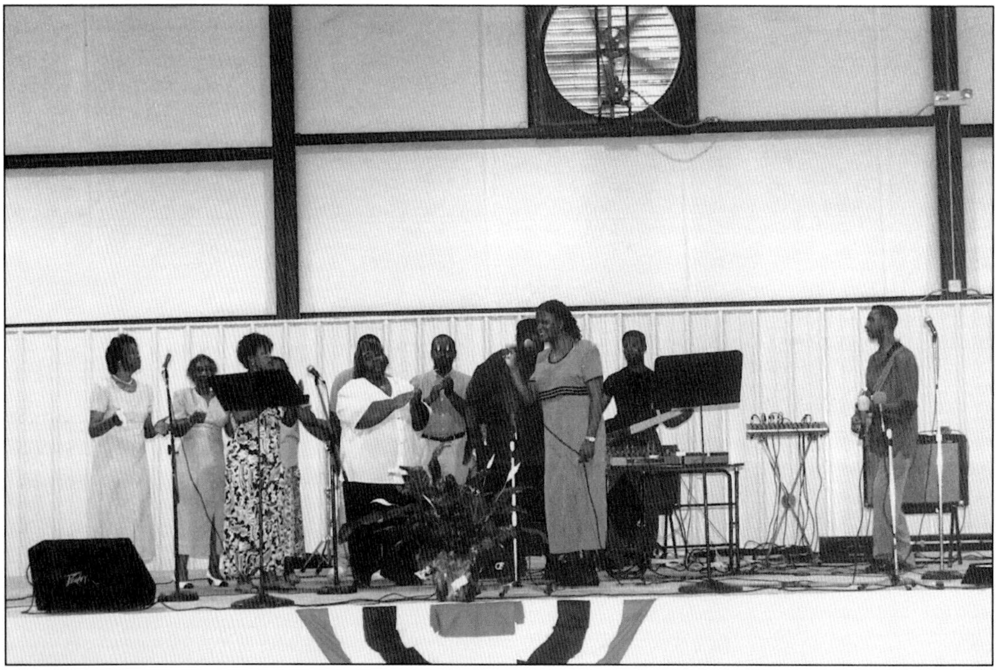

Members of Piney Grove's Progressive Choir donate their time and musical talents for a benefit to raise funds for a 12-year-old boy facing a liver transplant. Groups of volunteers, such as these, give encouragement to families who have to face medical expense. Among the volunteers pictured here are Eris Glenn, Elaine Ellis, Donald Johnson, Patricia Johnson, and Kathy Jones.

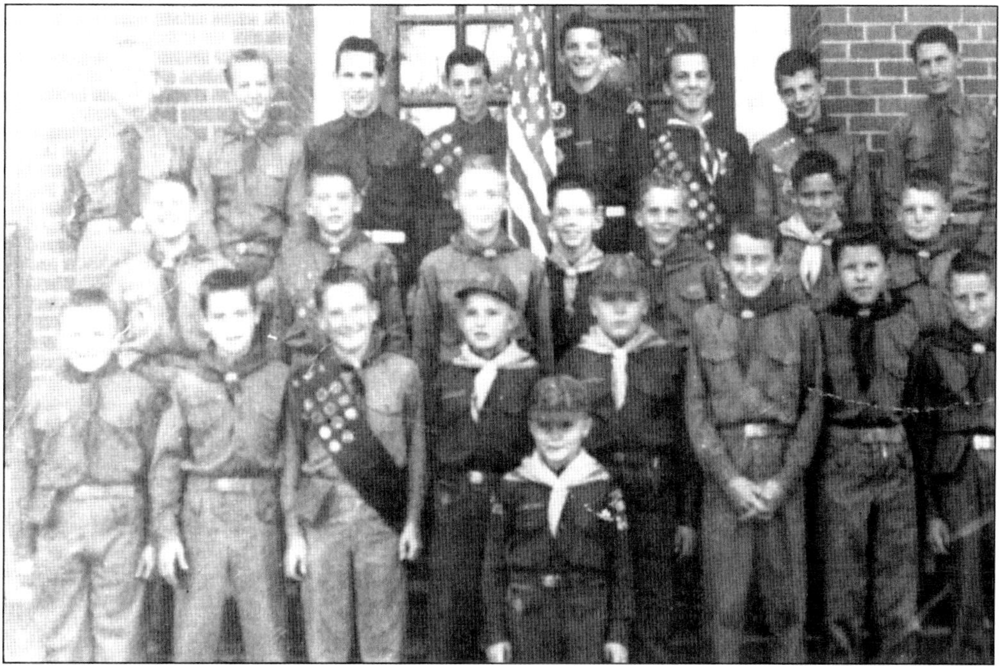

Boy Scout Troop No. 206 is pictured during the 1950s at Iva Elementary School. They are, from left to right, as follows: (first row) Craig Evans; Doug Wakefield; Archie Hicks; Bobby Bonds; John Rampey; Aaron Campbell; Levis Campbell; and Carlisle Evans; (second row) Charles Adams; Jake Swygert; Maxie Voyle; David McDonald; Wade Burdette; Bo Hayes; and Jimmy Cook; (third row) Fred McCoy, scoutmaster of Troop No. 85; Larry McMahan; Lee Patterson; Sammy Payton; Harper McNeace; Charles Evans; Bob Stone; and Carl Evans, scoutmaster of this troop.

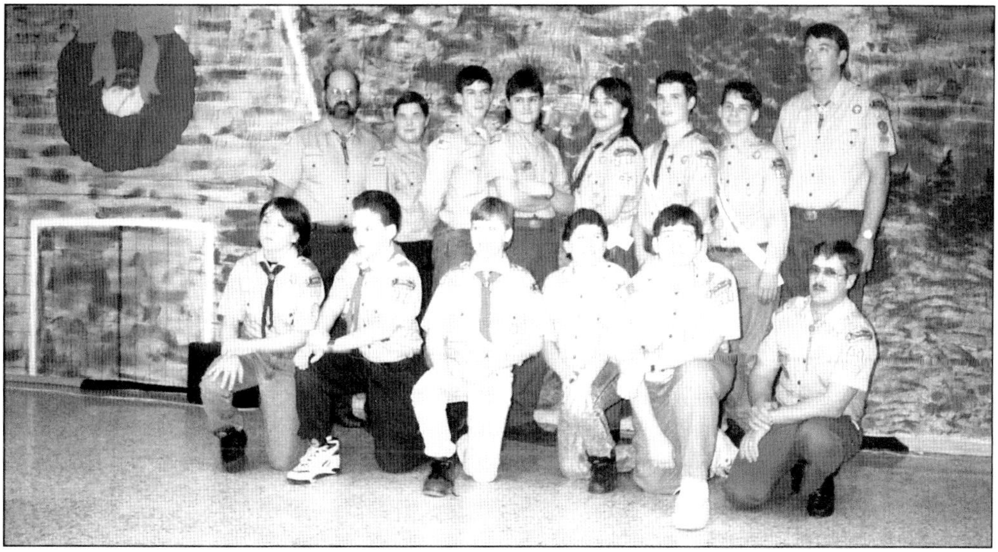

Boy Scout Troop No. 209 worked toward an Eagle Scout Award by doing community service on projects to assist REVIVA. Bridges were built over ditches at the millpond, and flower beds and two Bradford pear trees were planted. A mini park was also erected, complete with picnic tables nearby, for families of the community to enjoy when out walking.

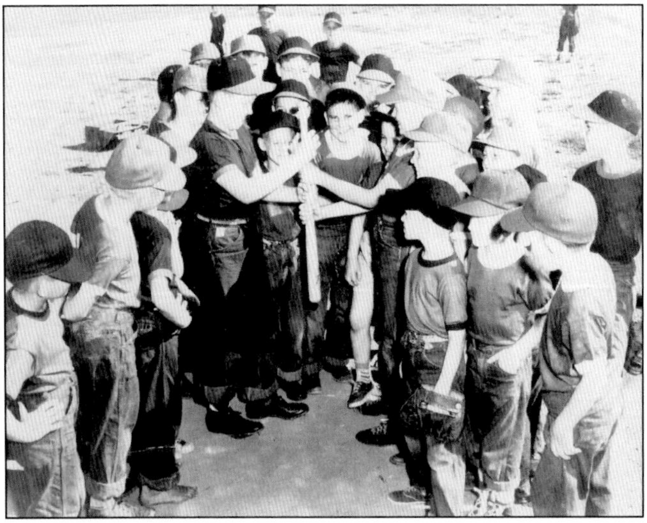

In this 1953–54 scene, ten-year-old Maurice Lopez Jr., the only player in shorts, takes part in "choosing up" teams for this baseball game at the site of the new Iva Library. Maurice grew up to be an educator in the Iva School area. Mr. Lopez retired from Anderson County District No. 3 in 1998, after serving his community as superintendent of Anderson County School District No. 3 for many years.

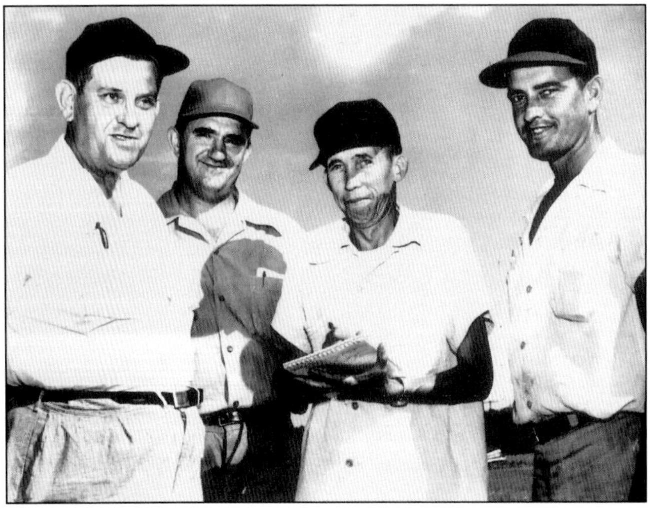

These little league coaches, from left to right, are M.K. Lopez, Hawk Evans, Joe Wilson, and S.L. Jones. Mr. Lopez was the owner and operator of the Iva Café. Mr. Evans was the owner and operator of the Evans Esso Station. Both Mr. Wilson and Mr. Jones were dedicated volunteers. S.L. Jones served as the "voice of the Tigers," announcing Crescent High School football games.

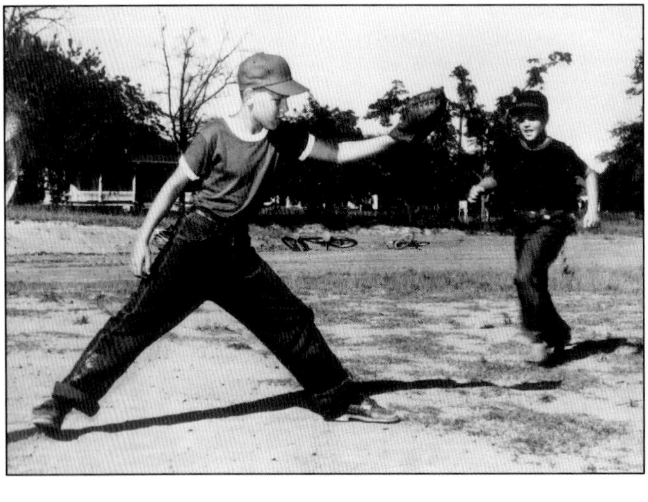

These two young unidentified Iva boys are pictured playing a serious game of baseball. Baseball was one of the favorite sports to play during the summer, even though it was not an organized sport in these days. It was played on back lots and any open pasture that could be found.

Mr. M.K. Lopez Sr. is seen umpiring Little League baseball during the 1950s. The job of umpire was not a very popular one, but due to Mr. Lopez's dedication to the youth, his spirit was never broken. Umpires held regular jobs, and so their time spent as umpire was donated.

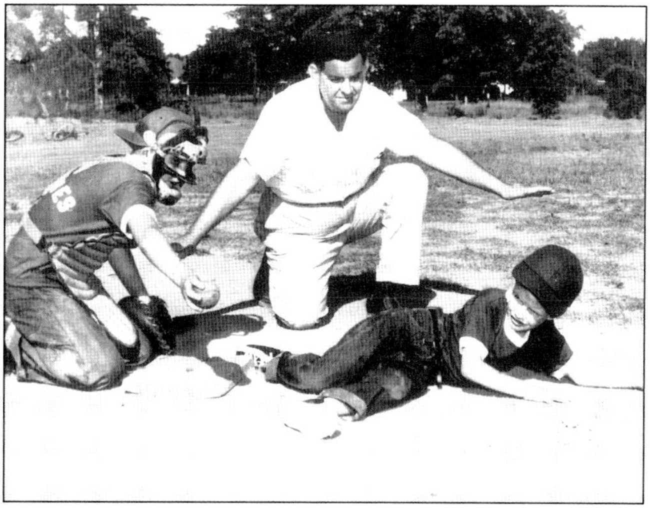

Four team members are sitting on the sideline waiting their turn at bat. For many years, businesses and organizations of the Iva community sponsored teams such as this one. The financial support provided the teams with identifying shirts, caps, and other equipment that they needed.

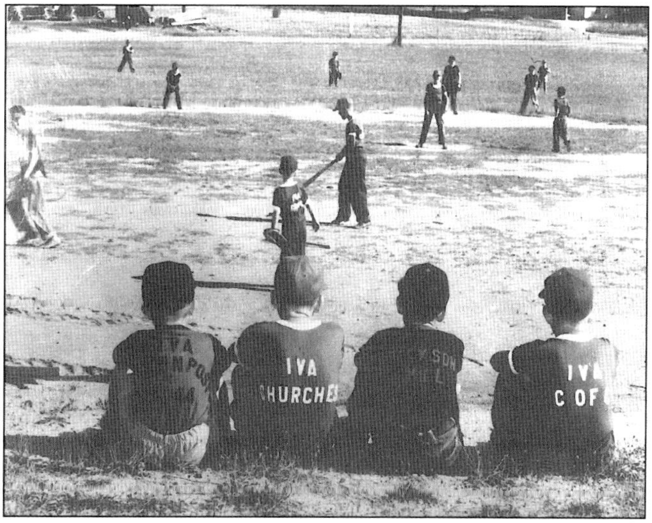

Students have the opportunity to learn the history of older homes in their community as they tour the town of Iva in 1997. These students are from Iva Elementary School. It took 12 children with joined hands to reach around this 100-year-old tree. This house, featured in chapter five and also on the cover, is now 100-or-more years old.

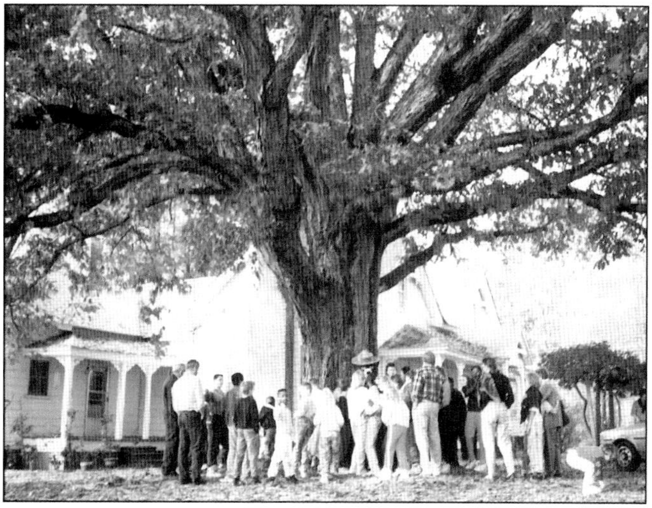

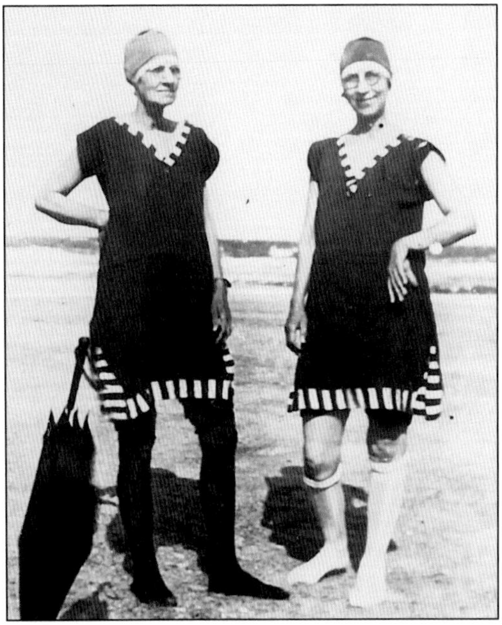

Mrs. Jesse (Mary Jones) Morris is pictured on the right with a friend. These ladies are enjoying a swim on a hot summer afternoon. The bathing suits are typical for this era (early 1900s). The long length of these bathing suits and stockings was proper fashion, as it was considered "not lady like" for women to have exposed skin.

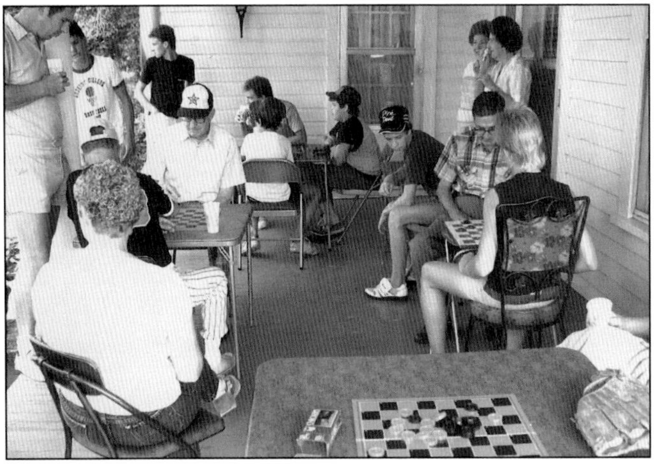

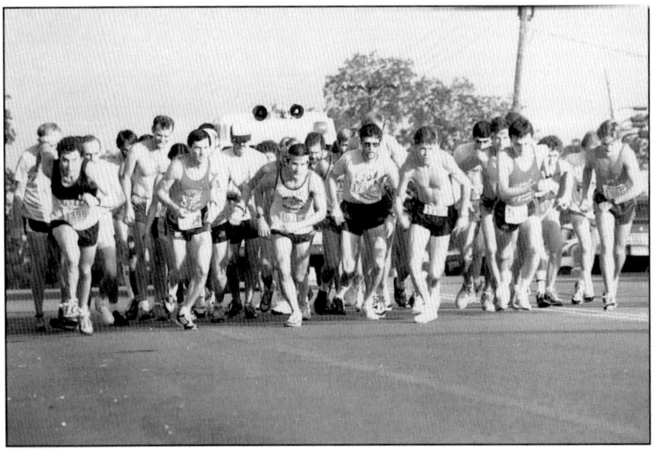

Summer Games were enjoyed by the entire town of Iva when the town was converted into a playing field. On this fun day, everyone could participate in some activity, instead of being just a spectator. People came from near and far, and even from other countries, to take part in the events. For this celebration, the winner of the Ping-Pong tournament was from France. Local families in the town loaned their porches for checkers, set back, and other games. Iva was once called the softball capital, and teams from all over the surrounding areas came here to play.

Everyone loves a parade! These vintage cars are pictured in an Iva Depot Days event in the 1990s. Many activities were enjoyed throughout the day. The vintage cars were brought from the surrounding areas, and awards were given in the judging contest of these cars.

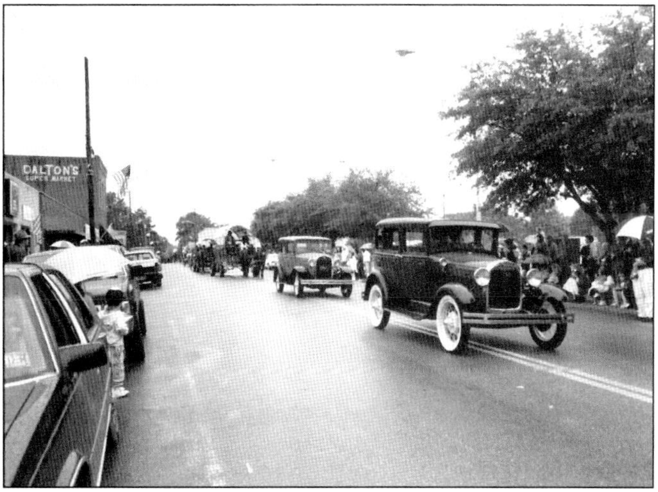

Horses and buggies were a big part of the Iva Centennial celebration parade in 1980. For the older people, this scene would have brought back memories of the time they used to travel this way. Horse-drawn buggies were mainly used for special occasions and Sunday travel.

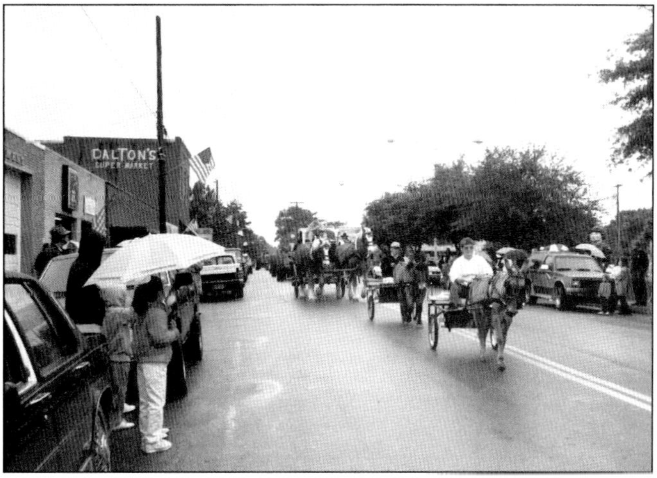

The Depot Days parade is pictured going through downtown Iva. Men really like to take part in a parade if they can drive their tractors, and there are many tractors to be seen in this parade. This was a fun day, and large crowds lined the street to watch and to cheer the participants.

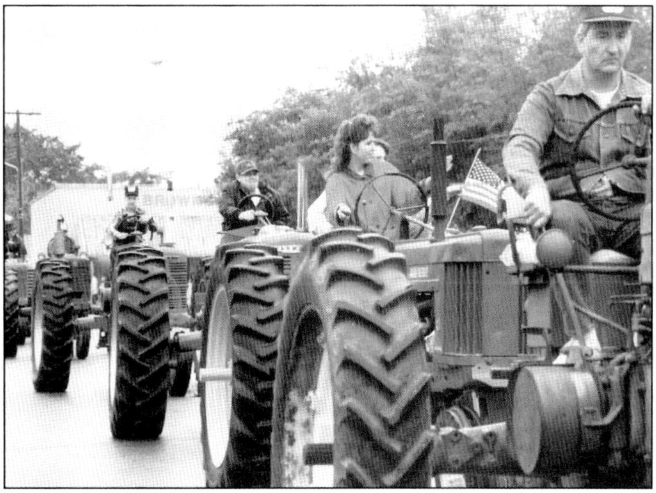

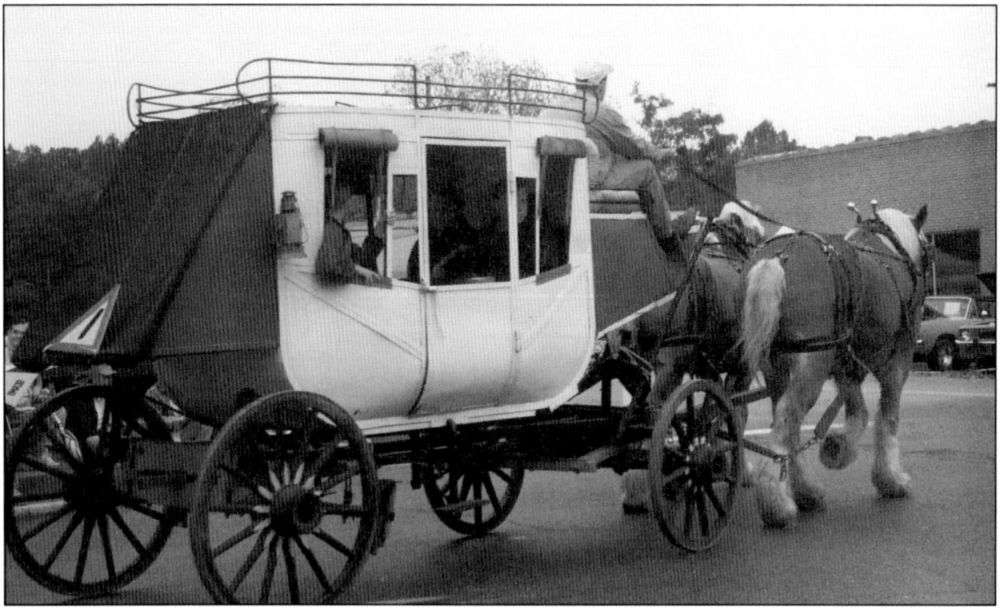

This horse-drawn coach was one of the many features in the Depot Days parade. Due to limited space, luggage was carried on top of the coach. In the 1800s and 1900s, blacksmith shops constructed vehicles and also kept them repaired. George W. Kelly of Lowndesville was one of these coach makers.

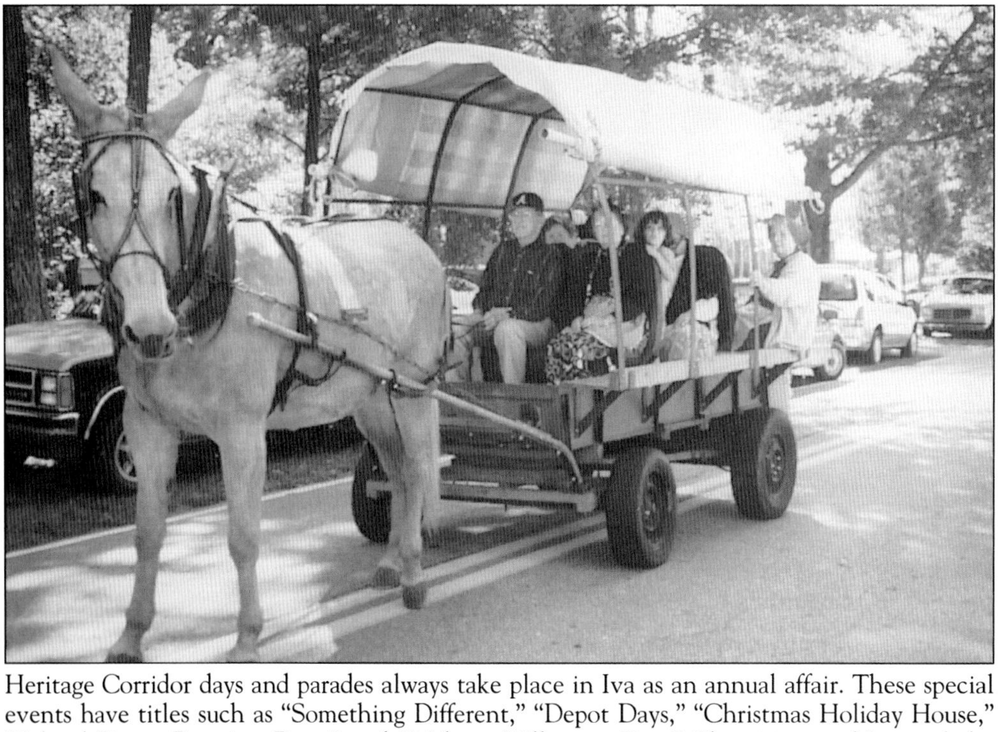

Heritage Corridor days and parades always take place in Iva as an annual affair. These special events have titles such as "Something Different," "Depot Days," "Christmas Holiday House," "School Days—Reunion Daze," and "Make a Difference Day." The citizens of Iva and the surrounding areas have always worked together to make these special days successful.

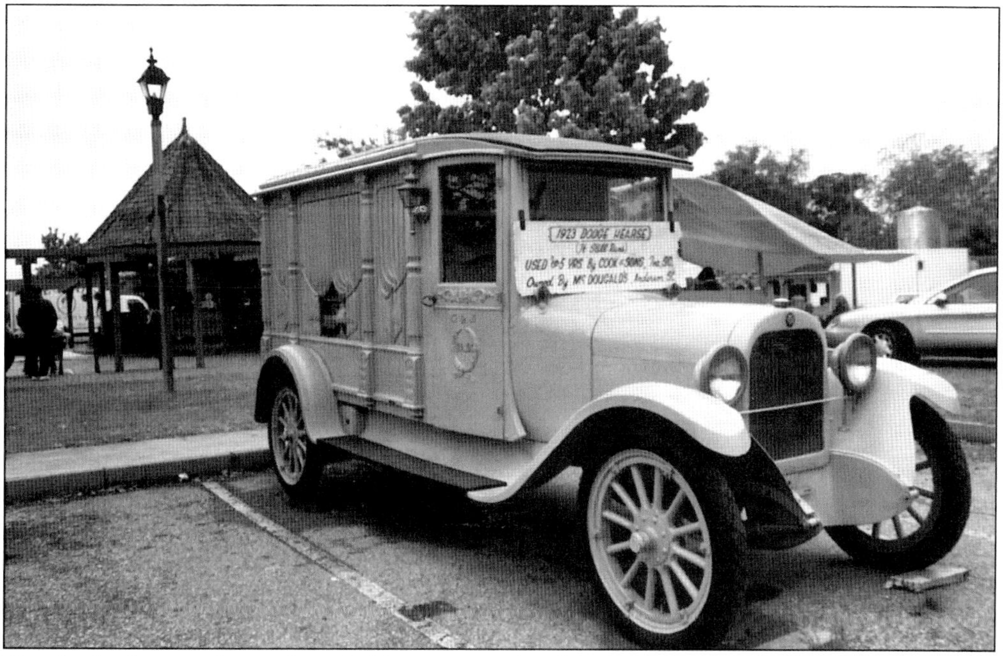

This Dodge hearse, dating from 1923, was owned and operated by the Cook and Jones Funeral Home in Iva. Pringle Cook and John J. Jones were the owners. The McDougald Funeral Home in Anderson bought the hearse from the Cook family. The two original lanterns from the front of the hearse are now in the Iva ARP Church archives.

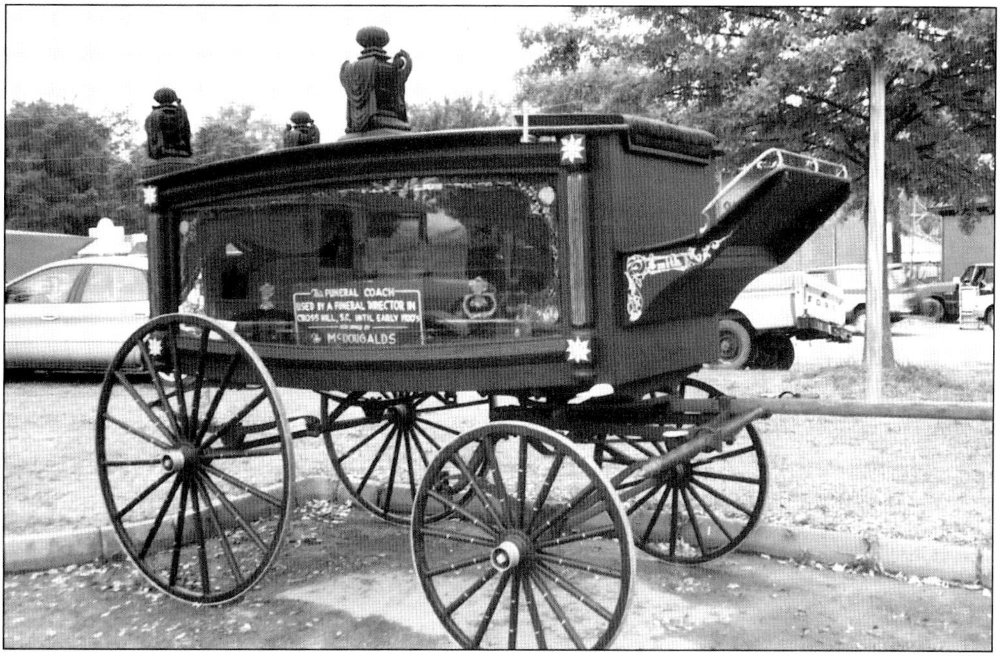

These funeral coaches date back to the Civil War. In those days, it was customary for a female to be carried by a white horse and a male to be carried by a dark horse. These coaches were on display during the Depot Days festival in Iva, courtesy of McDougald Funeral Home, which owns both of these exhibits.

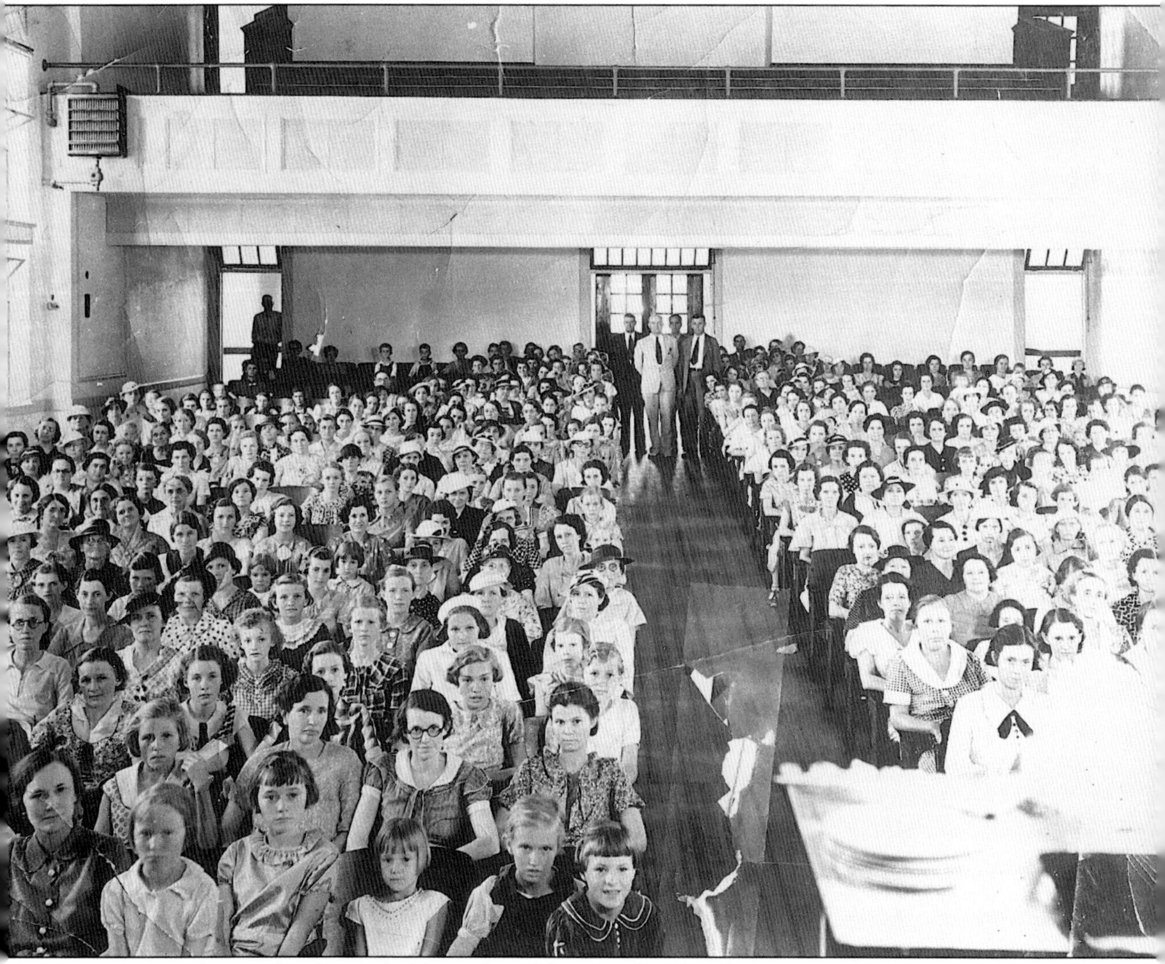

This cooking school was held in the old Iva School auditorium in the 1930s. The event was sponsored by the *Anderson Independent* newspaper. Recipes were given to everyone who attended, and dishes were prepared and given as door prizes. During the Great Depression years of the 1930s, people were uneducated, there was no means of employment, and very little was known about the benefits of proper food. The main diet, for some people, was black strap molasses, fatback, corn bread, and vegetables in season. People died of malnutrition, mostly from Pellagra, which is caused by a deficiency of vitamin A. Clemson University was, at that time, known as Clemson Agricultural College, and it developed yellow corn, which provided people with the vitamin A that they needed. The United States government created programs to teach people how to be more self-sufficient and to help boost the economy. The Home Demonstration Club for women was one of the many successful ones. This program taught ladies to sew, cook, preserve food, and ways to foster a healthier lifestyle. The government encouraged and supported cooking schools, like this one, all over the nation.

Nine

MILITARY

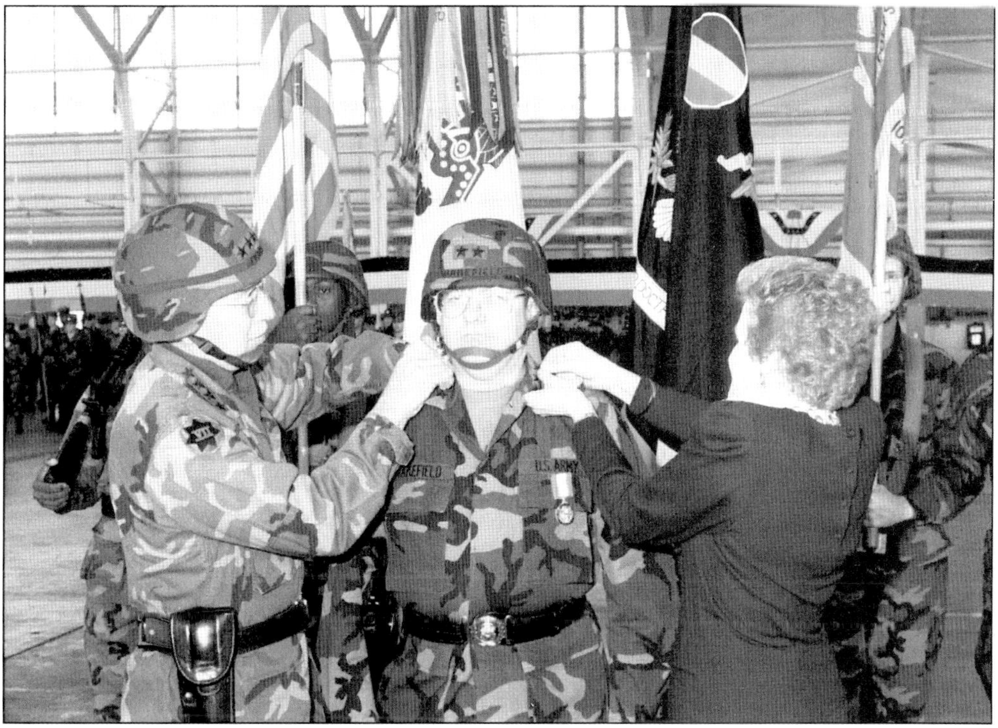

Sam Wakefield, a 1956 graduate of Iva High School and a native of the Iva-Antreville community, served 38 years in the U.S. Army at Fort Lee, Virginia. During this time, he earned promotion from major to a three-star general. He was awarded the Distinguished Service Medal with two Oak Cluster, the Legion of Merit, and the Defense Distinguished Service Medal. Lt. General Wakefield was a distinguished military graduate of The Citadel. He and his wife, Linda Bowen Wakefield, have two sons, Richard and Norris. His mother is Mary McAdams Wakefield.

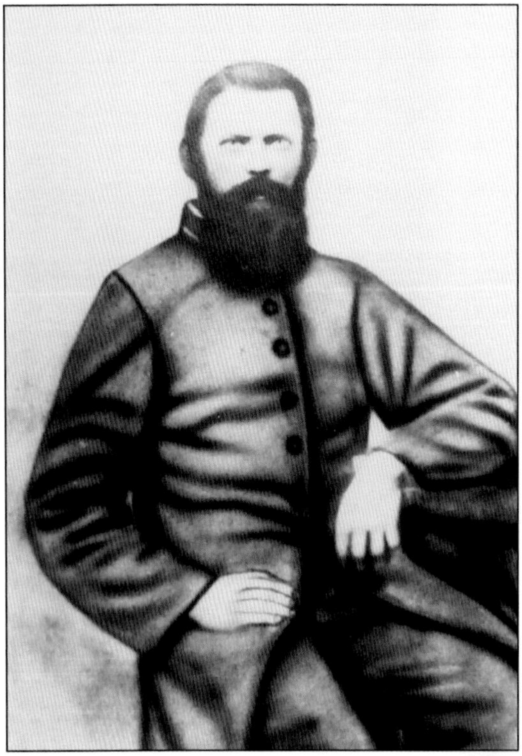

John Gregg Hall was a captain for the Confederacy and a defender of Charleston during the Civil War. Captain Hall married Jane Burriss, and their children were James, John Andrew, Lawrence, Will, Milford, Augustus, Julia, Lula, Matilda, and Palmyra. Captain Hall was one of the few officers to remain in South Carolina following the war.

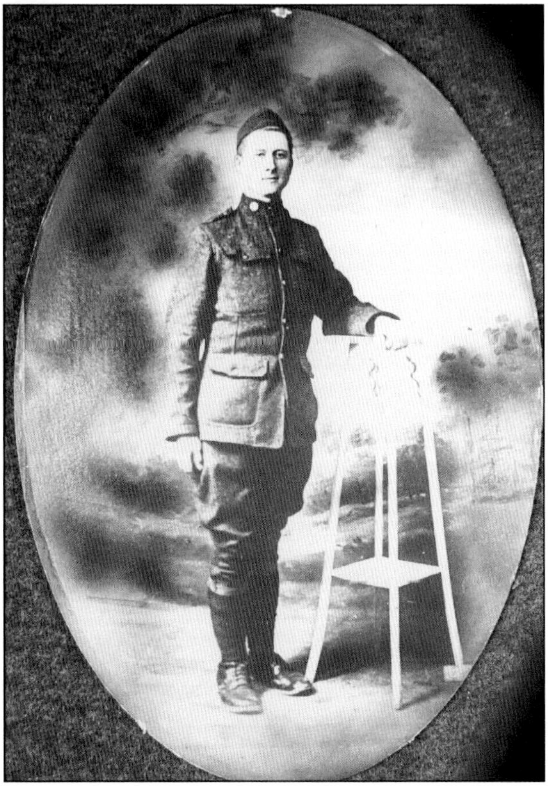

Leftridge C. Manning, pictured in military uniform, was born on August 12, 1895, and died on July 21, 1996. He entered the U.S. Army on July 25, 1918. He served in France and was discharged in 1919. He was married to Selma Burton in November 1920. They celebrated their 70th wedding anniversary in November 1990. This couple had six sons and one daughter. Mr. Manning faithfully served Union Baptist Church as an active deacon for 51 years.

Robert Barney Hutchinson served the Confederate States of America during the Civil War around 1862, lost a leg at Sharpsburg, Maryland, survived the war, and lived until 1906. He is buried in Providence Presbyterian Church Cemetery at Lowndesville.

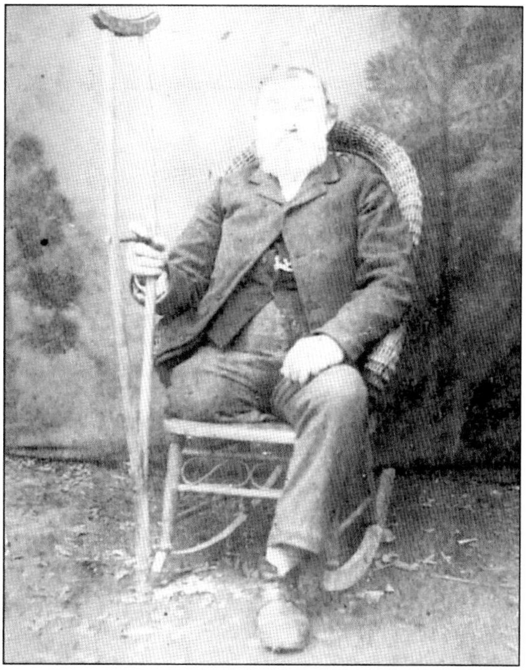

During World War II, the government had to ration certain items. These stamp-filled books were issued to each person. There were certain stamps for each scarce item, and this system assured everyone a fair share of the available supplies. "In 1942, gasoline rationing went into effect in 17 different states. Non-essential vehicles were allowed 3 gallons a week," according to the *Anderson Independent*.

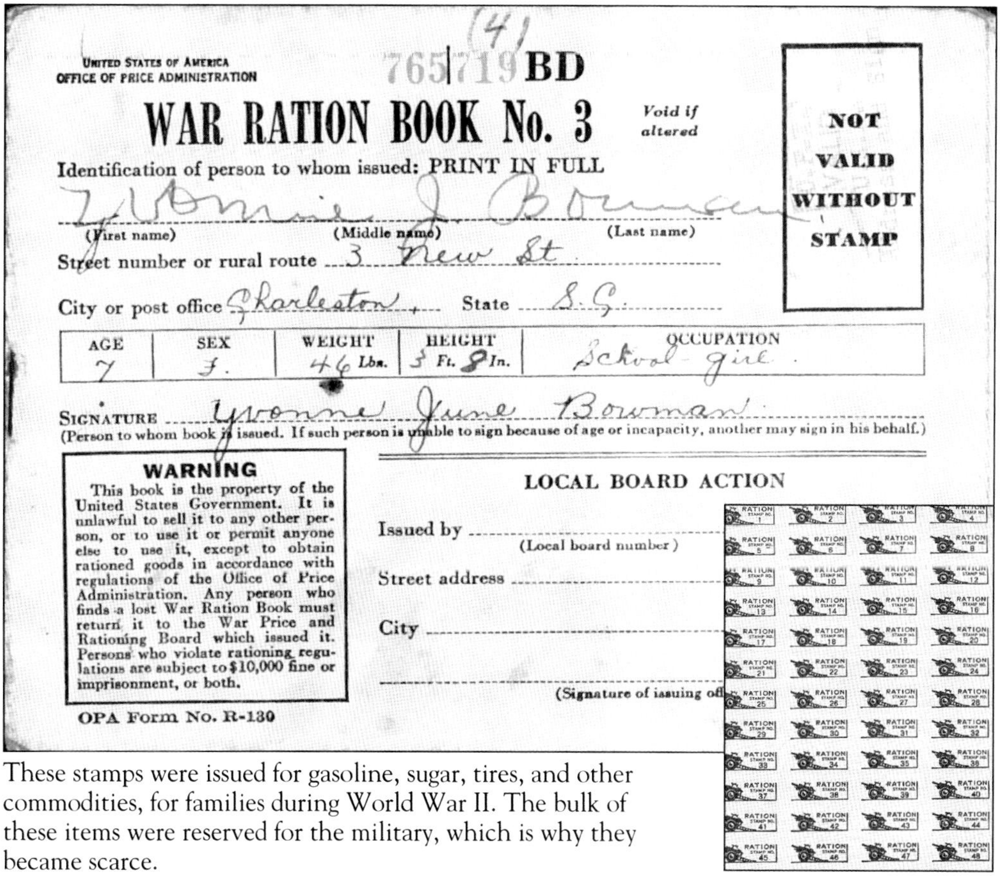

(4)

UNITED STATES OF AMERICA
OFFICE OF PRICE ADMINISTRATION

765719 BD

WAR RATION BOOK No. 3

Void if altered

NOT VALID WITHOUT STAMP

Identification of person to whom issued: PRINT IN FULL

Yvonne J. Bowman
(First name) (Middle name) (Last name)

Street number or rural route 3 New St

City or post office Charleston State S. C.

AGE	SEX	WEIGHT	HEIGHT	OCCUPATION
7	F.	46 Lbs.	3 Ft. 8 In.	School girl

SIGNATURE Yvonne June Bowman
(Person to whom book is issued. If such person is unable to sign because of age or incapacity, another may sign in his behalf.)

WARNING
This book is the property of the United States Government. It is unlawful to sell it to any other person, or to use it or permit anyone else to use it, except to obtain rationed goods in accordance with regulations of the Office of Price Administration. Any person who finds a lost War Ration Book must return it to the War Price and Rationing Board which issued it. Persons who violate rationing regulations are subject to $10,000 fine or imprisonment, or both.

OPA Form No. R-130

LOCAL BOARD ACTION

Issued by ....
(Local board number)

Street address ....

City ....

....
(Signature of issuing officer)

These stamps were issued for gasoline, sugar, tires, and other commodities, for families during World War II. The bulk of these items were reserved for the military, which is why they became scarce.

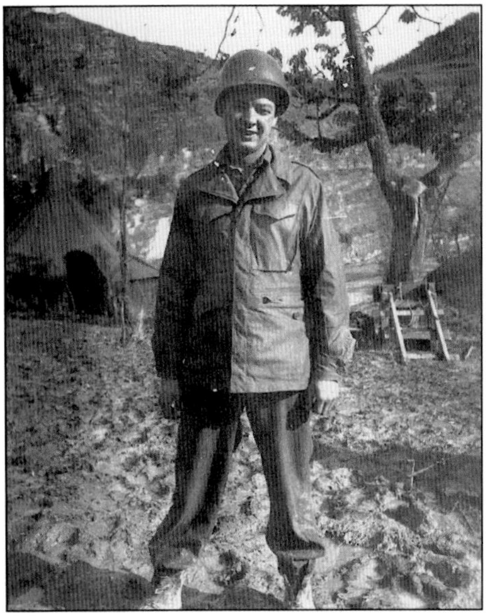

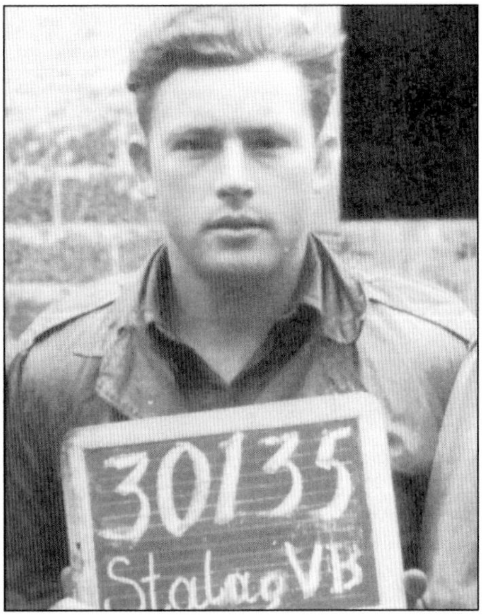

Left: Duane Gailey, while serving in Italy as a member of the Field Hospital during World War II, attended to the wounded on the front line. He was transferred to the Philippines when the German forces surrendered. By that time, the Japanese had surrendered. His company gathered equipment and flew to Japan to act as security. *Right:* Winston "Little Boy" Metz, with his Stalag prison number, worked at three different camps during his 27 months as a POW. He was captured in 1943 in Oran, North Africa, after being dug out of a foxhole that had collapsed, due to the weight of a German tank. He received the Purple Heart, EAMET Ribbon, and a Bronze Service Star.

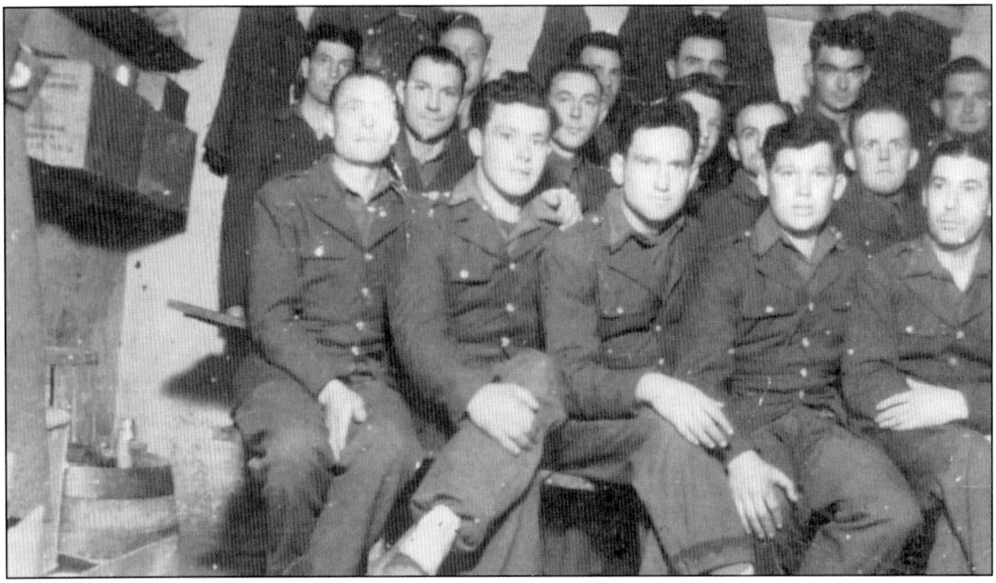

This German farm is situated near Mosine, Germany, 6 kilometers from the Polish border. Winston Metz of Iva, pictured second from the left on the front row, worked at this farm with these men for six months, during his imprisonment. Some of the other prisoners of war from Iva were Harold Bruce, James W. Ginn, Claude Manning, Chester McAdams, Herbert Dixon, and James Allred.

Ten

Along the Savannah River

Gregg Shoals and Harper's Ferry

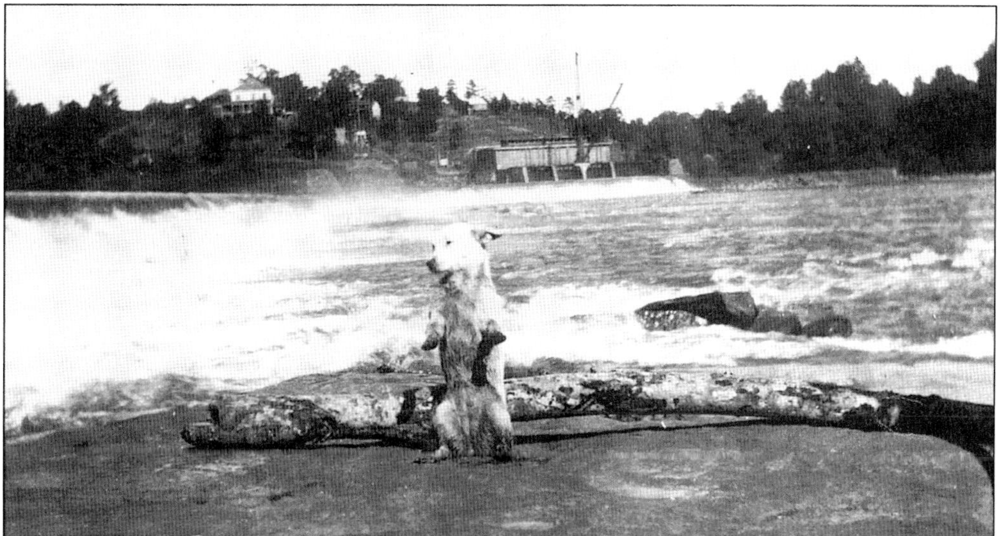

Gregg Shoals, 10 miles from Iva on the Savannah River, was the site of one of the Upstate's first hydroelectric plants. The plant was built in 1905 by the Savannah River Power Company to provide power for Anderson County and the surrounding communities. In 1954, the operation was outmoded by nuclear power plants. Seen in the background of this picture are the power plant (on the right) and "Big House" (on the left). "Big House" was home to the Metz, McMullan, Hill, and Dickerson families, who, along with other families, were in charge of plant operations.

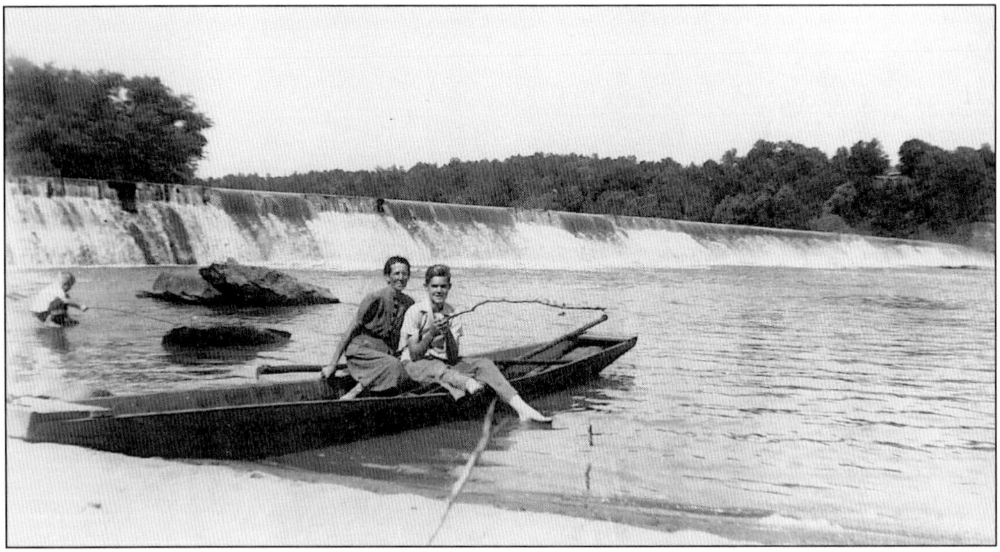

The Shoals was a popular place for boating, fishing, "fish fries," and picnics. Faye Hill Burriss, resident of Gregg Shoals, is pictured with her nephews. This was a popular spot during the early days of America, as the American Indians lived in this area. Tribes lived all along the Savannah River from the foothills to the coast, of what was to become the lovely state of South Carolina.

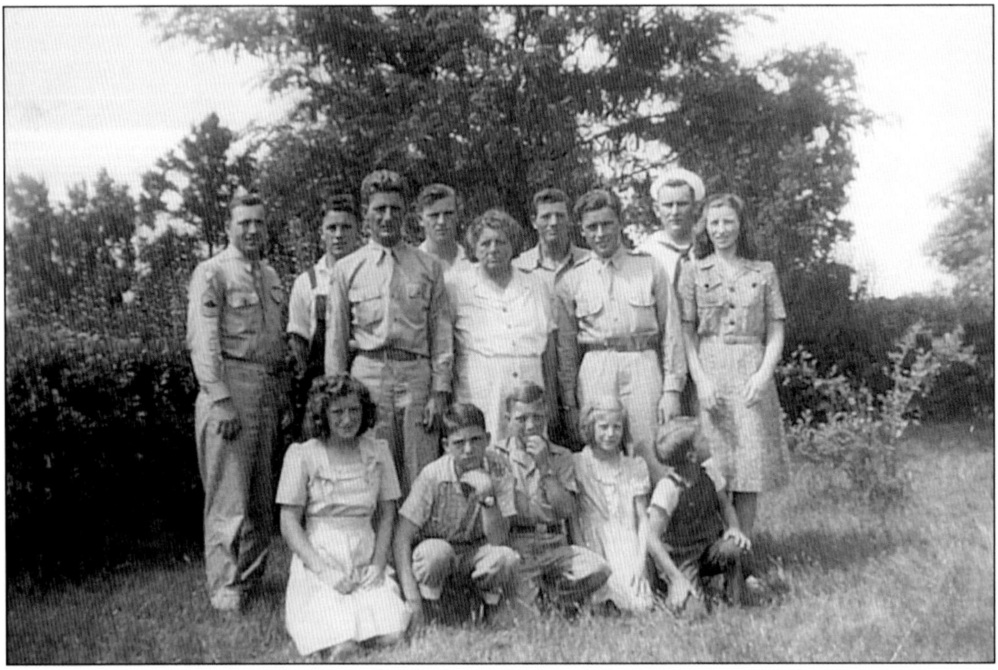

The Metz family lived at Gregg Shoals from 1924 until 1938, when Walter M. Metz, who worked at the power plant, died. He and his wife, Alberta, had 13 children, of which 5 sons fought in WW II. Mrs. Metz was awarded the Order of the Palmetto for having 5 sons in the service of their country.

The poem on the far left was part of a memorial service that paid tribute to the ten victims who drowned at Harper's Ferry on Easter Sunday, 1920. As they attempted to cross the swollen Savannah River, the cable post broke and the flat boat sank, sending its passengers into the swift current. The body of Charlie Meschine was never found. To the right of the poem is a listing of the victims that lost their lives at Harper's Ferry on Easter Sunday in 1920.

THE EASTER DROWNING IN SAVANNAH

In the spring of ninteen twenty
It had rained most every day
And the brooklets, creeks and rivers
1 Rushed in torrents on their way.
It was on the fourth of April,
In the Easter eventide
That eleven youngsters ventured
O'er Savanah wild and wide.

CHORUS
They have crossed , but not Savannah,
Yet beyond the veil of care
When their friends have crossed the river,
May they find their loved ones there.
CHORUS

Not a dream of lurking danger
Not a tear stood in their eye
Not a farewell kiss from mother,
2 Not a father's last goodby
Forth they went in quest of pleasure
As so often youngsters do,
In the bloom of youth and beauty
Brave young men and maidens true.

They had gone to Harper's Ferry
For they lived not far away
And the boatman's wife was teacher
3 of the district school they say.
Let us cross the brimming river,
Some one yelled in youthful glee,
It is well the others echoed
In a voice of ecstacy.

All were on and then the boatman
With his young and lovely bride,
When the flat was loosed from anchor
4 Started for the other side
Now a strong and goodly cable
Held the flat boat in its place,
But the rough and angry waters
Showed that time had left its trace

When they reached the mighty current
That with wonderous swiftness ran,
Then the cable post was broken,
5 Thus defied the works of man
As the flat swung down the river
Half restrained and partly free,
Then the air was rent with screaming
And with cries of agony.

Soon the goodly flat was sunken,
They must sleep, but not to dream
Eleven start, but ten are missing
6 One was left to tell the story,
Thomas Bradshaw is the name
But the rest will live forever
In our memory's hall of fame.

In that voyage across the stream.

Two of them were Misses Bradshaw,
They were sisters understand
Mannings three, two girls and a brother,
7 And a boy named Sutherland
Lester Waters, too, was missing,
With his young and lovely wife,
Charles Meschine and Alice also
Perished in that loss of life.

Easter night was swiftly falling
As the tragic news was borne
To the loved ones of the missing
8 And their friends who came to mourn.
After days of tireless searching
Through the sunshine, rain or chill,
In the bosom of Savannah
One of them is sleeping still.

Gone are they but not forgotten,
Change is wrought by fleeting time,
And the bloom of youth and beauty
9 Is the tempter's sweetest chime
Let us heed this note of warning
As the path of life we plod
Then my precious friend and reader,
Oh, prepare to meet thy God.

E. L. Fant
Author

DROWNED IN SAVANNAH RIVER AT HARPER'S FERRY.

5 MILES FROM LOWNDESVILLE, S. C.

EASTER SUNDAY
APRIL 4, 1920

Lester Waters
Oct. 25, 1894

Lollie S. Waters
Nov. 6, 1899

Alice Meschine
Aug. 7, 1906

Charlie Meschine
Feb. 4, 1904

Albert Sutherland
June 27, 1904

Robert Manning
June 12, 1900

Inez Manning
May 23, 1897

Annie Manning
Mar. 18, 1904

Allie Bradshaw
Dec. 28, 1907

Lucy Bradshaw
Mar. 14, 1903

The body of Charlie Meschine was never found

Buried at
PROVIDENCE PRESBYTERIAN CHURCH CEMETERY
Lowndesville, S. C.

Memorial Service
EASTER SUNDAY 1980

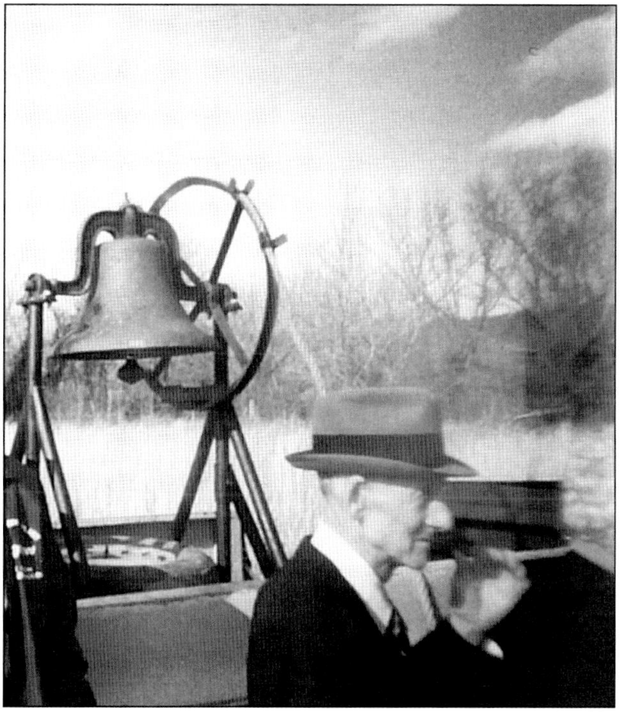

This old bell was rung at Harper's Ferry Crossing, on the Savannah River where the cable ferry crossed. This was at the scene where the 1920 Harper's Ferry Easter tragedy occurred, and ten young people drowned. L.C. Manning was brother to several of the young victims. A monument can be found at Providence Presbyterian Church, in Lowndesville, which lists the names of the victims.

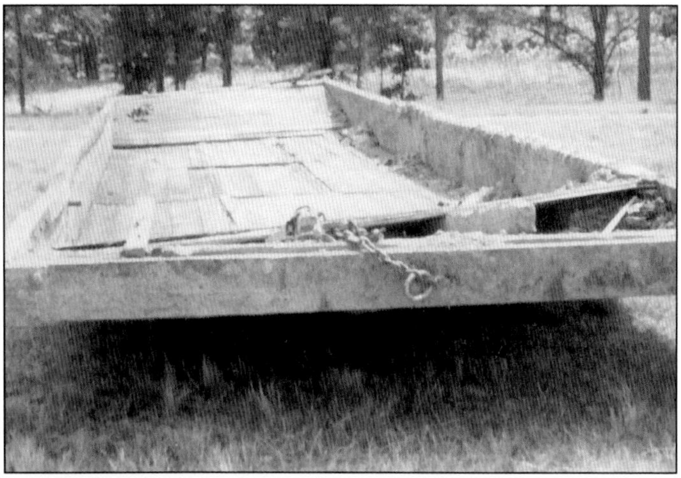

This old ferry was owned by Mr. Hailey of Hartwell, Georgia. It was found buried in the mud at Gregg Shoals, and was recovered when Lake Russell was being built. The ferry is now preserved in a pond at McCalla State Park, near Lowndesville. It once transported people and goods back and forth across the Savannah River from South Carolina to Georgia, near what is now the Smith McGee Bridge.

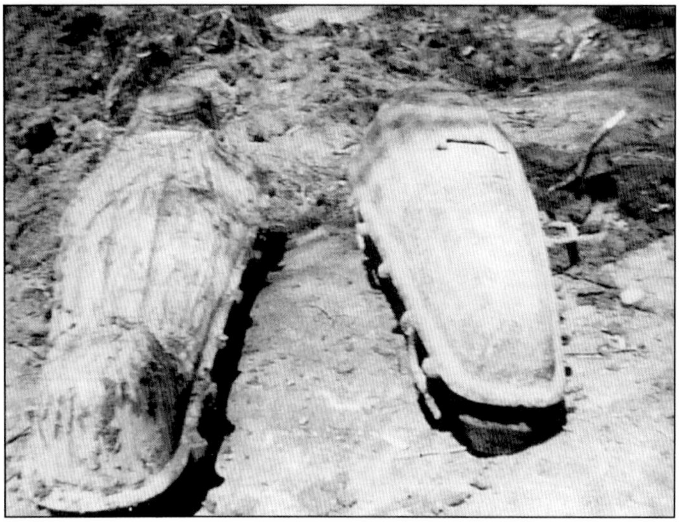

Two unidentified children's coffins were unearthed during the excavation for the building of Lake Russell during the 1980s. One coffin was engraved with the date 1856. These were metal coffins, indicating that the victims were from a wealthy family.

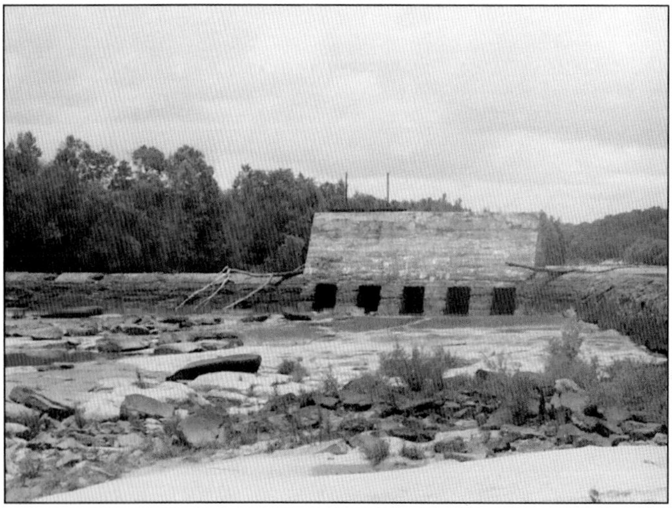

Old bulkhead and retaining walls were all that was left of the Gregg Shoals dam after it was dynamited in 1955. This was the first time in 50 years fish had been allowed to swim "upstream." This section is now under the waters of Lake Russell, which is one of a chain of lakes, built by the U.S. government's Corps of Engineers, along the Savannah River over the last four decades.

Eleven

History in the Making

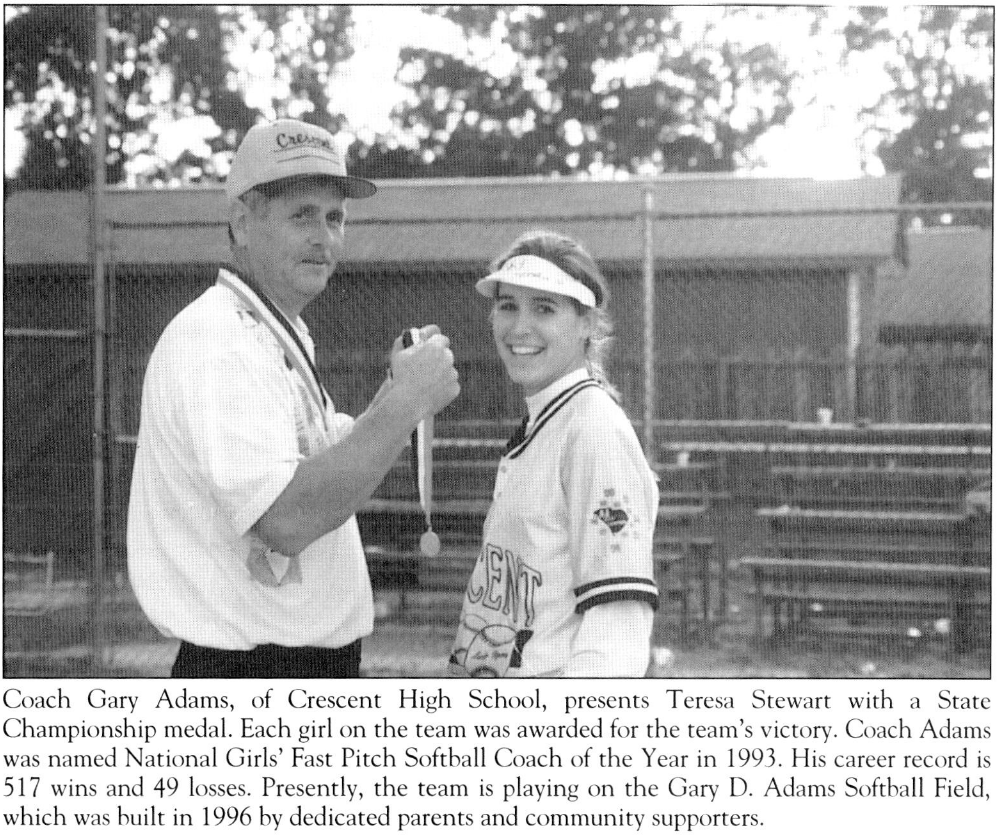

Coach Gary Adams, of Crescent High School, presents Teresa Stewart with a State Championship medal. Each girl on the team was awarded for the team's victory. Coach Adams was named National Girls' Fast Pitch Softball Coach of the Year in 1993. His career record is 517 wins and 49 losses. Presently, the team is playing on the Gary D. Adams Softball Field, which was built in 1996 by dedicated parents and community supporters.

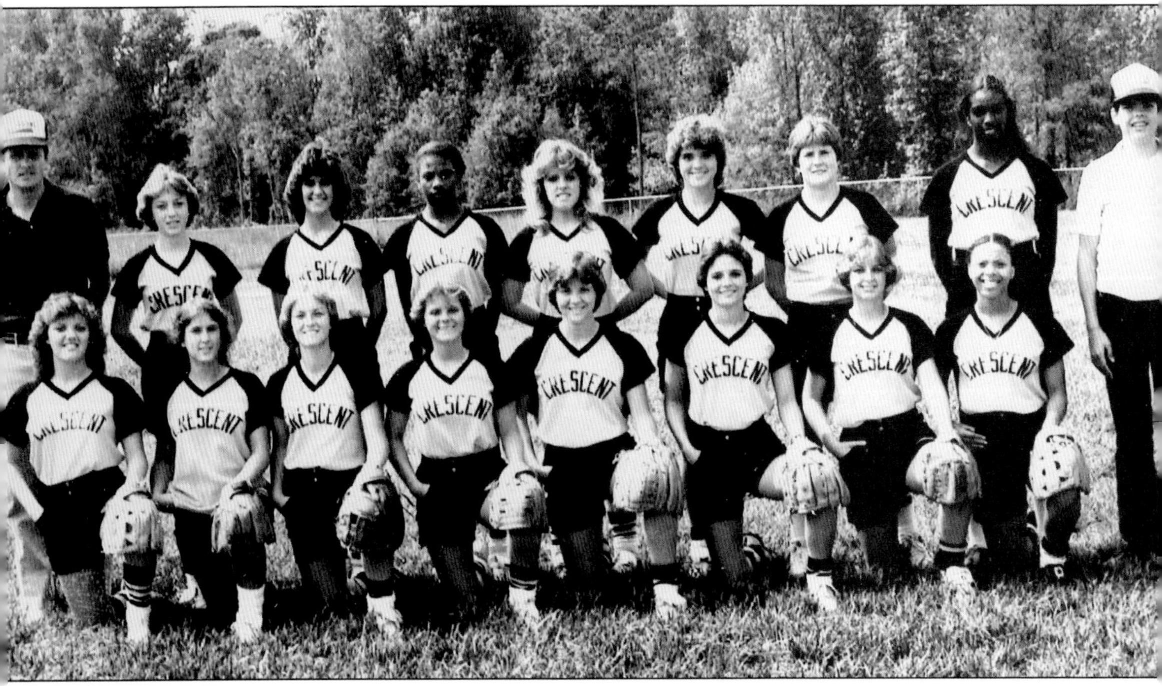

In 1982, the Crescent High School girls' fast pitch softball team won their first 2-AA State Championship. The two national records are for "Most Wins at 15" and "Most Consecutive Wins at 11." Pictured, from left to right, are as follows: (first row) Pam Richardson, Sheryl McGee, Kathy Dickerson, Gay Burke, Jan Bundy, Donna Isom, Beth King, and Theresa Chenault; (second row) Coach Gary Adams, Robin Powell, Marla Young, Frankie Norris, Susan Davis, DeeAnn Roberts, Tracie Cronk, Evelyn Boston, and manager Mac McCalla.

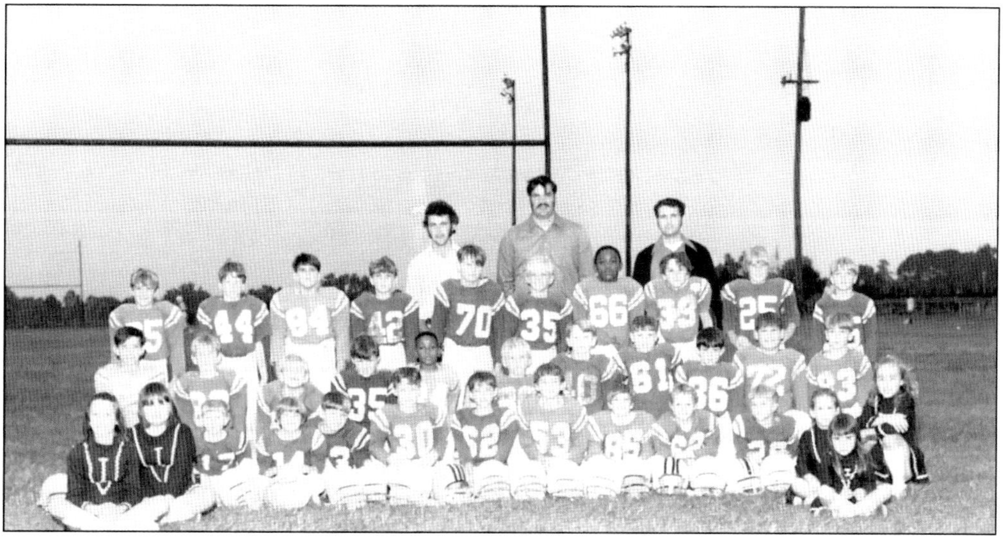

Iva's 11-Under 1973 State Football Championship team set many records. They played together for three years and had won 44 straight games on their way to the state championship, after which they were challenged by two undefeated teams from Georgia, winning over Athens 20-0 and Atlanta 48-13. The coaches were Robert Powell, Roscoe Powell, and Jack Wiles.

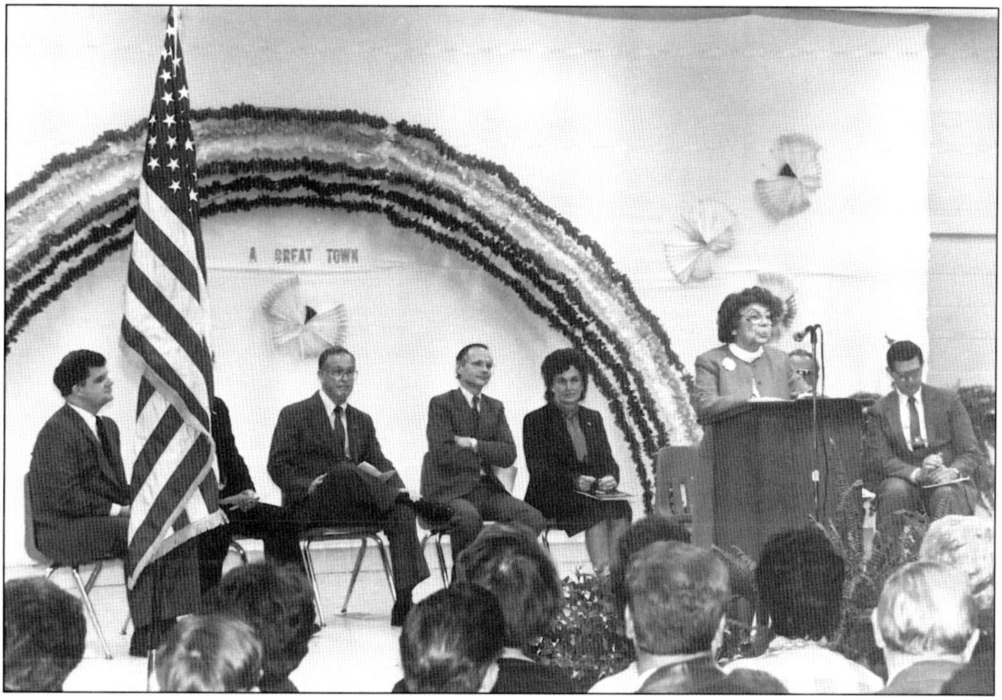

Iva officially became a "Great Town" in 1985! This was the beginning of one of many honors that were awarded to REVIVA (revitalize Iva) over the years. REVIVA member Elsie Evans speaks during the awards presentation. Pictured, from left to right, are the following: Reverend Ted Hagan, pastor of Good Hope Presbyterian Church; Mickey Walker, of the South Carolina Development Association; Richard Riley, South Carolina governor; Yvonne McGee, coordinator of REVIVA; and Reverend Jerry Laughter, pastor of Iva First Baptist Church.

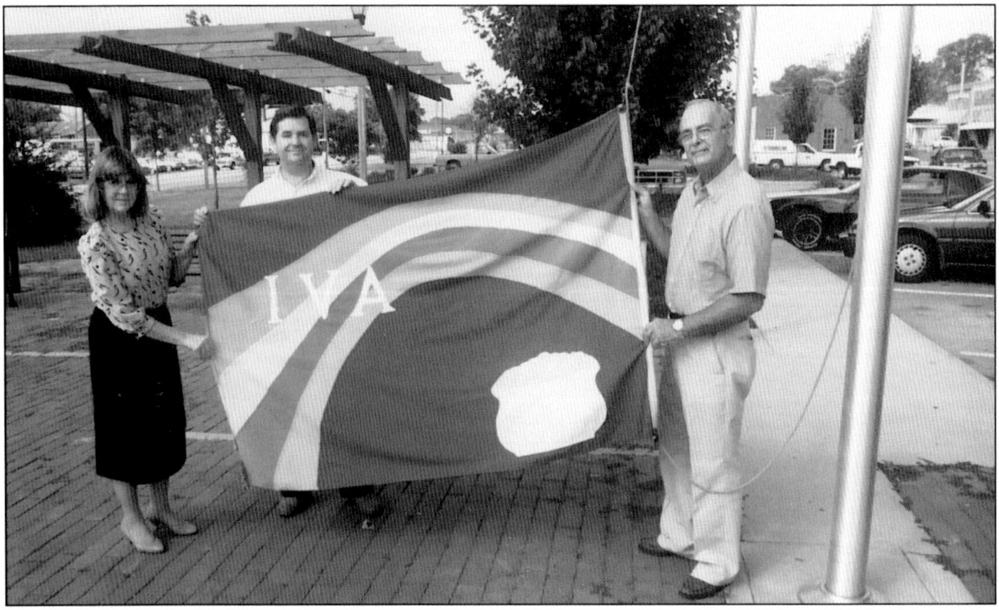

Iva citizens took pride in designing their own town flag. Four flagpoles were erected on the downtown square—one for the American flag, the state flag, the town flag, and the Tree City, USA flag, which was received for the town's Arbor Day accomplishments over the years. Pictured, from left to right, are the following: Elaine and Julian Maxwell, makers of the flag; and Mr. Art Stezin, who designed the flag with his wife.

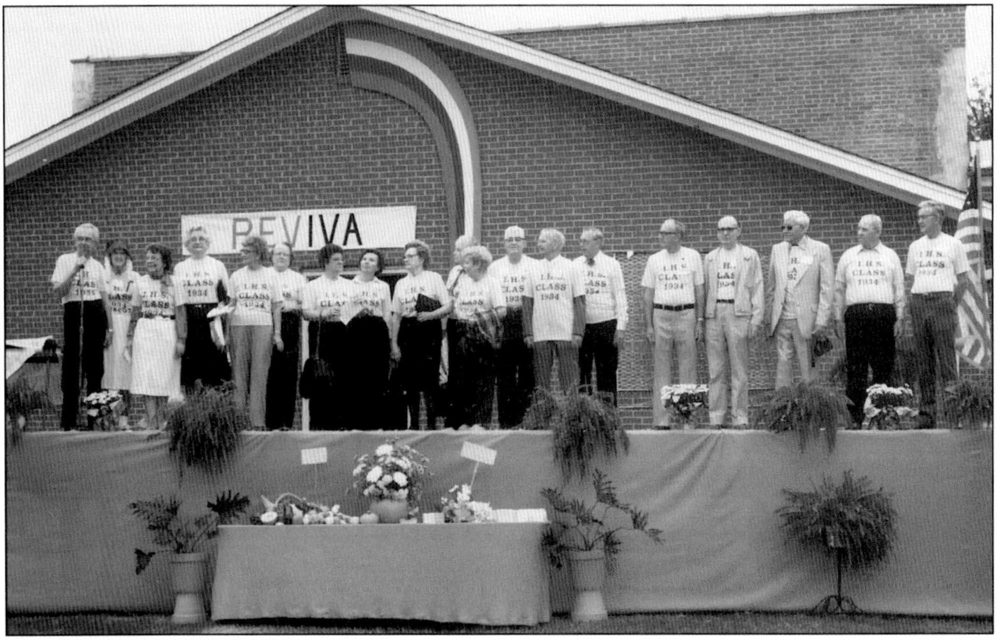

The graduating Class of 1934 is shown in this photograph. The first High School Homecoming Reunion, sponsored by REVIVA, was held on September 2, 1984, the date that marked the 50th anniversary of this graduating class. Mr. Sam Martin, a member of the class, ordered special shirts with "Class of 1934" printed on them, for the class members to wear for this important occasion.

Doris Ligon Shirley, wearing one of the first basketball uniforms for girls at Iva High School, is pictured during the 1920s. Doris played basketball throughout her high school days. The team played on outdoor courts and had emblems of "I.H.S." (Iva High School) on their suits, as can be seen here. Note that the style of this suit is quite different from the girls' uniforms of today.

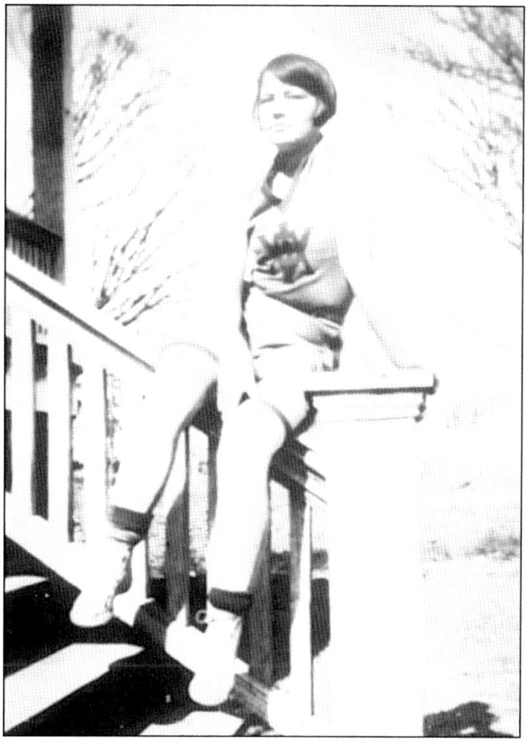

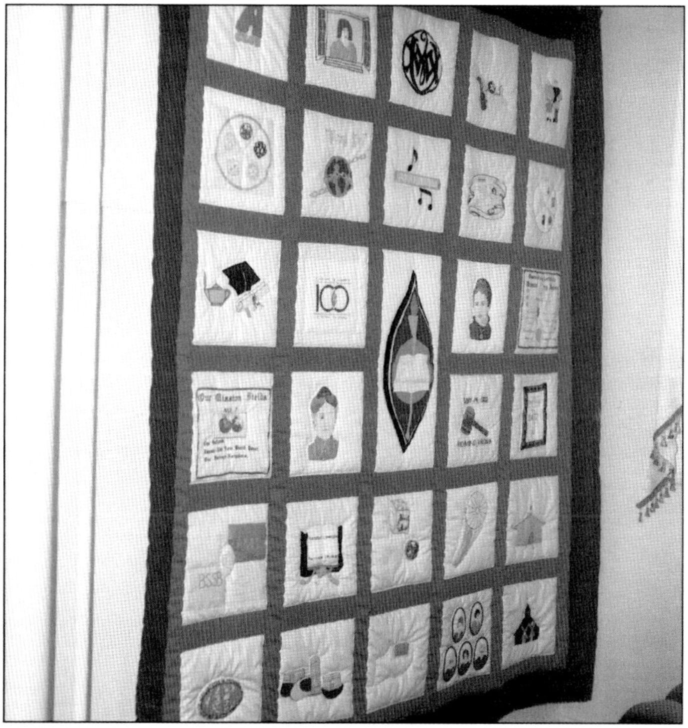

This beautiful quilt was made by the Women's Missionary Society (WMS), of the Iva First Baptist Church, to commemorate the WMS's 100th anniversary during the 1980s. The quilt is now on display in a room to the right of the vestibule. Each lady completed a square, which was then used by Mrs. Hugh Hayes and Mrs. Betsy Latham to put the quilt together.

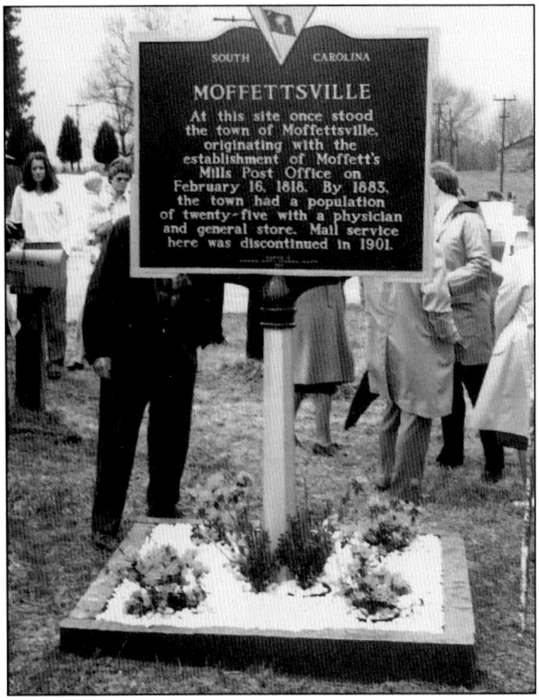

This historical marker is all that remains of Moffettsville, 2.5 miles west of Iva. Originally, the town was known as Moffett's Mill, after being named for Colonel John Moffett around 1780. The town included a store, cotton gin, a tannery, two grain mills, and a post office. The first postmaster was James H. Davidson, and the last postmaster was W.T.A. Sherard. Colonel Moffett established the Moffett Academy, a school for boys, near the Generostee ARP Church.

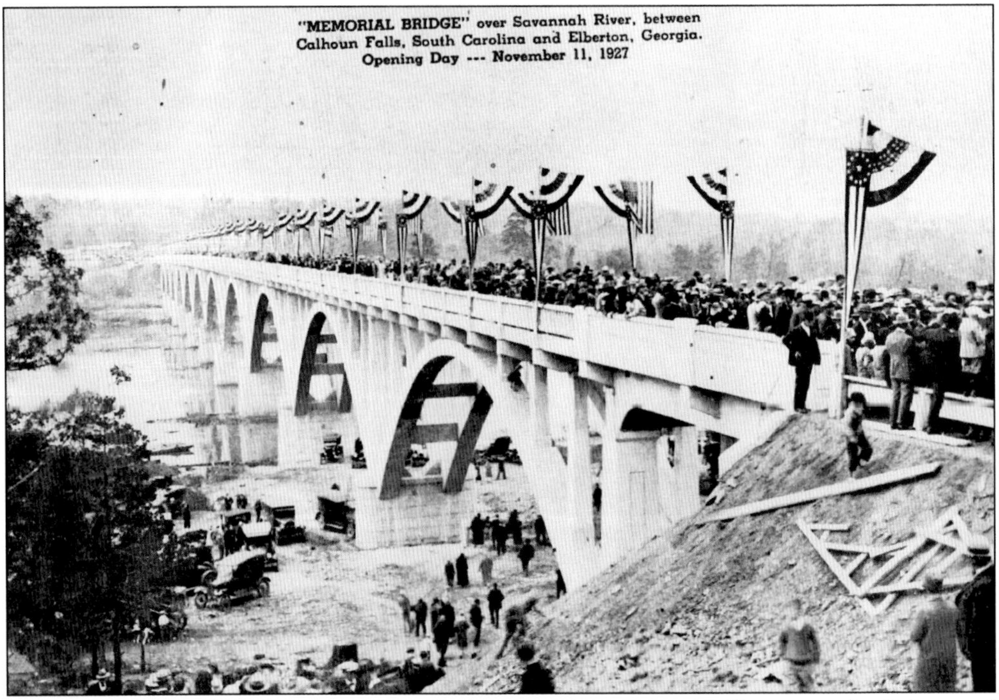

This handsome bridge over the Savannah River no longer stands. Known as the "Memorial Bridge," it was built in honor of the soldiers killed in World War I. The bridge was dedicated on Armistice Day, 1927, and was christened with a bottle of ginger ale by Ida Calhoun, a descendant of John C. Calhoun. The bridge was submerged when Russell Lake was constructed, and was replaced by a new, higher bridge.

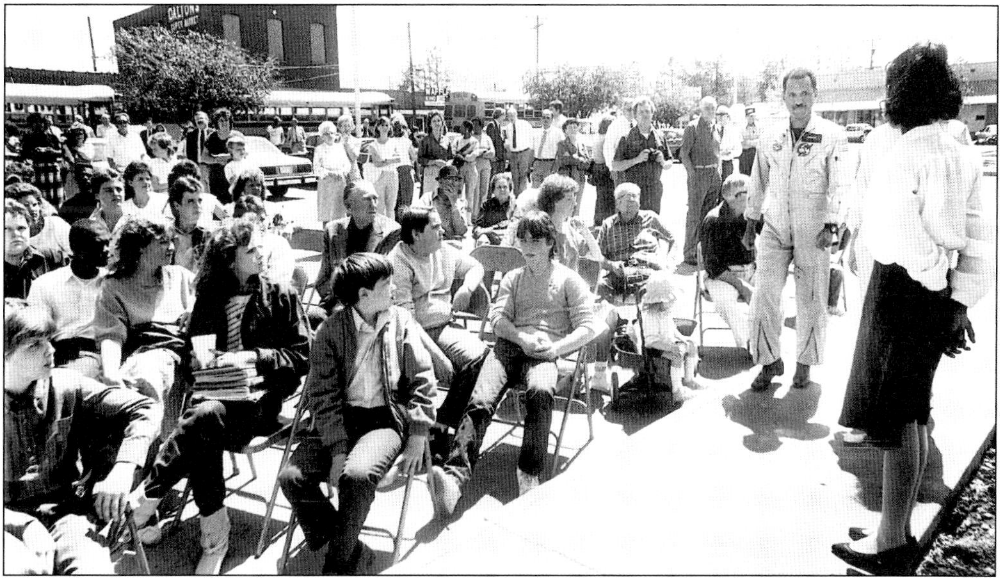

Iva experienced a once-in-a-lifetime event in April of 1987. Astronaut Charles Bolden visited the schools and community and participated in the dedication of seven trees. These trees had been planted on the town square in December 1986 as a living memorial to the astronauts and teacher of the *Challenger* disaster. Bolden had served as pilot of the space shuttle *Columbia* during earlier space flights.

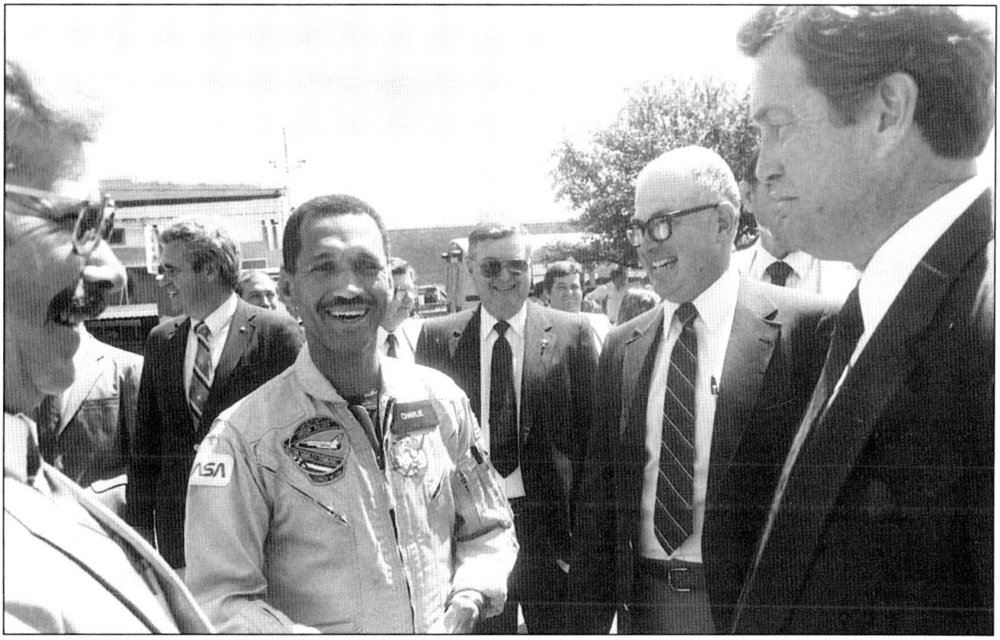

NASA astronaut Charles Bolden is pictured surrounded by county and town officials. He is seen talking with, from left to right, Mayor Elmer Powell; Roy Herron, superintendent of Iva-Starr Schools, who was responsible for getting Bolden to visit the area; and J.R. McGee, CEO and president of The Peoples Bank of Iva, who was also the REVIVA member responsible for welcoming Bolden to this special event. April 9 and 10, 1987, were two very special days for Iva.

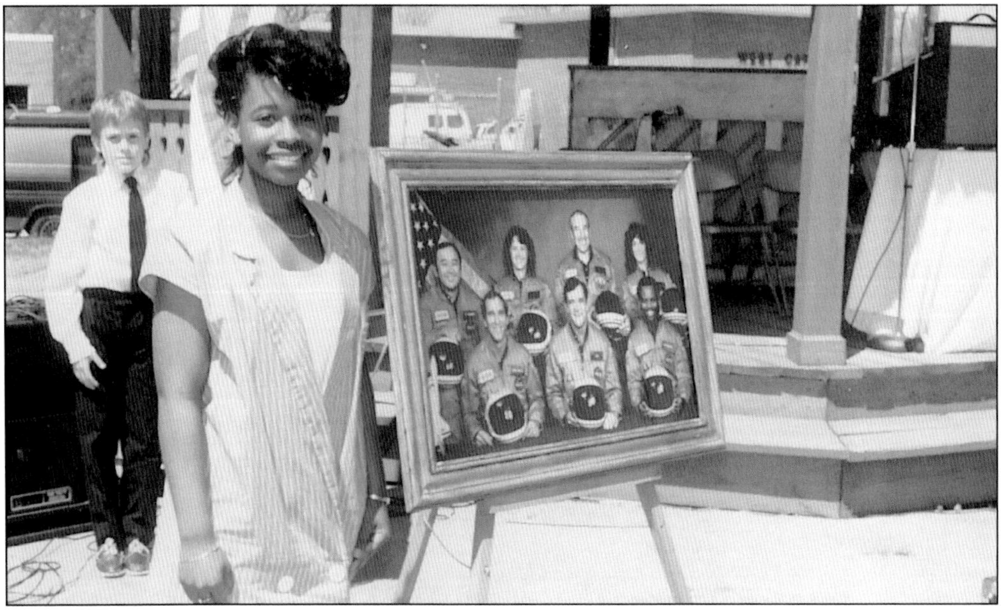

This photograph of a portrait of the *Challenger* crew was taken during memorial services in April 1987 on Iva town square, where seven trees were planted. Student Martsney Johnson, positioned beside the portrait, and Jarrett Davis, by the flag, represented the Iva-Starr Schools. The *Challenger* crew, from left to right, are as follows: (front row) Mike Smith, Dick Scobee, and Ron McNair; (back row) El Onizuka, teacher Christa McAuliffe, Greg Jarvis, and Judy Resnik. The crew lost their lives on January 28, 1986, at 11:38 a.m., when the tragedy of the *Challenger* happened.

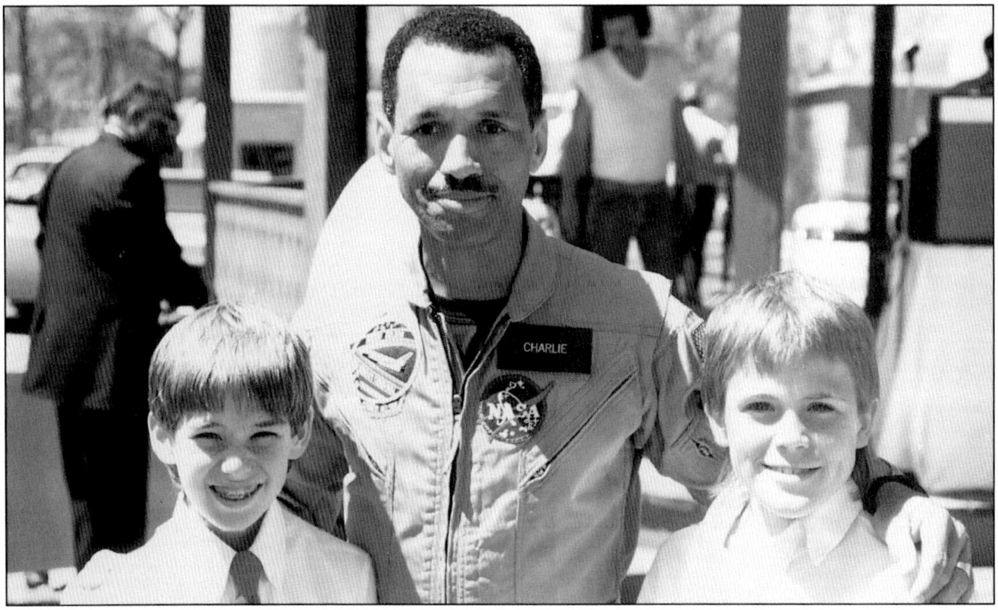

Two young Iva elementary students, Josh Gray and Jarrett Davis, are proud to be Americans on this special day. They were honored to meet astronaut Charles Bolden, who is a native of South Carolina. Josh Gray is the son of Ricky and Connie Gray, and Jarrett Davis is the son of Danny and Sharon Davis.

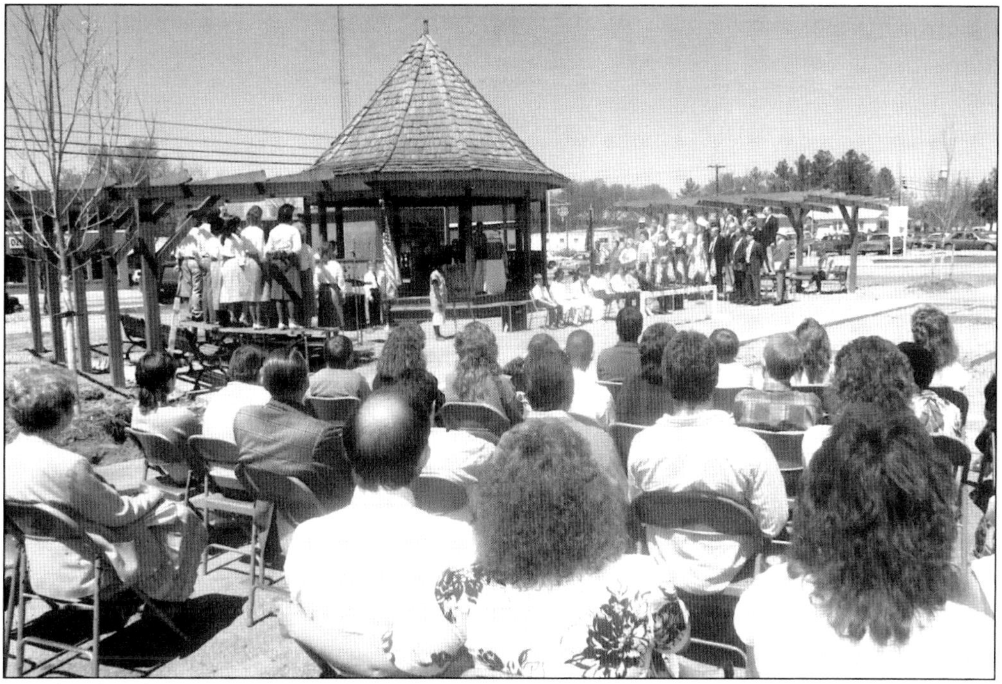

On the day that astronaut Charles Bolden came to Iva, approximately 500 people, including more than 300 Starr-Iva students, were in attendance. Mr. Bolden placed U.S. flags beside seven golden maple trees, which had been purchased with money raised by the students.

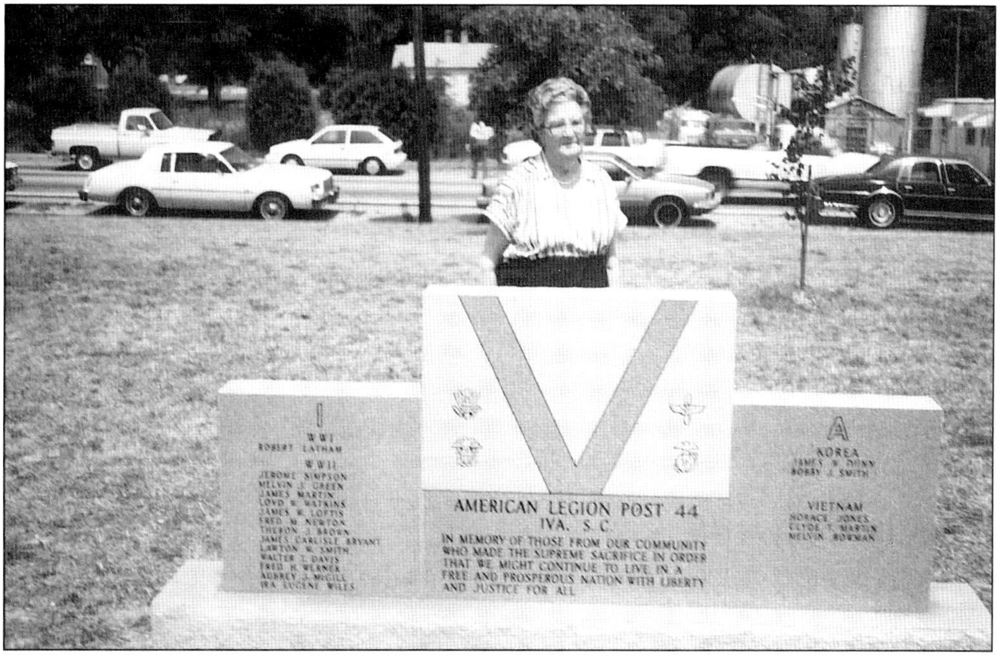

Mrs. Ora Dunn stands at the American Legion monument during a patriotic ceremony that was held in Iva Square. This monument lists servicemen who died for our country in WW I, WW II, the Korean War, and the Vietnam Conflict. Mrs. Dunn is one of several Gold Star Mothers (one who has lost a son or daughter in service during a war) living in our area.

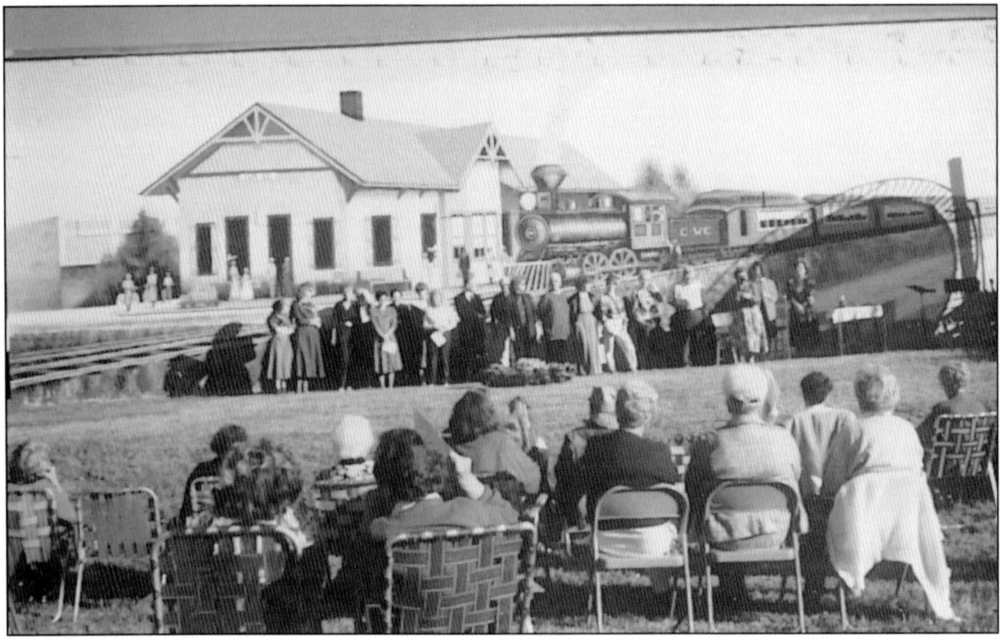

This picture shows the dedication program for the Railroad Depot mural, which was painted on the side of Brown's 5 & 10¢ store by artist Oscar Velasquez. The Iva depot, which was once on the town square, was moved to another location and made into a private home, which was a REVIVA community project. REVIVA also commissioned Velasquez to do prints of the depot, the fountain, and the gazebo, to make available to the public.

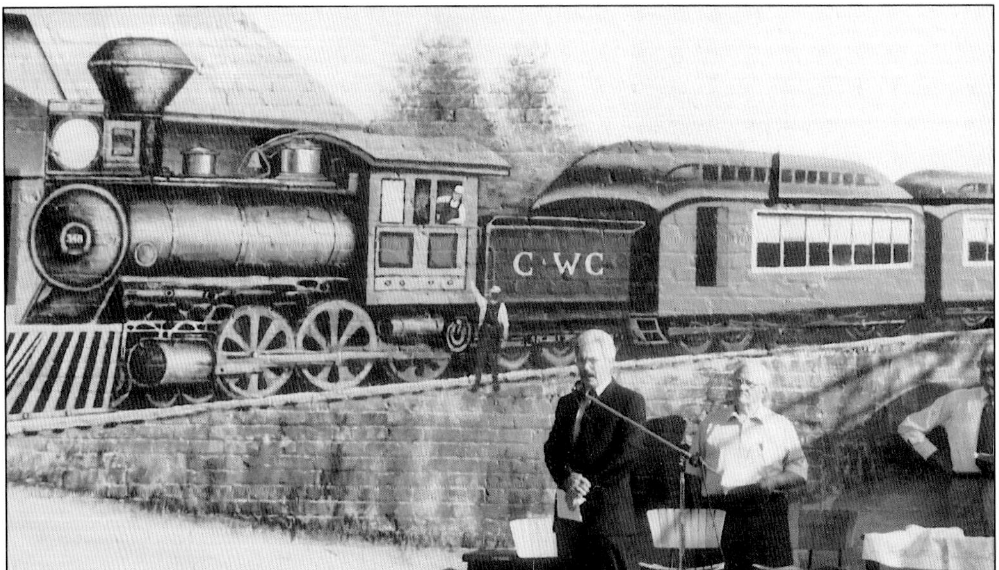

This lifelike mural of the C & WC Railroad train and a likeness of the engineer was painted on the side of Brown's 5 & 10¢ store in downtown Iva. Mayor Elmer Powell, "Hawk" Evans, and Hoyt Ozmint took part in a dedication service for this mural by artist Oscar Velasquez.

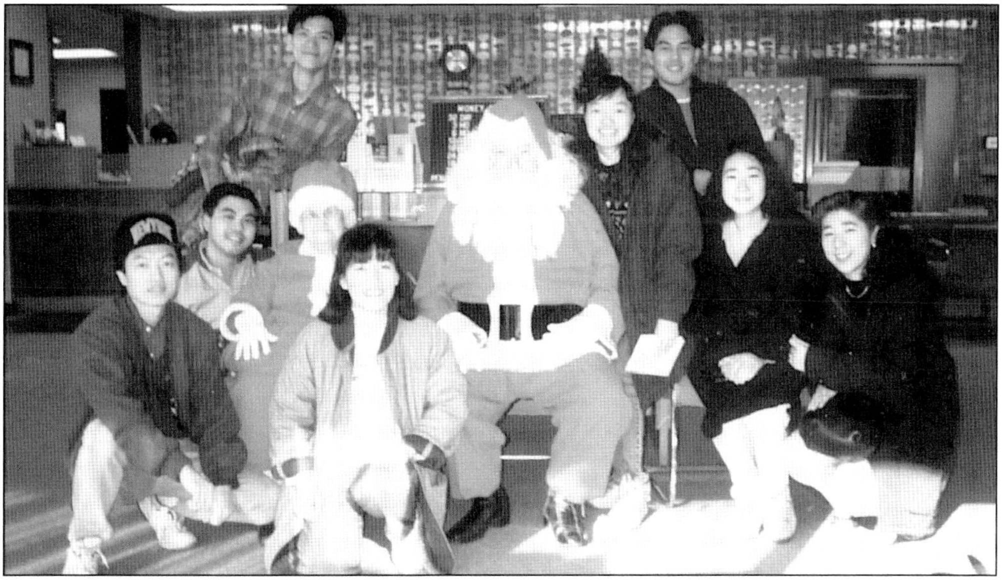

"Friendship House International" (FHI) was sponsored by Iva First Baptist Church and "Christmas House International" by Good Hope Presbyterian, who hosted college students from other countries who are studying in the U.S.A. and cannot go home for Christmas. Many countries are represented. Local folks open their homes and have students live with their families during the two to three weeks of the Christmas and New Year holidays.

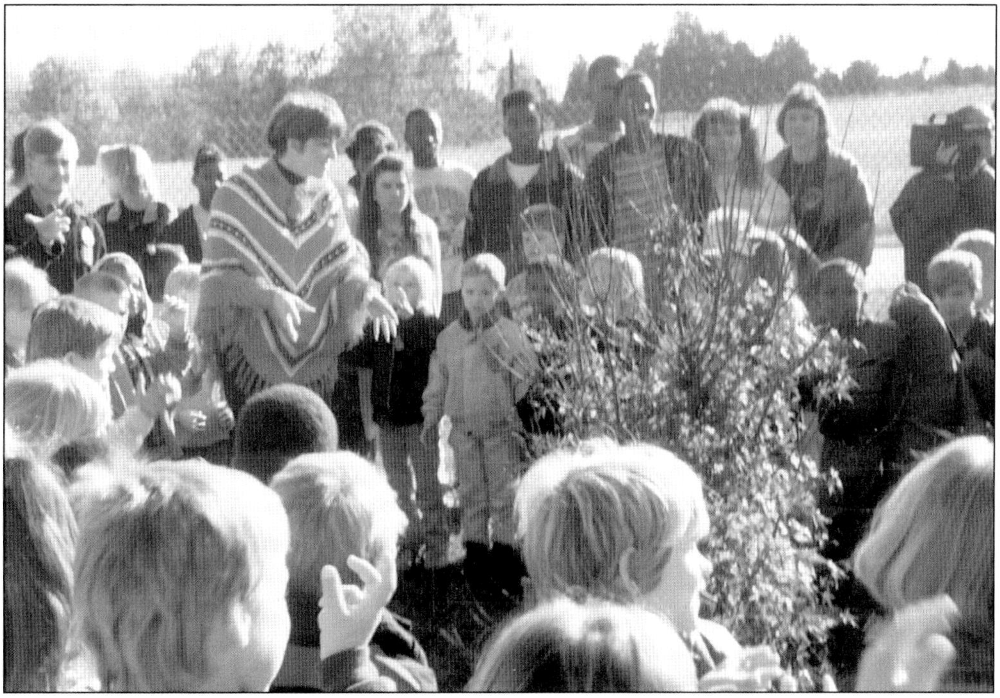

Arbor Day is celebrated in Iva on the first day of December each year. Grade students of Iva and Starr Elementary Schools each plant a tree at Crescent High School during this event. They will watch their trees grow, and then see how big the trees have grown in 12 years, when they graduate.

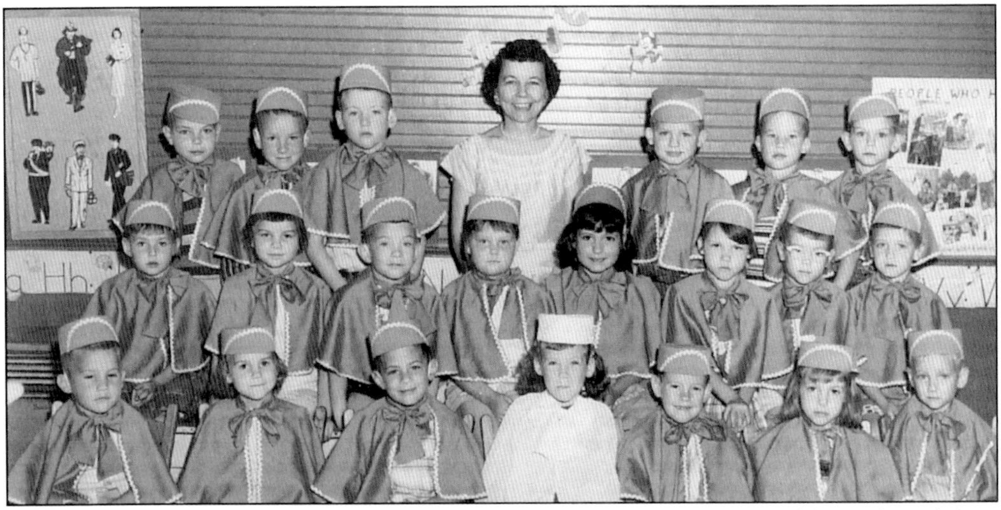

Miss Elsie Evans taught kindergarten classes in Iva for 28 years. Pictured here, from left to right, are the following: (first row) Lee Woolbright, Rita Faye Simpson, Guy Epstein, Karen Burdette, Tommy Purdy, Claire Hall, and Gerry Campbell; (second row) Debbie Burdette, Marsha Atkins, George Kelley, Jean Baugus, Anne Holley, Rhonda Willis, Terry Jane Loftis, and Jackie Jones; (third row) Mike Hanks, Gerald Jordan, Randall Shirley, teacher Mrs. Elsie Evans, Lindsay Craft, Tim Eaves, and Danny Drennon.

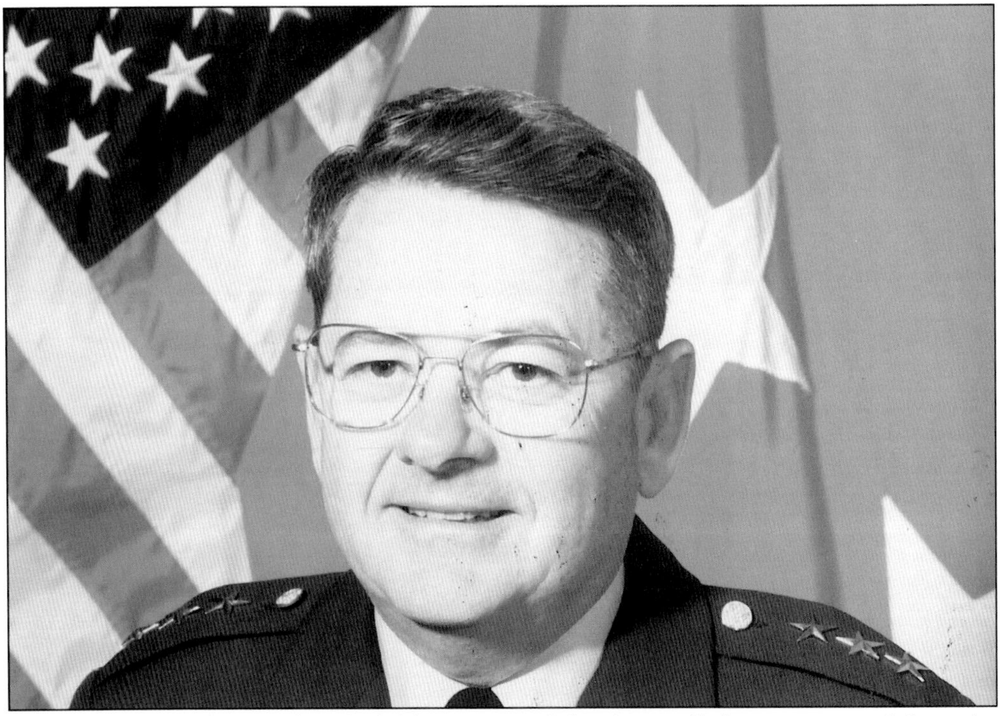

Lieutenant General Samuel Wakefield, a native of the Antreville/Iva area, retired from the army on June 27, 1994, as a three-star general. He is the son of Sam and Mary McAdams Wakefield and the grandson of Sam and Ada McAdams. Mr. McAdams was one of the earliest mail carriers in 1901, delivering mail on horseback or on foot. Lieutenant General Wakefield now resides with his family at Savannah Lakes in McCormick.

In the 38th Annual Lions Club Convention in Atlantic City, New Jersey, Marie Bowie and her husband, Parker Bowie, represented Iva and South Carolina in the parade. Mr. Bowie had made special clocks for the Lions Club. The clocks were constructed with special chimes so that blind people would be able to know the time of day. He also made beautiful furniture for his home.

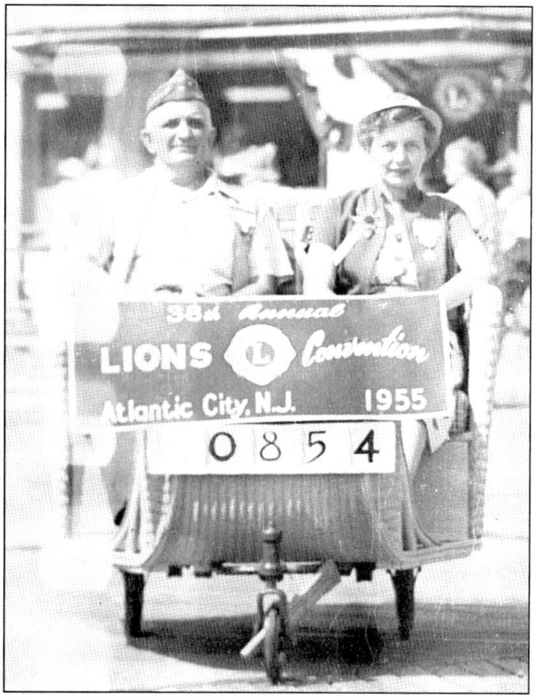

Dr. W. Parker Bowie was born near Iva, South Carolina, on June 28, 1901, the only son of Luther Edwin and Lucia Parker Bowie. He was a farmer and philanthropist who worked with the Lions' Club Sight Conservation program, Shriners' Hospital, and other worthy charities. He was a state agricultural leader who won the South Carolina Farm Bureau's Distinguished Service Award in 1968. He contributed financing as well as his time and oversight for the extensive renovation of the Iva Associate Reformed Presbyterian Church. In 1983 he and his wife, Dr. Marie Thomason Bowie, gave funds for the construction of Bowie Divinity Hall and its furnishings, including a two manual 14-rank Wicks pipe organ in the Marie T. Bowie Chapel. At that time it represented the largest single gift ever contributed to Erskine College and Theological Seminary, or any institution or agency of the Associate Reformed Presbyterian Church.

Dr. Marie Thomason Bowie, only daughter of Melvin A. and Eddie Terry Thomason, was born January 5, 1913, near Honea Path, South Carolina. She served as a teacher in the Iva District Schools for 35 years. She joined her husband in all his charitable endeavors and continued to give generously to her church and community after his passing in 1986. A special interest in the fine arts, combined with a keen interest in the work of Erskine College, led her to fund the construction of the Bowie Arts Center on the Erskine campus. The Bowies were enthusiastic collectors of antique furniture and clocks, and these, as well as items handmade by Dr. W. Parker Bowie, are featured items of the Bowie Arts Center collection.

Mr. and Mrs. Luther Edwin Bowie, Parker's parents, established the Bowie farm which is still thriving today. His wife, who took over the farm after his death, was an active member of the Iva Associate Reformed Presbyterian Church and its women's organizations.

Dr. and Mrs. Parker Bowie contributed much to the Iva community and to nearby Erskine College. Mr. Bowie is now deceased. Mrs. Bowie is a retired teacher from Crescent High School, and she still resides in their home on Parker Bowie Road in Iva. She continues to contribute to her community with her generous giving.

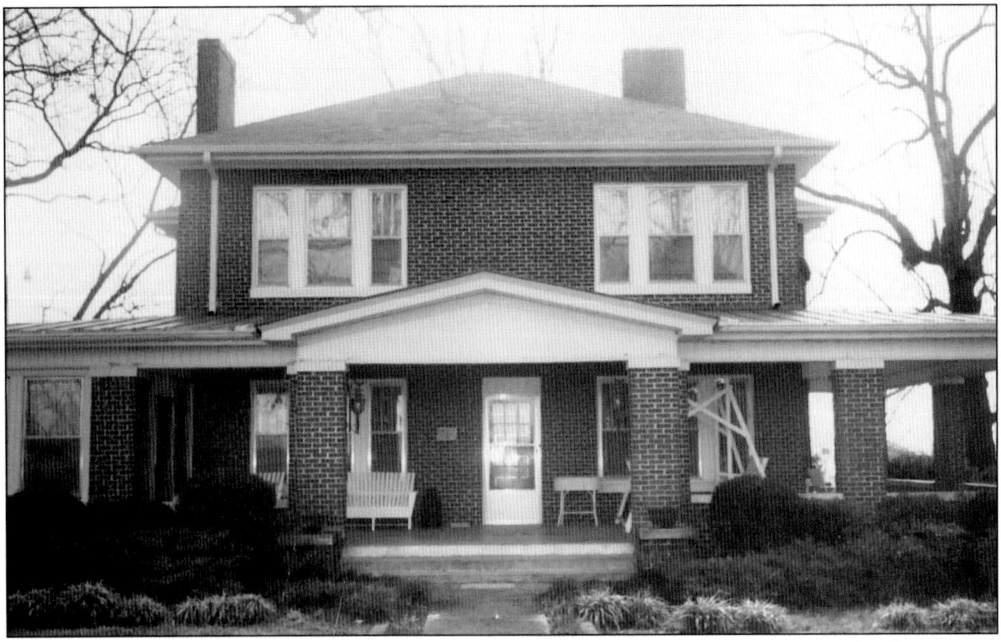

The home of Marie Thomason Bowie is located on Parker Bowie Road in Iva. This house was built in 1923, and at that time, very few houses were built with brick. Trees were plentiful, so lumber was available, and more practical, to use for housing. Luther and "Miss Lucia" Bowie, the parents of Dr. Parker Bowie, built this house.

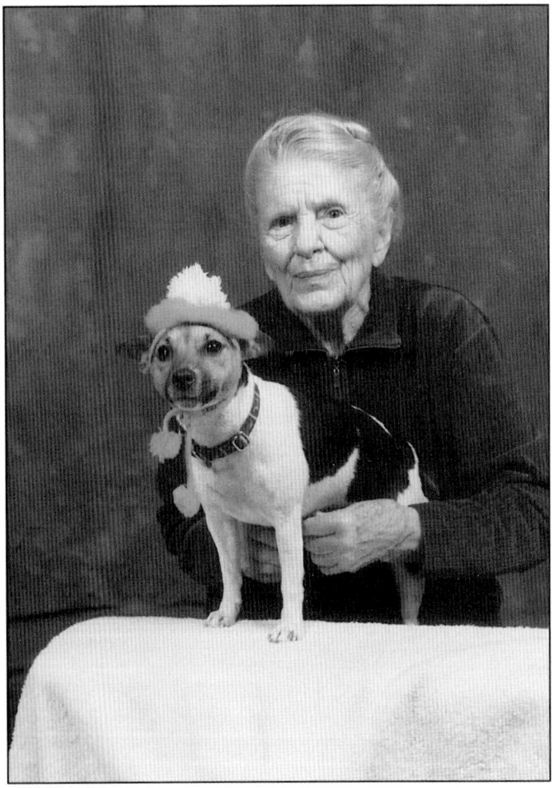

Marie Thomason Bowie is pictured with her Jack Russell Terrier, named "Trixie." Mrs. Bowie has established the "Thomason-Bowie Outdoor Educational Foundation" on her 788-acre farm. It was named in honor of her late husband, Dr. Parker Bowie, and late brother, Dr. Houston Thomason. This land is to be operated as an agricultural and environmental laboratory for the region's children.

This old Standard Oil Pump is a relic that can be seen on the Bowie farm. The pump used no electricity when it was in operation; instead, it had a handle at its base for pumping the gas up into the glass tank on top. This tank was marked by downward gallons. The handle could be locked to its base.

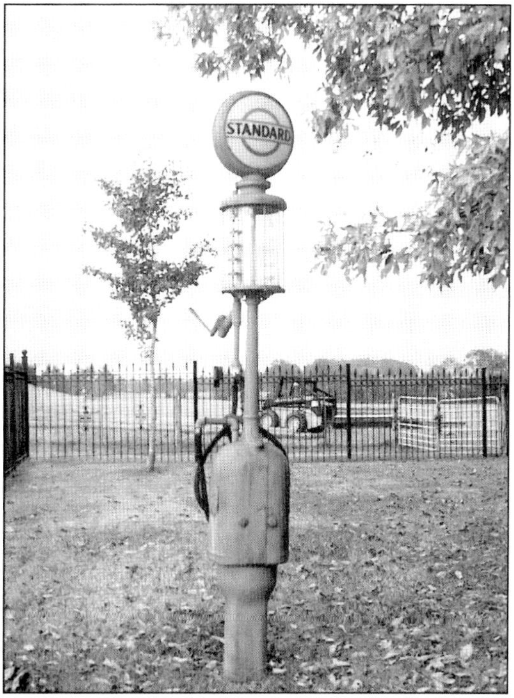

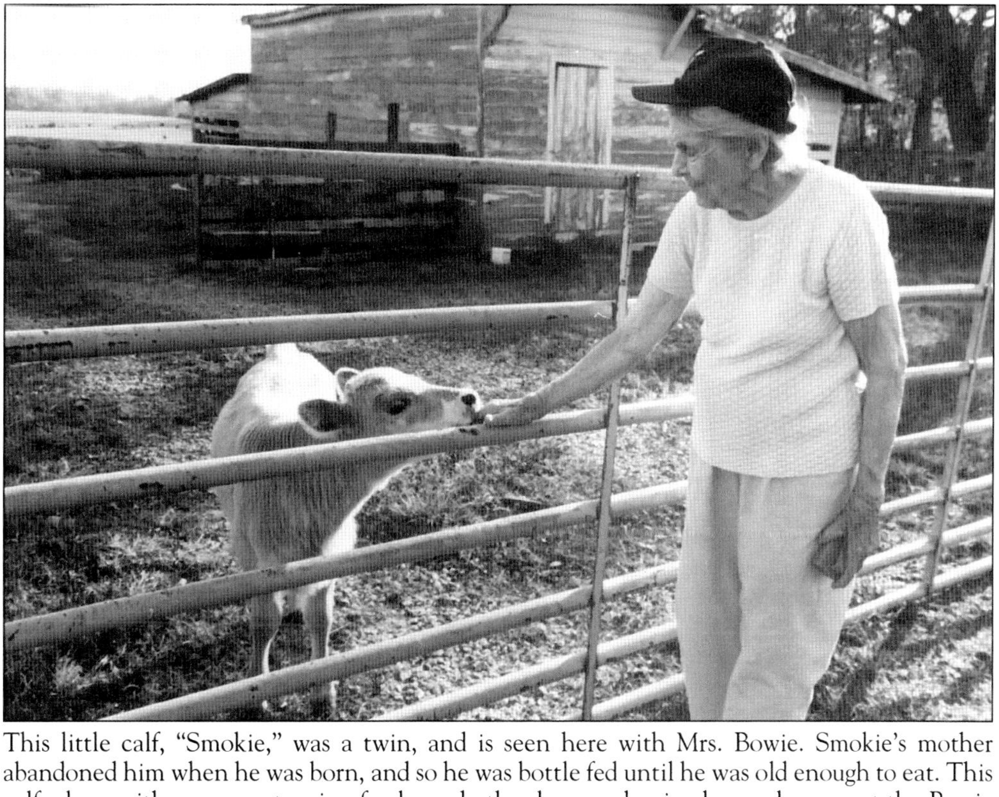

This little calf, "Smokie," was a twin, and is seen here with Mrs. Bowie. Smokie's mother abandoned him when he was born, and so he was bottle fed until he was old enough to eat. This calf, along with cows, goats, pigs, fowls, and other barnyard animals, can be seen at the Bowie Thomason Educational Foundation.

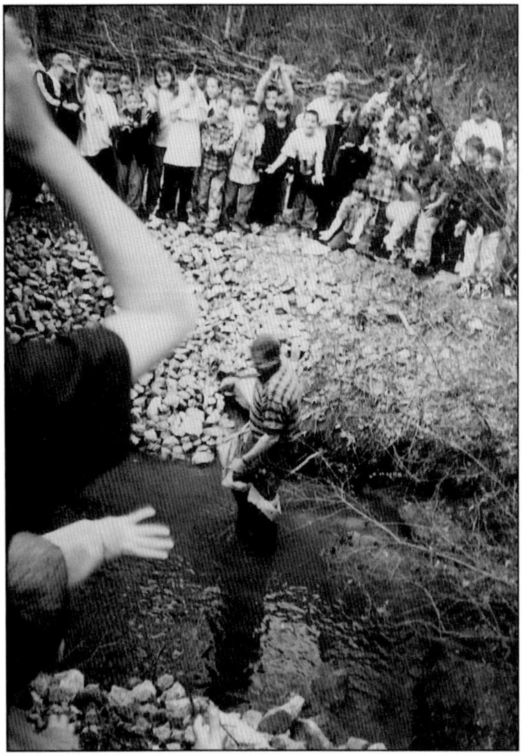

These students are involved in a "learning experience" at the Thomason-Bowie outdoor educational classroom setting on the creek. William "Rockie" English, of the Clemson University Extension Center, is in the stream showing the children how bugs can tell us if the water is polluted. He also scooped up salamanders, crawfish, and mayflies, and then explained what their presence indicates about water quality.

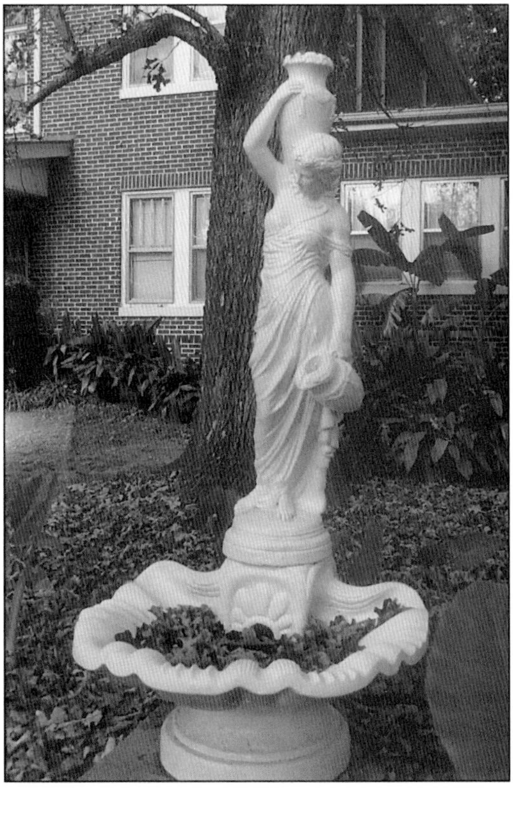

"Rebekah" is seen holding her water jug. This very eye-catching fountain, depicting "Rebekah at the Well," can be seen at the Outdoor Educational Foundation. The fountain was originally intended for the foyer of the Bowie Arts Center at Erskine College in Due West, South Carolina. Unfortunately, due to its size, it was not suitable for the college. The fountain graces a flower bed at the entrance to Mrs. Bowie's home.